14 -

9116

2

Sam Choy's Island Flavors

Sam Choy's

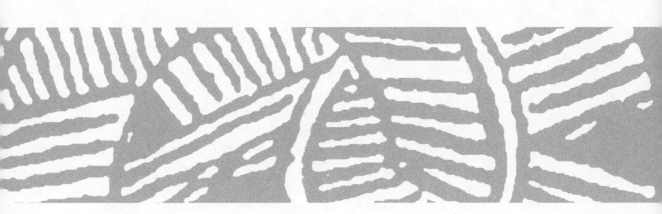

Island Flavors

Written by **Sam Choy**

with U'i and Steven Goldsberry

Photographs by Douglas Peebles

HYPERION

NEW YORK

LIBRARY OF CONGRESS CATALOGING-IN-PUBLICATION DATA

CHOY, SAM.
SAM CHOY'S ISLAND FLAVORS / SAM CHOY. — 1ST ED.
P. CM.
INCLUDES INDEX.
ISBN 0-7868-6474-5
1. COOKERY, HAWAIIAN. I. TITLE.
II. TITLE: ISLAND FLAVORS.
TX724.5.H3C4815 1999   98-44345
641.59969—DC21   CIP

BOOK DESIGN BY
BARBARA M. BACHMAN

FIRST EDITION
10 9 8 7 6 5 4 3 2 1

To my parents,

Clairemoana and Hung Sam Choy,

for instilling in me a powerful

work ethic and a love for

creating good food.

Mahalo, oʻu makua aloha.

Contents

Acknowledgments   ix

Introduction   1

How to Use This Book   4

Working with Fish and Shellfish   9

Appetizers   13

Salads   55

Soups and Stews   95

Shellfish   117

Fish   147

Poultry   177

Beef   209

Pork and Lamb   231

Side Dishes   251

Desserts   277

Drinks   303

Menus   313

Glossary   317

Index   327

Acknowledgments

It is a Hawai'i tradition to thank everyone who helps on a project, be it making a canoe, building a house, writing a book, or lending support and kokua (help) along life's winding path.

There are so many—family, friends, employees, staff, professional acquaintances, and folks who have challenged and encouraged me—that I need to thank. So to all of you good people who have helped me along my life's path, mahalo nui loa (thank you so very much).

I want to first thank my parents, Clairemoana and Hung Sam Choy, for their support and love. Thank you to my brother, Patrick, and my sisters, Wai Sun and Wai Lin, for their patience and help. And most important, aloha nui (much love) and mahalo (thank you) to my wife, Carol, for working so hard to support me and raise our two sons, Sam Jr. and Christopher, into the fine young men they have become.

Thank you to my business partner, James Lee; my agent, Laurie Liss; and Bennett Hymer of Mutual Publishing, who have helped me realize my dream of sharing the foods and flavors of Hawai'i with the world. A special mahalo to my executive assistant, Renee Dyer, for all of her long hours spent organizing my hectic schedule, and to my promotional chef, Troy Terorotua, a jack-of-all-trades.

For their constant encouragement and professionalism, on this project in particular, thank you to my writers, U'i and Steven Goldsberry; my editor at Hyperion, Will Schwalbe, his assistant, Halley MacNaughton, and production editor Adrian James; photographer Douglas Peebles; food stylist Faith Ogawa; and to Dolores Simon, copy editor extraordinaire.

Mahalo to the people of Hawai'i, those who live on the Islands and those who hold the Islands close to their hearts, for being a part of the magic that makes this paradise our home.

Sam Choy's Island Flavors

Introduction

*I*n the Islands we have a saying: *"Lucky you live Hawai'i."*

That's how I've always felt. I grew up on the North Shore of O'ahu in a little fishing village called La'ie. My lucky upbringing centers on my family, especially my parents. My dad, Hung Sam Choy, and my mother, Clairemoana Choy, wanted to introduce their children to a wide variety of foods. They shared the cooking responsibilities in our home, and stressed the principles of freshness and flavor and, most important, tradition.

Every holiday, they prepared a special meal. Thanksgiving, Christmas, New Year, and Chinese New Year dinners were spectacular, but so were the Easter and Halloween meals, and Kuhio Day. Our birthdays were the best, though. I could never tell if it was the love for celebration, or their aloha for cooking that made their food so 'ono (delicious).

My dad was of Chinese descent, born and raised in Hawai'i. I loved listening to him talk about his "small-kid" days. His parents were taro farmers. Folks tell me that my grandfather, Hong Lai Choy, used to be one of O'ahu's "taro kings." He and my grandmother grew their own vegetables—watercress, ong choy, Chinese parsley (cilantro), green onions, and many different types of squash—right there on the farm. Of course they had an abundance of taro and taro leaves (lu'au).

Dad learned to cook by helping his mother, Yuk Kiew Lee, in the kitchen. Every day, she prepared all the meals for the people who worked on the taro farm. She was an excellent cook who knew how to create classic Chinese and Hawaiian dishes, using ingredients she gathered from her garden. My dad said he took it all in—the sights, smells, and tastes of everything she made. The magic of his mom's kitchen became a family legacy, a blessing that he wanted to share with his own children.

My dad is gone now, but I'll always remember him whipping up everything from oxtail soup, chow mein, and gun lo mein noodles, to traditional Hawaiian dishes like lomi salmon and squid lu'au. He just flat-out loved to cook!

My mother, Clairemoana, is part German, but mostly Hawaiian. When she was a young girl, she was sent to a missionary finishing school, where she received formal training in Western etiquette, like serving high tea and all that fancy stuff. She brought the flavors of European cooking and the elegance of fine dining to our family table. My parents, together, are the blend that made me who I am—a chef who enjoys turning traditional, home-style cooking into the drama of haute cuisine.

Hawai'i, a tiny group of islands in the middle of the Pacific, has a multicultural society that has grown in strength through the immigration of people from all corners of the world. They brought with them their food, their families, their traditions, and their personalities, and have melded these into what we call "local-style."

This "local-style" is so essential to our Island culture that unless someone labels something as Japanese or Chinese or Hawaiian, we don't ever think about it as coming from somewhere else. When I was little I remember sitting with some friends at a lu'au. We were talking about how good the food was, and one guy said, "I don't like the Japanese stuff. You know, the raw fish things, and the kim chee" (pickled cabbage with hot peppers).

One of my friends who is part Japanese said, "Hawaiians always ate raw fish, like poke. And kim chee is Korean, brah, not Japanese."

The conversation went on about teriyaki being from Japan, and lemon chicken from China, and kal bi steak from Korea.

I was amazed. It never occurred to me that the foods I'd grown up with and learned to love were from different countries. To me, they were just "local-style" food, Hawaiian food.

As I got older, I paid more attention. Our cultural mix in the Islands comes from a wonderful blend of people from all over Asia and Polynesia, as well as Europe and America, and it has evolved to make Hawai'i a gourmet "gathering place" where today's talented, award-winning chefs practice their eclectic craft. The festive culinary possibilities are endless.

Very few places on earth are as beautiful as Hawai'i, and nowhere do you find such an abundance of great food—fresh fish from our reefs and open ocean, fruits and crisp vegetables from mineral-rich volcanic soils, beef and poultry from upcountry ranches, and seaweed and crustaceans from our aquafarms.

What we do with this food—how we cook it—is unique. And really exciting. I think the foods themselves and the power of this place make our cuisine what it is. "Hapa hybrid," someone called it. "Hapa" is Hawaiian for "half-half, or part," a mixing of races, as most of our children are. As I am.

Our hapa hybrid cooking manages to be regional and international at the same time. Whether you say it's "local-style," "Island-style," "Hawaiian-style," or whatever, it is a distinct and increasingly popular cuisine. I like to call it Island cuisine.

We've borrowed so many cooking methods and ingredients in this crossroads of the Pacific that it's easy to lose track of the origin of each element. Sometimes when I try to explain my ideas for preparing a certain dish I find myself saying things like, "Well, the Chinese cook chicken like this, but the spice mixture is from Fiji, the side dishes are European, Italian, and Spanish, the presentation is Hawaiian, and the garnish Australian."

I am sure of my own influences as an Island chef.

My mother's Hawaiian ancestors used ingredients they found in the rain forests, in the sea, and in their sweet potato patches and lo'i (taro ponds). Their lives were slow, and blended into the balm and beauty of the 'aina (land).

Mom's German side brought heavier foods to our family, the gravies and sausages, the strong vinegars.

My father's Chinese relatives cooked with more spice and quick fire, more hot Asian flamboyance.

And our friends and cousins and aunties and uncles ranged far across the culinary landscape.

That's me as a chef: easygoing Hawaiian, focused German, wild Chinese, and Island boy to the max.

I hope you enjoy this book. I wanted to show every home chef, no matter what part of the country you're from, how easy and fun it is to cook Island flavors. Most of the time you can use ingredients at hand. I've called this a "somma" cookbook because usually all you need is "somma this" and "somma that."

How to Use This Book

C ooking is really very simple. The trick is to know your ingredients—their properties, their flavors, their ability to blend. The rest is just technique and creativity. Art exists when there is a balance between ingredients and technique, with a whole lot of love thrown in.

I used to think that I was happiest when I was cooking. That's still true most of the time, but it runs a close second to the joy I get from sharing the exotically simple cuisine of Hawai'i. Watching people's eyes sparkle when they take a bite of one of my new dishes, or when they let a "Wow!" sneak out through a mouthful of my 'onolicious cooking—it's a real pleasure.

I hope these recipes will make you feel the joy of the Islands. But before you begin this new adventure in cooking, let me quickly explain a few things.

Building a Dish

I like to compare building a dish to building a house. You start with a strong foundation (your main ingredient), add walls and a roof (the marinades, pastas, or vegetables), then, at the very end, you decorate it and make it yours (the sauce and/or garnish).

I construct a dish starting with a very basic layer—the main ingredient. Again, it's important to use the sweetest, freshest fish, beef, pork, chicken, or seafood you can find. I create either a dry or liquid marinade with a hint of seasoning—very basic salt and pepper, or a blend of garlic and ginger—then add the rice, pasta, or stir-fried vegetables.

The final layer is the sauce. The goal here is the marriage of flavors. This layer is the finishing touch, the blending element. The sauce titillates the palate and allows the flavors of the marinade, the main ingredient, and the vegetables to come through. It smooths out the edges and allows the magic to happen.

When I was learning the art of fine cooking, a friend of mine said, "You know, Sam, there are some cooks who make food that is really good, but you can't eat much of it. The flavors are too dense, too rich. They saturate the palate too quickly. When you cook, the goal is for your guests to want that seventh and eighth bite. The flavors should gently coax, not overpower."

When you eat, an interesting phenomenon occurs. As you take the food into your mouth, the flavors build with each bite, becoming stronger. That is why I marinate for a very short time, and am careful never to overcook anything. In the overall enjoyment of a meal, texture is just as important as taste.

Ingredients

Make sure your ingredients are absolutely fresh. The best of all scenarios, of course, is to gather herbs and vegetables from your garden. I know that's not always possible, but you get the idea. Some of my recipes call for fruits and vegetables that aren't available fresh in many parts of the country. In these cases, as when liliko'i (passion fruit) juice is needed, it's acceptable to use a concentrate. The thing to remember is that the fresher the ingredients, the bolder the flavors.

There may be some ingredients that sound unfamiliar, like *sambal oelek* or *black goma*. You can find all of them in your local Asian market. I've done cooking demonstrations around the world, and often people write to tell me they tried one of my more unusual recipes. They bought each of the strange-sounding ingredients, made the dish, loved it, and now something like *dau see* is a staple in their kitchen, right next to the fusilli and cumin.

A common question is "What brand of soy sauce is best?" Some soy sauces are very salty. Kikkoman brand is strong and may be better in marinades than for table use. Yamasa is a good, high-bred soy sauce with a little sugar added. Each brand has a distinctive flavor. Try the one that is most easily available in your part of the country. And the next time you are in your local Japanese, Chinese, Korean, Vietnamese, or Thai restaurant, ask what type of soy sauce they use. If you like it, pick it up at the local Asian market and try it at home.

Substitutions

Some of the suggested ingredients may be difficult to find in your area. Don't panic. I've included substitutions in the Working with Fish and Shellfish section, pages 9–12, and others within the body of each recipe, and in the Glossary (page 317)—for example, use corn husks instead of ti leaves, use spinach instead of lu'au (taro) leaves, use any firm white fish in place of ono or 'opakapaka. All of the Asian ingredients can be found in an Asian market. Trust me, the flavor experience that these exotic condiments and spices bring to a meal makes it worth hunting them down. Most of the recipes, however, require only ingredients that can be easily found in any local supermarket.

Marinades

I use marinades quite often. They infuse the flavor of the meat, fish, shellfish, or tofu with the essence of the marinade ingredients. A marinade allows you to capture the piquancy of garlic or the toasted flavor of sesame oil without overwhelming the palate. I love using a marinade bath to season the meat lightly before I begin cooking.

I also use marinades to seal the meat before grilling. If you place fish on the barbecue without a quick marinade bath, it will dry out and burn. The marinade locks the juices in and allows the meat a chance to cook to moist, tender perfection.

Sauces

Included with each recipe is a corresponding sauce designed to crown your entree. When you get used to the flavor of the sauce, use your creativity. Try different sauces with different dishes. Remember, once you have the technique down, it's time to create the art.

Decorating the Dish

A good meal involves as many of the senses as possible. Most of my restaurant guests begin their dining experience the minute they read the menu or hear the names of the specials. Some of our return customers say they start to salivate when they make their reservations, because they already know what to expect.

The names of the dishes you serve should be pleasant to hear and descriptive enough to whet the appetite. And when the food is brought to the table, the aroma of the dish should captivate the sense of smell. The way the dish is presented—garnished with fresh herbs, interesting pasta shapes, ti leaf wraps, or edible flowers—should be a pleasing sight. And the flavors and textures of the meal should satisfy the senses of taste and touch. It's all important.

Remember, though, that everything on a serving plate should contribute to the flavor, including the garnish. The herbs or edible flowers are there to enhance the taste of the dish, as well as please the eye.

Never Overcook

All of us have had the unfortunate experience of sitting down to a meal where the vegetables are mushy, the meat is tough, and the gravies and sauces look like dense pudding. It's not a pretty sight. Here are a few tips to ensure that the food coming from your kitchen is "broke da mouth" perfect—the vegetables are brightly colored and crisp, the meat is moist, and your sauces drizzle in light, creamy streams.

If you want your vegetables to retain their bright, fresh color and crunchy texture after they're cooked, shock them in a basin of ice water. I prefer to steam my veggies (if I'm not stir-frying them), and when they're done, I remove the entire steamer basket and plunge it into the icy water. It quick-chills the veggies and stops the cooking process.

I do the same thing with shrimp. Food continues to cook even after you have removed it from the heat source. Shrimp tends to get rubbery when cooked too long. So, after I boil the shrimp, I throw them into an ice-plunge. They come out perfect every time.

People have a tendency to cook fish until the meat is solid. At that point, it's rubbery and tough: ruined. All fish should be cooked through, but not overcooked. As I said, food keeps on cooking even when removed from the heat source. I cook my fish to the point right between rare and done. I remove the meat when its center is still slightly pink, and let the cooking process continue on the serving plate. This method takes a lot of practice to get the timing right, but when my guests cut into the fillet, the fish is cooked through, moist and tender, and really juicy. I'm not recommending that you present your guests with partially cooked fish that is raw in the center. Watch your cooking closely, make sure the meat is cooked through before serving, and don't overcook it.

It's a good idea, when first starting out, to follow the "Canadian rule"—for each inch of meat thickness, cook 10 minutes, whether on the grill or under the broiler, steamed, boiled, or baked in the oven at 450°F. Also, add 5 minutes for each inch if the baked fish is stuffed or prepared in a sauce. Boil or steam mollusks (mussels, clams, or oysters) for 4 to 6 minutes once the cooking liquid begins to bubble.

Menus

I've included eight menus in this book, from an intimate dinner for two to a tailgate meal for those autumn afternoons before the big game. The menus are just suggestions, a starting point to give you some ideas for dish combinations. Some of the menus are exotic, some are just fun, and all are packed with delicious food.

Tropical Drinks

One day, while sitting in my Diamond Head restaurant compiling the recipes for this book, I watched our bartender prep the bar. He pulled out all of the umbrellas and swizzle sticks, then polished up the glasses, and restocked the liquor. I thought then what a great idea it would be to include some of our favorite drinks, complete with garnish and decoration suggestions.

These drinks are really a joy to make, and they come out looking as if a professional bartender from the tropics whipped them up. The liquor is optional; the drinks taste great "virgin."

My hope is that you'll try these recipes the first time as they are written, just to get used to this new type of cuisine. Then feel free to change any spice, garnish, or flavoring you don't find appealing. Or just drop it out of the recipe.

Most chefs are pretty rigid. They want you to use exactly what they use, with certain amounts of each ingredient and all ingredients included. Maybe it's the Hawaiian way I was brought up, but that never seemed right to me. Everyone has different tastes and should feel free to mix things the way they like. That's how we do food in the Islands. So maybe these aren't recipes I'm giving you, but guidelines for how to make dishes that are like the dishes I've had success with.

Anyway, take the challenge, be creative, and above all, HAVE FUN.

Aloha a me hau'oli (Have a good time).

Working with Fish and Shellfish

Selection and Purchase of Fresh Fish and Shellfish

Fish and shellfish are such interesting ingredients. They are loved and hated, feared and embraced. They are both the most healthful of meats (rich in beneficial minerals and oils), and the most dangerous (because of pollutants and their highly perishable nature).

Included here are some tips for selecting and purchasing raw fish and shellfish, and a listing of viable fish substitutions. The first and most important tip is to buy your fish and shellfish from a well-established and reputable source. Stay away from roadside stands, and get to know your local fishmonger. He should be able to answer questions like where the fish or shellfish comes from, how fresh it is, whether it was previously frozen, how long it will keep at home, and how it can be prepared. A good fishmonger should be able to produce a certification tag that verifies that the bivalve shellfish he sells was gathered in government-tested waters. The other guidelines are quite simple. Just use your senses of sight, smell, and touch.

Sight

When shopping for fresh seafood, pay attention to the way the fish and shellfish are displayed. The most important factor is temperature. Fresh seafood should always be kept at temperatures as close to 32°F as possible, and frozen seafood below 0°F. Fish fillets and steaks should be in separate pans set on and surrounded by (but not directly touching) ice or be stored in a well-refrigerated display case; whole fish should be smothered in crushed ice with just part of the head showing; live mussels, crabs, clams, and oysters should nestle in crushed ice with the melting ice water constantly draining; and cooked shellfish and fish salads must be kept in separate containers from raw fish.

Whole fish must feature gleaming, shiny skin, tight scales flat to the skin, and clean, bright red or pink gills; fish fillets or steaks should have firm flesh that is moist and translucent. Avoid any meat that looks dull, dry, or opaque. The meat of shucked shellfish—such as scallops, which are rarely in their shells when sold to consumers—should look like plump pillows with a white, light orange, tan, or pinkish hue. Avoid any shellfish meat that is yellowish or brown around the edges.

Smell

Fresh fish smell like the sea and have a sweet odor. A store maintaining quality sanitary standards will smell like virgin surf—and so should the fish you buy. Avoid fish with an ammonia odor or a fishy stench; these may be in the first stages of spoiling. If the fish is prewrapped, smell it anyway. The fumes of bad seafood are usually strong enough to cut through cellophane.

Touch

The flesh of fresh fish bounces back when pressed with a finger.

Be sure to purchase live bivalves that are relatively free from debris and have intact shells. If you find a mussel that is cracked or has a broken shell that stays shut, it is probably still alive and okay to use. Live clams close their shells completely when they are tapped or squeezed.

Sashimi/Poke-Quality Raw Fish

The guidelines for selecting fresh fish also apply when purchasing the high-quality raw fish needed for sashimi and poke. Buy your meat from a fishmonger who has a good reputation for superb quality and high standards of sanitation. Try to buy fish on the day they are hauled off the boat. Your fishmonger can tell you when the fishing boats are coming in and when he's picking up the catch.

Again, the first indication of freshness is a pleasing, mild aroma. Select moist steaks or fillets that look freshly cut, and avoid those that are dry or brown around the edges. Firm flesh will spring up to its original contour after being pressed. Fish has lost its freshness if the meat is loose or pulling away from the bone.

Before buying your selection, examine the whole fish on display in the market. It serves as a reliable barometer of the overall freshness of the catch. The eyes of the whole fish will be clear and full if fresh, and cloudy or sunken if the fish is starting to spoil. The skin should be shiny with distinct markings.

I want to stress the importance of using fish on the day it is caught when preparing sashimi, poke, or raw fish recipes of any kind. When working with raw fish, one day of aging can be the difference between serving a meal that is just okay (or even worse, a waste of time and money), and having a brilliantly successful culinary evening.

Fish Substitutions

I was quite young when I started cooking fish, and I learned to identify them by their Hawaiian names and the flesh texture. As I worked with mainland fish, I found that their flavors and textures were quite similar to the fish I grew to know.

What I've discovered is that there are two general rules for fish substitutions. First, all firm fish with white meat can be easily interchanged in a recipe. I might get into a little trouble for this one, but, really, if the texture is similar, it should be fine. The flavor will differ depending on whether you use a bold-tasting fish in place of a mild-tasting one. But even within the culinary community, there is discussion about whether a fish is mild, moderate, or bold in flavor. If you need to substitute fish in my recipes, choose one with a similar texture.

Second, taste the dish and experiment. Once you've decided on a substitution, make the recipe and see if you like it. Remember, if the recipe calls for a mild-tasting fish with a firm texture, choose a substitute with like qualities. Your chances of success increase.

Listed below are the fish used in my recipes and some acceptable substitutions:

- **'ahi (yellowfin, bigeye, or albacore tuna)**
  Substitute sea bass, red snapper, swordfish, marlin, or mahimahi.
- **butterfish (black cod)**
  Substitute herring, mackerel, smelt, salmon, or rainbow trout.
- **ehu (orange snapper)**
  Substitute sea bass, yellowfin tuna ('ahi), trout, cod, haddock, halibut, pollack, ocean perch, rockfish, or tilefish.
- **hapu-upu-u (grouper or sea bass)**
  Substitute rainbow trout, yellowfin tuna ('ahi), red snapper, or mahimahi.
- **mahimahi (dolphinfish)**
  Substitute yellowfin, bigeye, or albacore tuna, red snapper or any other snapper, trout, or halibut.
- **marlin (nairagi)**
  Substitute barracuda, striped bass, bonito tuna, swordfish, or whiting.

- onaga (red snapper)
  Substitute sea bass, yellowfin tuna ('ahi), trout, cod, haddock, halibut, pollack, ocean perch, rockfish, or tilefish.
- 'opakapaka (pink snapper)
  Substitute sea bass, yellowfin tuna ('ahi), trout, cod, haddock, halibut, pollack, ocean perch, rockfish, or tilefish.
- ono (wahoo or large mackerel)
  Substitute herring, mackerel, smelt, salmon, or rainbow trout.
- opah (moonfish)
  Substitute herring, mackerel, smelt, salmon, or rainbow trout.
- swordfish (broadbill)
  Substitute barracuda, striped bass, bonito tuna, or whiting.
- uku (gray snapper)
  Substitute sea bass, yellowfin tuna ('ahi), trout, cod, haddock, halibut, pollack, ocean perch, rockfish, or tilefish.

Please remember that this list is not complete, and that these are very general substitution guidelines. Work with what's available from your local fishmonger or supermarket fish department. Buy whatever is freshest. Always buy the highest quality. Then come home and experiment with the flavors.

It's really nothing to change the amount of salt in a recipe or omit an ingredient you don't particularly care for, or one that is not readily available. Experiment with the flavors and textures of the fish and find combinations that you love and that are uniquely yours.

Appetizers

In the old days, when our sugar plantations were running full-bore, the workers carried their lunches in "kaukau" tins—covered, triple-layer containers with narrow metal handles. The midday whistle meant kaukau time, and everyone gathered and put all their main dishes in the middle of a circle. Each person held a bowl of rice in one hand and chopsticks in the other, and plucked the food out of the little tin buckets. That was how the traditional pupu (finger food) carried over into modern Hawai'i—everyone sharing their small contributions of unique cultural flavors.

The word *pupu* dates back to ancient Hawai'i. It means shell, or any tight round thing, and is also the name for any morsel of fish, chicken, or banana.

Of course, the variety of ingredients used for pupus has changed over the years, but the concept is the same—mixing and blending a medley of tastes in a sampler presentation.

Pupus have always been associated with casual dining, and they are perfect for all occasions—a snack to take on a hike or a dish for an office party. And they work especially well as dinner hors d'oeuvres. Appetizers set the tone for the evening. These will tickle the palate and prepare people for the wonderful flavors of the coming feast.

One of the most frequently served pupus is poke (POE-kay). It's not the same as poky (slow), or Pake, the Hawaiian word for Chinese, and it doesn't mean to poke something. The poke I'm talking about is a Hawaiian dish much like a seviche. It usually consists of sliced raw fish, limu (seaweed), fresh red chili pepper, Hawaiian sea salt, and 'inamona (roasted, ground, and salted kukui nuts).

Poke has become so popular that every year we sponsor the Sam Choy/Aloha Festivals International Poke Recipe Contest. We get hundreds of entries from all over the world. Famous chefs, regular folks, and old fishermen prepare their favorite poke dishes for a panel of judges. We even have a celebrity competion. It's amazing to me that people from as far away as the East Coast on the mainland have poke recipes.

I've included a couple of poke recipes in this chapter. Do make sure to read my comments on pages 10–11 on how to ensure the fish you use is high enough quality for poke. Come, try.

Baked Brie with Macadamia Nuts

(Serves 4)

Brie cheese, combined with the rich flavor of macadamia nuts, has become vastly popular in the Islands. I like to serve this baked treat with spicy mango chutney or poha berry preserves. Poha berries, very similar to ground cherries (cape gooseberries) found in the continental United States, grow along the volcanic slopes of the Big Island of Hawai'i.

2 small rounds of Brie cheese, 4½ ounces each
1 tablespoon all-purpose flour
1 large egg, lightly beaten
½ cup macadamia nuts, finely chopped
½ cup panko (Japanese-style crispy bread crumbs) or fine dry bread crumbs
Spicy Mango Chutney (see recipe on page 16)

Garnish:
Lavash, toasted pita, or other thin crisp bread
1 apple, thinly sliced

Cut each Brie round in quarters, and coat with flour. Dip in egg. In a shallow dish, combine macadamia nuts and panko. Coat the Brie well on all sides with the macadamia nut mixture, patting the mixture on to help it adhere. Chill for 30 minutes.

Preheat the oven to 400°F. Arrange the Brie in a pie pan or an ovenproof dish and bake for 10 minutes or until the crust is golden brown. Transfer carefully to a platter, and serve hot with spicy mango chutney, lavash, and apple slices.

Spicy Mango Chutney

(Makes 2 cups)

2 mangoes, 1 pound each
2 teaspoons minced fresh garlic
2 teaspoons peeled and minced fresh ginger
2 tablespoons cider vinegar
½ cup packed dark brown sugar
½ cup golden raisins
1 tablespoon fresh lime juice
2 teaspoons coarse Dijon mustard
¼ teaspoon salt
⅛ teaspoon hot Asian chili paste, such as sambal oelek

Peel the mangoes, dice the flesh into small cubes, and set aside.

Simmer the garlic, ginger, vinegar, and brown sugar in a small saucepan for 10 minutes. Add mangoes, raisins, lime juice, mustard, salt, and *sambal oelek*. Continue to simmer for 20 minutes. Refrigerate. (This chutney will keep refrigerated for up to 1 week.)

Crab-and-Shrimp-Stuffed Shiitake Mushrooms with Mango Béarnaise Sauce

(Serves 16)

Fresh shiitake speaks for itself. It's the best mushroom in the world. With crab and shrimp—'onolicious!—it doesn't get any better. You can top off the dish with any sauce. Béarnaise just happens to be my favorite.

16 large fresh shiitake mushrooms, about 1 pound
1 cup heavy cream
½ cup chopped fresh spinach
2 tablespoons chopped shallots
½ cup coconut milk
1 cup Ritz cracker crumbs
¾ cup cooked crabmeat, picked over well
¼ cup chopped cooked shrimp
¼ teaspoon salt
¼ teaspoon black pepper
Pinch of fresh dill
Mango Béarnaise Sauce (see recipe on page 18)

Garnish:
3 tablespoons grated Parmesan cheese

Preheat the oven to 350°F. Wipe the mushrooms and remove their stems (they can be set aside for another purpose).

In a saucepan over medium-low heat, cook the cream and spinach together until the cream is reduced by half. Stir in the shallots and cook for 1 minute. Remove from the heat and stir in the coconut milk, cracker crumbs, crabmeat, shrimp, salt, pepper, and dill.

Stuff the mushroom caps with the crab-shrimp mixture. Place the caps in a shallow baking pan. Put ½ tablespoon of the béarnaise sauce on each stuffed mushroom. Bake 8 to 10 minutes. Remove from the oven and sprinkle tops with Parmesan cheese.

Mango Béarnaise Sauce

(Makes 1½ cups)

1 tablespoon canola oil
12 tablespoons (1½ sticks) butter
2 shallots, finely chopped
2 or 3 sprigs fresh tarragon, chopped
2 sprigs fresh parsley, chopped
½ cup diced fresh mango
⅔ cup vinegar
3 egg yolks, at room temperature
2 tablespoons cold water
Salt and pepper to taste

In a saucepan, heat the oil and 1 tablespoon of butter. Add shallots, half the tarragon, half the parsley, ¼ cup of the mango, and the vinegar. Cook over gentle heat for 20 minutes or until only 1 tablespoon of liquid remains. Strain through a fine-mesh sieve.

To clarify butter, melt the remaining 11 tablespoons of butter in a double boiler over hot water. After several minutes, milk solids will settle to the bottom. Pour the clear butter into a bowl, leaving the milky residue behind.

To finish the béarnaise, combine the egg yolks and the vinegar mixture in a double boiler over hot water. Whisk well. Gradually incorporate the cold water, salt, and pepper, continuing to whisk vigorously until the mixture becomes creamy. Remove the double boiler from the heat and continue whisking while adding the clarified butter in a thin stream.

Stir the remaining tarragon, parsley, and mango into the mixture. Use béarnaise immediately or reserve in a double boiler over hot but not boiling water.

Mochi Mochi Chicken

(Serves 8)

This dish is 'ono (delicious) with rice—crisp outside and juicy inside. I use mochiko, a very tasty Japanese rice flour, to give the marinade a distinctive flavor. Serve this with hot sticky rice.

Mochi Mochi Marinade (see recipe below)
5 pounds boneless, skinless chicken thighs, cut into large cubes
Vegetable oil for deep-frying

Prepare mochi mochi marinade, and marinate chicken overnight in the refrigerator.

When you're ready to start cooking, drain the marinade from the chicken pieces. Heat about 2 inches of oil in a wok or a deep, heavy pot over medium-high heat until it registers 350°F to 365°F on a deep-fry thermometer. Fry the chicken pieces in batches, without crowding, until deep golden brown and just cooked through. This will take two to three minutes, depending on the size of the cubes. Allow the oil to return to 350°F before adding a new batch. Drain on paper towels.

Mochi Mochi Marinade

(Makes 2½ cups)

½ cup mochiko (Japanese glutinous rice flour)
½ cup cornstarch
½ cup granulated sugar
½ cup chopped scallions or green onions
½ cup soy sauce
4 large eggs, beaten
4 cloves fresh garlic, minced
1 teaspoon salt

Combine marinade ingredients in large bowl and set aside.

Spicy Chicken Wingettes

(Serves 4 to 5)

This is a great finger food. It's easy to prepare and even easier to eat. Great for parties. And very addictive. You can't eat just one or two or three. I'd like to say it's "finger lickin' good," but I know it's even better than that.

½ cup soy sauce
½ teaspoon white pepper
1 tablespoon minced fresh garlic
½ teaspoon peeled and minced fresh ginger
1 cup sherry
3 pounds chicken wing drumettes (the meaty first joints),
    rinsed and dried
1 cup all-purpose flour
½ cup mochiko (Japanese glutinous rice flour)
½ cup cornstarch
Vegetable oil for deep-frying
Spicy Chicken Sauce (see recipe on page 21)

Garnish:
Sprouts or lettuce leaves

In a large bowl, mix together the soy sauce, white pepper, garlic, ginger, and sherry. Add the chicken to the soy sauce mixture and marinate for 1 hour. Mix together the flour, mochiko, and cornstarch. Remove the chicken from marinade and dredge in the flour mixture until coated, or shake the pieces in a plastic bag containing the flour mixture.

Heat 2½ to 3 inches of oil in a wok or a deep, heavy pot over medium-high heat until it registers 350°F to 375°F on a deep-fry thermometer. Add the chicken pieces a few at a time and fry for 3 to 4 minutes, or until golden brown. Do not drain the wingettes after frying; instead, lift them with tongs and place directly in the spicy chicken sauce for about a half minute. Remove and arrange on a serving platter over a bed of sprouts or lettuce leaves.

Spicy Chicken Sauce

(Makes 4 cups)

2 cups soy sauce

1 cup water

1 cup pineapple juice

1½ cups granulated sugar

1 cup minced scallions or green onions

1 teaspoon peeled and minced fresh ginger

1 tablespoon red chili pepper flakes

1 tablespoon sesame oil

In a large mixing bowl, combine all the ingredients and whisk until the sugar has completely dissolved. (You can make the sauce ahead of time, if you like.)

"Pau Hana" Hot Chicken with Cold Ginger Sauce

(Serves 4)

In Hawai'i, when you are done with work, it's "pau hana" time. Literally it translates to mean pau = finished, hana = work. For some people, it's the reason for the workday—a cold beer, some tasty pupus (appetizers), and a good talk-story session. The next time you and your co-workers get together for a pau hana party, take along this chicken treat. You can make it ahead of time and put the chicken in the microwave to heat it up before serving. If you don't have pau hana gatherings at your job, it may be time to start a new tradition.

> *2 cups water*
> *½ cup chopped fresh cilantro*
> *1-inch piece fresh ginger, peeled and crushed*
> *½ teaspoon salt*
> *6 boneless, skinless chicken breast halves*
> *Cold Ginger Sauce (see recipe on page 23)*

In a medium saucepan, combine the water, cilantro, ginger, and salt. Bring to a boil and add the chicken; reduce heat and simmer for 6 to 8 minutes, or until tender. Remove chicken from water. Cut into 1-inch strips and arrange on a platter. Top with cold ginger sauce.

Cold Ginger Sauce

(Makes ½ cup)

2 tablespoons granulated sugar

⅓ cup lemon juice

2 tablespoons soy sauce

1 tablespoon peeled and finely grated fresh ginger

3 tablespoons sherry

3 tablespoons chopped scallions or green onions

3 tablespoons chopped fresh cilantro

Mix sugar and lemon juice until sugar dissolves. Add soy sauce, ginger, sherry, green onion, and cilantro. Let stand for 1 hour, covered in refrigerator.

Hot, I Mean Hot, Miniature Beef Kabobs

(Serves 4)

The usual way of making kabobs is to string a bunch of vegetables and meat on a skewer, then cook them over hot coals. You can't really improve on something so simple and good. I like to make kabobs spicy, and cook them medium rare. But remember, you are the artist and can create whatever you like. A nice touch when you have guests over is to sear the kabobs right at the table on a hibachi.

Hot Kabob Marinade (see recipe on page 24)

20 ounces flank steak

1 pound mushrooms

2 onions

Teriyaki Glaze (see recipe on page 25)

Prepare the marinade, then thoroughly massage into the beef for 2 to 10 minutes. Let sit for 45 minutes to marinate. Cut the meat into ½-inch chunks.

 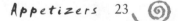

Remove mushroom stems from caps, clean the caps, and set aside. Cut the onions into ½-inch cubes, and set aside.

Alternately string chunks of beef and chunks of onion on bamboo skewers, starting and ending with a mushroom cap.

Grill each side for 2½ minutes (for medium-rare) over hot coals or on a flat-top grill. Serve with teriyaki glaze.

Hot Kabob Marinade

(Makes 2 cups)

½ cup soy sauce

½ cup salad oil

½ teaspoon sesame oil

2 tablespoons dry roasted sesame seeds

2 tablespoons brown sugar

1 tablespoon minced fresh cilantro

1 tablespoon minced fresh garlic

1 tablespoon peeled and minced fresh ginger

¼ teaspoon white pepper

1 teaspoon red chili pepper flakes, or 2 small fresh
    hot peppers, minced

Combine all ingredients in a glass bowl and mix well.

Teriyaki Glaze

(Makes 1 cup)

1 cup soy sauce
½ cup mirin (Japanese sweet rice wine)
½ cup water
¼ cup packed brown sugar
1½ teaspoons peeled and minced fresh garlic
1½ teaspoons peeled and minced fresh ginger
1 tablespoon cornstarch
2 tablespoons water

In a small saucepan, combine all ingredients except cornstarch and water and bring to a boil. Blend cornstarch and water to make a smooth paste, then add to mixture in pan. Reduce heat and simmer, stirring frequently, until thickened.

Sam's Coconut Sweet Pork

(Serves 6 to 8)

Because of my Asian background, I like to marinate meat so that a nice flavor is embedded in it. And because of my Hawaiian roots, I like to use Island fruit in my recipes. This dish represents influences from both sides of my heritage—Chinese sweet pork and Hawaiian coconut—combining them in a beautiful blend of flavors, while at the same time keeping it simple.

¼ cup rock or kosher salt
½ cup plus 2 tablespoons soy sauce
¾ cup minced fresh garlic
1 tablespoon peeled and minced fresh ginger
1 whole pork butt (3 to 4 pounds), deboned, cut into strips
*   1 inch thick, 2 inches wide, and about 5 inches long*
2 cups packed brown sugar
2 tablespoons light salad oil
½ cup coconut syrup
Hot Mustard Dip (see recipe on page 27)

Garnish:
1 to 2 cups shredded cabbage

Combine rock salt, 2 tablespoons of soy sauce, garlic, and ginger. Massage mixture into the meat for 5 to 10 minutes. Refrigerate for 3 to 4 hours.

Remove pork from refrigerator. Blend brown sugar with ½ cup of soy sauce and pour over the pork. Massage again for another 5 to 10 minutes. Return to the refrigerator and let marinate overnight.

The next day, in a small mixing bowl, combine salad oil with coconut syrup and set aside.

Preheat the oven to 350°F. Place a rack in a roasting pan and arrange the strips of marinated sweet pork on it. Bake for 30 minutes at 350°F. Reduce heat to 250°F and bake for 1 hour, or until pork is done. It is very important to cook pork well, so when you think it's done, slice the thickest piece and make sure no pink juice runs out.

Using a pastry brush, baste the meat three times with the oil-coconut syrup mixture during the last hour.

This can be served hot, warm, or cold, sliced thick or very thin (but it is easier to slice when it is cooled).

Serve on a bed of shredded cabbage with hot mustard dip.

Hot Mustard Dip

(Makes ¼ cup)

2 tablespoons hot mustard powder
1 tablespoon water
Soy sauce

Blend mustard powder and water, then add soy sauce until it reaches a nice dipping consistency.

"Catch of the Day" Crispy Seafood Basket

(Serves 12)

Wasabi, the Japanese version of horseradish, has an extremely strong, sharp flavor that causes unsuspecting people to gasp for water. If you happen to get too much wasabi in one mouthful, don't drink water—eat rice. The sugars in the rice will comfort your burning mouth and throat.

> 1 pound scallops
> 2 pounds clams, shelled
> 1 pound shrimp, shelled and deveined
> Tempura Batter (see recipe on page 29)
> 4 cups panko (Japanese-style crispy bread crumbs) or
>   fine dry bread crumbs, or as needed
> 3 tablespoons minced fresh cilantro
> 1½ teaspoons whole celery seeds
> 1½ teaspoons chopped fresh thyme leaves or ¾ teaspoon dried
> Honey Wasabi Sauce (see recipe on page 29)
> 3 or more cups vegetable oil

Rinse the scallops and clams in cold water. Drain well, pat dry with paper towels, and set aside with the prepared shrimp.

Prepare tempura batter, and set aside. Toss together the bread crumbs, cilantro, celery seeds, and thyme in a 2-inch-deep pan to make the breading. Dip seafood into tempura batter; coat well. Let excess drip off, then coat with crumbs. Place breaded seafood on parchment-lined baking sheets sprinkled with crumbs. Cover lightly with waxed paper and refrigerate. Make honey wasabi sauce and set aside.

Heat 2½ to 3 inches of oil in a wok or a deep, heavy pot over medium-high heat until it registers 365°F to 370°F on a deep-fry thermometer. Add 4 or 5 pieces of seafood at a time and fry for 2 to 3 minutes or until golden brown; drain on paper towels. Allow the oil to return to 365°F before adding a new batch. Serve in a parchment-lined basket with honey wasabi sauce on the side.

Tempura Batter

(Makes about 2½ to 3 cups)

2 cups all-purpose flour
1 cup cornstarch
Salt and pepper
1 tablespoon baking powder
1 egg, beaten
1½ cups cold ale or beer

Combine dry ingredients, then add egg and ale. Whisk batter until smooth.

Honey Wasabi Sauce

(Makes 1 cup)

1 tablespoon wasabi paste (Japanese horseradish)
¼ cup honey
1 cup mayonnaise
3 tablespoons sour cream
Salt and pepper to taste

Combine all ingredients and mix well.

Deep-Fried Mahimahi Macadamia Nut Fingers

(Serves 8)

his elegant pupu (appetizer) features foods that capture the essence of the Islands—mahimahi, macadamia nuts, pineapple, papaya, even cane sugar. For best results, roast the macadamia nut bits on a dry baking sheet for 3 or 4 minutes in an oven preheated to 300°F.

3 pounds mahimahi (dolphinfish) fillets, cut into
    2 × 3-inch pieces
Seafood Soy Sauce Marinade (see recipe on page 31)
1½ cups macadamia nuts, minced
Vegetable oil for deep-frying
Tropical Marmalade (see recipe on page 31)

In a large mixing bowl, marinate the mahimahi "fingers" in the seafood soy sauce marinade for 10 minutes. Drain. Dip the fish pieces in macadamia nuts to coat.

In a wok or deep heavy kettle, heat 2½ to 3 inches of oil on medium-high heat until it registers 365°F on a deep-fry thermometer. Fry fish fingers a few at a time until golden. Drain briefly on paper towels and serve with tropical marmalade.

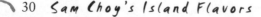

Seafood Soy Sauce Marinade

(Makes ½ cup)

2 eggs, beaten
1 green onion, minced
1 tablespoon peeled and minced fresh ginger
1 tablespoon soy sauce
1 teaspoon sherry
1 teaspoon granulated sugar
1 teaspoon cornstarch
Salt and white pepper to taste

Combine all ingredients.

Tropical Marmalade

(Makes about 1 cup)

2 cups diced fresh pineapple
3 cups diced fresh papaya
½ cup fresh cape gooseberries (ground cherries) (optional)
6 tablespoons granulated sugar, or to taste
Fresh mint or spearmint, chopped
⅛ teaspoon prepared horseradish or to taste (optional)

In a saucepan, combine all ingredients except the mint. Bring to a boil, then simmer—stirring every 5 minutes to avoid scorching—for 1 hour or until the mixture reaches jam consistency. Cool. Last, fold in the fresh mint to taste. Horseradish may be added if desired.

Poke Patties

(Serves 4)

The Hawaiian word poke (pronounced POE-kay) means to slice or cut crosswise into pieces. Poke is a dish of raw fish cut into cubes, marinated in a special sauce, and seared. It has become so popular that every year we sponsor the Sam Choy/Aloha Festivals International Poke Recipe Contest. We get hundreds of entries from all over the world. Poke is usually served raw. We sear the fish in this recipe, yet on the inside it's rare, with traditional poke-style seasoning.

> *Poke Patty Mixture (see recipe on page 33)*
> *Panko (Japanese-style crispy bread crumbs) or fine dry*
>   *Italian bread crumbs*
> *¼ cup canola oil*
> *Traditional Poke Seasoning Sauce (see recipe on page 33)*
>
> *Garnish:*
> *2 cups chopped cabbage*

Make poke patties and press in crumbs to coat. In a frying pan, heat the oil over medium-high heat. Gently place the patties in the pan and brown on both sides, keeping the inside of the patties medium rare.

To serve, arrange poke patties on a bed of chopped cabbage and drizzle with the seasoning sauce.

Poke Patty Mixture

(Makes 4 patties)

2 cups 'ahi (yellowfin tuna) or aku (skipjack tuna),
    cut into ¼- to ⅜-inch cubes (see page 11)
½ cup minced maui or globe onion
½ cup minced green onions
2 eggs
¼ cup chopped ogo seaweed (optional)
¼ cup soy sauce
2 teaspoons sesame oil
Salt and pepper to taste

Combine all ingredients and form into 4 patties.

Traditional Poke Seasoning Sauce

(Makes ½ cup)

½ cup sliced mushrooms
4 tablespoons (½ stick) butter
2 teaspoons soy sauce
2 teaspoons oyster sauce
1 teaspoon chopped fresh cilantro

Sauté mushrooms in butter for 2 minutes. Add the remaining sauce ingredients and cook for 1 minute.

Sam Choy's World-Famous Fried Marlin Poke

(Serves 4)

When I cook fish I do it Chinese-style, by searing it on high heat to seal in flavor and moisture; it's one of the secrets that make the fish I serve at my restaurants taste so good. You have to be careful when using this technique, though, because if you don't remove the fish quickly from the hot pan it will overcook. Basically, you just slap the fish in the pan, sizzle it on all sides, and remove. You need to add enough oil to coat the bottom of your wok or skillet so the fish won't stick, and heat the oil until it's almost smoking before you add the fish. I serve 1,000 pounds of this poke in my Kona restaurant each week, and I'm not kidding when I say it's world famous.

*1 pound marlin fillets (no other fish works as well in this recipe),
    cut into ¾-inch cubes (see pages 10– 11)*
4 teaspoons soy sauce
1 cup chopped globe onion
4 teaspoons chopped green onions
1 cup chopped ogo seaweed (optional)
4 teaspoons sesame oil
4 tablespoons vegetable oil, for searing

Garnish:
Bean sprouts
Chopped cabbage
Salad greens
Ogo seaweed

Place marlin cubes in a mixing bowl with the soy sauce, onions, ogo seaweed, and sesame oil. Mix well.

In a wok, heat the vegetable oil (or enough to cover the bottom of the pan) on high heat. Sear the marlin mixture while tossing. Don't cook for more than a minute or two, as you want the center raw.

Serve on a bed of bean sprouts, chopped cabbage, salad greens, or ogo seaweed.

Seafood-Stuffed Nori Fish Rolls with Tomato Lomi

(Serves 4)

*T*his appetizer is easy to make, but your guests will think you spent hours. The nori wrap makes it look kind of like sushi, but this is a cooked dish. The Tomato Lomi ("lomi" means to massage or mix) is like a very chunky salsa-type sauce. A little dollop goes a long way.

> *4 sheets nori (dried seaweed sheets)*
> *8 (¼-inch-thin) horizontal slices of firm, white-meat fish fillets of*
> *   your choice (onaga or red snapper, ono or mackerel)*
> *Seafood Stuffing (see recipe on page 36)*
> *½ cup all-purpose flour*
> *2 eggs, for egg wash*
> *3 cups panko (Japanese-style crispy bread crumbs) or*
> *   fine dry bread crumbs*
> *Vegetable oil for deep-frying*
> *Tomato Lomi (see recipe on page 36)*
> *Spicy Citrus Dressing (see recipe on page 37)*

Lay a sheet of nori on a flat surface (preferably a bamboo mat). Place a slice of fish on the nori (skin side down) and spread the fish with ¼ of the seafood stuffing. Top with another slice of fish (skin side up) and roll up tightly. Repeat with the remaining fish and stuffing.

Put the flour in a shallow bowl. Beat the eggs with 1 tablespoon of water in another shallow bowl. Put the bread crumbs in a third bowl.

Dust the nori-wrapped stuffed fillets with flour, then dip them in the egg wash. Roll in the bread crumbs. Wrap each roll tightly in plastic wrap and place in the refrigerator for at least 1 hour to firm.

Heat 2 to 3 inches of oil in a wok or a deep, heavy pot over medium-high heat until it registers 365°F on a deep-fry thermometer. Fry the fish rolls in two batches for 4 or 5 minutes, until golden brown; drain on paper towels.

Slice the rolls in half crosswise, then slice each half into 4 pieces. Arrange on a platter; serve with a bowl of tomato lomi and a bowl of spicy citrus dressing.

Seafood Stuffing

(Makes about 4 cups)

2 tablespoons butter
¼ cup minced globe onion
¼ cup minced celery
½ teaspoon minced garlic
¾ cup shrimp meat, finely chopped
¾ cup scallops, finely chopped
½ cup crabmeat, finely chopped (imitation crabmeat can be used)
½ teaspoon paprika
¼ cup all-purpose flour
¼ cup heavy cream
Salt and pepper to taste

Heat the butter in a frying pan. Sauté the onion, celery, and garlic. Add the seafood and paprika, and mix. Add flour and blend. Last, pour in heavy cream, and cook for 3 to 5 minutes, stirring constantly. Add salt and pepper to taste. Let cool before using.

Tomato Lomi

(Makes about 1 cup)

½ medium onion, cut into ¼-inch dice
3 medium tomatoes, cut into ¼-inch dice
¼ cup chopped green onions
1 tablespoon chopped fresh cilantro
½ teaspoon minced fresh garlic
Salt to taste
¼ teaspoon red chili pepper flakes
Juice of 1 lemon

Mix all ingredients together. Chill for 1 hour.

Spicy Citrus Dressing

(Makes 1½ cups)

½ cup soy sauce
½ cup cider vinegar
½ cup orange juice
2 tablespoons sesame oil
½ cup granulated sugar
1 teaspoon red chili pepper flakes
Salt and pepper to taste

Mix ingredients together until sugar is dissolved.

Furikake-Crusted Sashimi

(Serves 4)

Sashimi, brought to Hawai'i by Japanese immigrants, are extra-thin slices of raw tuna, sea bass, halibut, or other fish arranged atop shredded carrot and snowy daikon, and served with a wasabi paste. This simple dish has crossed all cultural boundaries, and is served throughout the state at parties, neighborhood gatherings, office functions, and everywhere people are having a great time.

1 tablespoon wasabi paste (Japanese horseradish)
2 tablespoons soy sauce
2 pounds 'ahi (yellowfin tuna) or swordfish fillets,
    cut into 2 × 2-inch squares (see pages 10–11)
¼ cup furikake (dried seaweed flakes and sesame seeds) or
    sesame seeds
Sweet-and-Sour Cucumber Vinaigrette (see recipe on page 39)

Garnish:

Organic field greens

In a small bowl, combine the wasabi and soy sauce. Marinate the fish in this mixture for 30 minutes. Roll the fish in furikake. Heat a heavy skillet until very hot, coat with cooking oil spray, and quickly sear the fish for about 15 to 30 seconds on each side. Slice sashimi-style (in ¼-inch-thin strips).

Arrange sashimi on a bed of fresh field greens and drizzle with some of the cucumber vinaigrette.

Sweet-and-Sour Cucumber Vinaigrette

(Makes 2 cups)

1 cup white wine vinegar
½ cup water
¾ cup granulated sugar
Pinch of salt
1 cup grated cucumbers
½ tablespoon peeled and grated fresh ginger

Blend all ingredients until sugar dissolves. Chill.

Ginger-Marinated Seared Sashimi

(Serves 4 to 6)

I've given this classic Japanese sashimi dish a "Choy" twist. Some of my restaurant customers didn't appreciate the texture of raw fish, so I decided to marinate, then sear the sashimi. At first it was a way to introduce a dish I love, and then it turned out to be a whole new style of preparation.

> *2 pounds 'ahi (yellowfin tuna) or swordfish, cut into*
> * 2 × 2-inch squares (see pages 10–11)*
> *Ginger Marinade (see recipe below)*
> *Spicy Sashimi Dipping Sauce (see recipe on page 41)*
>
> *Garnish:*
> *Shredded cabbage (won bok, head cabbage, or*
> * red cabbage) or sprouts*
> *2 teaspoons black goma (black sesame seeds)*

Marinate 'ahi in the ginger marinade for 45 minutes to 1 hour. After marinating, place fish on a hot hibachi or barbecue grill, searing very quickly (about 10 seconds, or less) on all sides. Slice fish as thick or as thin as you like, then arrange on an appetizer platter over a bed of shredded cabbage or your favorite sprouts. Garnish with black sesame seeds, and serve with the dipping sauce.

Ginger Marinade

(Makes ½ cup)

> *2 teaspoons peeled and minced fresh ginger*
> *½ cup soy sauce*
> *1 tablespoon brown sugar*
> *½ teaspoon sesame oil*
> *2 hot chili peppers, finely minced*

Combine ingredients and stir until sugar is dissolved.

Spicy Sashimi Dipping Sauce
(Makes 1½ cups)

¼ cup peeled and minced fresh ginger
½ cup chopped fresh cilantro
¼ cup minced green onions
2 cloves fresh garlic, minced
½ cup light salad oil
1 teaspoon red chili flakes
Salt and white pepper to taste

Process ingredients in a blender for 30 seconds, then adjust seasoning with salt and white pepper. (Do not substitute black pepper.) Pour into serving bowls or small individual dipping containers.

Ono Carpaccio with Hot Ginger-Pepper Oil
(Serves 4)

*T*his recipe developed when I tried to spice up some sashimi. The combination had a sweet, fresh medley of flavors. Then I said it needed a kick, so I poured spicy oil on top. Ho! It's a *winner*!

1-pound block very fresh ono (wahoo) fillet (see page 12)
Hot Ginger-Pepper Oil (see recipe on page 42)

Garnish:
1½ cups raw vegetables (cabbage, carrot, jicama, or beet),
  finely shredded

Cut the raw fish into 2½ × 1¾-inch strips that are about ¼ inch thick.
Arrange raw ono slices on a small platter over a bed of shredded vegetables. Spoon hot ginger-pepper oil over the fish.

Hot Ginger-Pepper Oil

(Makes ¾ cup)

¾ cup canola oil

¼ cup peeled and minced fresh ginger

¼ cup minced shallots or green onion

¼ cup lightly packed minced fresh cilantro

½ teaspoon red chili pepper flakes

¼ teaspoon salt

⅛ teaspoon white pepper

Heat the oil in a small saucepan. Stir in ginger, shallots, cilantro, chili pepper flakes, salt, and white pepper. Strain. Serve hot.

'Ahi Cakes with Wasabi Aioli

(Serves 2)

You can use these tuna cakes in a number of ways once they're cooked. They are wonderful in sandwiches, as party finger food, or as the grand topping for a cool summer salad.

1 (8-ounce) 'ahi (yellowfin tuna) fillet, minced

2 tablespoons mayonnaise

1 tablespoon chopped green onion

1 tablespoon chopped ogo seaweed (optional)

1 tablespoon soy sauce

1 teaspoon sesame oil

2 tablespoons panko (Japanese-style crispy bread crumbs) or fine dry bread crumbs

1 tablespoon chopped fresh dill

2 tablespoons all-purpose flour

2 tablespoons light olive oil
1 cup Wasabi Aioli (see recipe below)

Garnish:
1 cup mixed salad greens

Mix 'ahi, mayonnaise, green onion, ogo, soy sauce, sesame oil, panko, and dill. Shape mixture into 4 small cakes. Dust with flour. Heat olive oil in a skillet and sauté the cakes about 2 minutes on each side, until golden brown. Place on a platter garnished with salad greens, and drizzle with wasabi aioli.

Wasabi Aioli

(Makes 1 cup)

2 tablespoons wasabi paste (Japanese horseradish)
1 cup mayonnaise
1 tablespoon light olive oil
Salt and pepper to taste

Whisk all ingredients together.

'Ahi and Shrimp Candy

(Makes 6 skewers)

You can substitute swordfish, marlin, or any other tuna for the 'ahi in this recipe. The marinade has a distinctive Asian flavor. Soak the large 'ahi cubes and shrimp in the thick mixture, then sear quickly. It will give the outside a golden, caramelized sugar-shoyu crust.

> 6 whole jumbo shrimp (16 to 20 count), shelled and deveined
> 6 'ahi (yellowfin tuna) blocks, 3 ounces each
> Five-Spice Marinade (see recipe below)

On each of 6 thin sticks or skewers (bamboo, chopsticks, carrot sticks, or other vegetable sticks), thread 1 shrimp and 1 'ahi block. Marinate skewered seafood in five-spice marinade for 30 minutes. Grill over hot coals until done, about 4 to 5 minutes. Remove shells before serving.

Five-Spice Marinade

(Makes 2¾ cups)

> 1½ cups packed brown sugar
> ½ cup soy sauce
> 3 tablespoons chopped green onions
> 2 tablespoons peeled and chopped fresh ginger
> ½ teaspoon sesame oil
> ⅛ teaspoon Chinese five-spice powder

Combine all ingredients.

Coconut MacNut Shrimp with Guava Sweet & Sour Sauce

(Serves 4)

I love dishes that successfully blend a variety of textures, flavors, and aromas. This one's a real winner. Adding the coconut flakes makes all the difference. They crisp up into spiny-looking prongs that crackle when you bite into them.

24 extra-large shrimp (21 to 25 count)
⅓ cup all-purpose flour
3 eggs
1 cup coconut flakes
1 cup toasted macadamia nuts, crushed
1½ cups panko (Japanese-style crispy bread crumbs) or
  fine dry bread crumbs
4 cups vegetable oil
Sam Choy's Guava Sweet & Sour Sauce (see recipe on page 46)

Shell and devein the shrimp and pat them dry with paper towels. Put the flour in a shallow bowl. Beat the eggs in another shallow bowl. Mix the coconut flakes, macadamia nuts, and bread crumbs together in a third bowl.

Dust the shrimp with flour, shaking off excess, then dip them in beaten egg. Roll them in the coconut–macnut mixture. Let stand on a rack until all are breaded. Meanwhile, heat 2½ to 3 inches of oil in a wok or a deep, heavy pot over medium-high heat until it registers 365°F on a deep-fry thermometer.

Fry the shrimp, 4 or 5 at a time, for about 3 minutes or until golden brown; drain on paper towels. Allow the oil to return to 365°F before adding a new batch.

Serve with the guava sweet & sour sauce.

Sam Choy's Guava Sweet & Sour Sauce

(Makes 3 cups)

½ cup ketchup
½ cup white wine vinegar
½ cup water
2 teaspoons soy sauce
½ cup granulated sugar
¼ cup frozen guava concentrate, undiluted
1½ teaspoons minced fresh garlic
¼ teaspoon hot pepper sauce
¼ cup pineapple juice
¼ cup cornstarch mixed with 3 tablespoons water, for thickening

In a medium saucepan, combine all ingredients except cornstarch mixture. Blend well, bring to a boil, then add cornstarch mixture. Reduce heat and simmer, stirring frequently, until thickened.

Steamed "'Onolicious" Shrimp

(Serves 3 to 4)

T he type of steamer you use doesn't really matter. It's the steam and/or the liquid in the pot that does the cooking. If you don't have a steamer, you can remove the tops and bottoms of three or four tuna (or similar-sized) cans, arrange them on the bottom of a large saucepan with a tight-fitting cover, and place a rack or heatproof plate on top of the cans. Pour about 1 inch of water into the pan, cover, bring to a boil, and you're in business.

> *12 extra-large shrimp (21 to 25 count)*
> *¼ cup sherry*
> *Salt and white pepper to taste*
> *1 egg, beaten*
> *1 teaspoon cornstarch*
> *½ cup diced smoked ham*
> *½ cup minced green onions*
> *1 tablespoon peeled and minced fresh ginger*
> *2 tablespoons minced globe onion*
> *½ teaspoon granulated sugar*

Shell and devein the shrimp. Place in a bowl with the sherry, salt, and pepper and marinate them for 1 hour. Discard the marinade. Add the egg and 1 teaspoon cornstarch to the shrimp and stir to coat. Arrange the shrimp in a dish, place the dish in a steamer, and sprinkle with ham, green onions, ginger, and onion. Season with sugar and steam until the shrimp are pink (6 to 8 minutes).

Wok-Barbecued Shrimp with Pepper-Papaya-Pineapple Chutney

(Serves 4)

I "fire up" my wok-cooked shrimp by marinating them in the zesty flavors of fresh ginger and Asian chilies. Pour the stir-fried shrimp over a bed of hot rice with the spicy chutney on the side for dipping. The exotic flavors are a crowd pleaser every time.

> 1 pound jumbo shrimp (16 to 20 count)
> Wok Barbecue Marinade (see recipe below)
> 1½ tablespoons canola oil
> Pepper-Papaya-Pineapple Chutney (see recipe on page 49)

To prepare shrimp, shell and devein them but leave the tails attached. Marinate them in the wok barbecue marinade for 30 minutes. In a wok, heat the oil and stir-fry the shrimp over high heat for 4 to 5 minutes. Do not overcook. Serve with pepper papaya-pineapple chutney.

Wok Barbecue Marinade

(Makes 1 cup)

¼ cup canola oil

2 tablespoons soy sauce

2 tablespoons peeled and minced fresh ginger

2 tablespoons chopped fresh cilantro

1 tablespoon minced fresh garlic

½ teaspoon granulated sugar

1 chili pepper, seeded and chopped (or ⅛ teaspoon red
    chili pepper flakes)

Combine ingredients and mix well.

Pepper-Papaya-Pineapple Chutney

(Makes 1½ cups)

1 small fresh pineapple, peeled, cored, and chopped
1 medium fresh papaya, seeded, peeled, and chopped
1 tablespoon peeled and minced fresh ginger
6 tablespoons granulated sugar
1 tablespoon hot Asian chili paste, such as sambal oelek

In a medium saucepan, combine all the ingredients except the chili paste. Cook uncovered over medium heat for 1 hour or until the mixture has a syrupy consistency. Fold in the chili paste.

Chinese Scallops with Chili-Ginger Oil and Black Beans

(Serves 4)

Hot, spicy chili-ginger oil really brings out the flavor of these large scallops. The stir-fried vegetables and black beans give the dish a real Chinese flair. And as a bonus, it's a colorful dish that tastes as good as it looks.

2 tablespoons peanut oil
½ cup peeled and thinly sliced fresh ginger
1 pound sea scallops
3 tablespoons preserved black beans, rinsed well
½ large red bell pepper, cut into julienne
½ large yellow bell pepper, cut into julienne
Chili-Ginger Oil (see recipe on page 50)

Garnish:
2 cups fresh spinach leaves, rinsed and dried

Heat peanut oil in a wok over moderate heat. Add the ginger and scallops. Cook for 2 minutes, stirring constantly. Add the black beans and bell peppers. Cook for 1 more minute, stirring constantly. Remove the scallop mixture from the heat and arrange on fresh spinach leaves. Drizzle with the chili-ginger oil. Serve immediately.

Chili-Ginger Oil

(Makes 1½ cups)

½ cup peanut oil
4 fresh hot chili peppers, split and chopped
½ cup peeled and minced fresh ginger
2 cloves fresh garlic, thinly sliced
2 tablespoons sesame oil
2 tablespoons soy sauce

Heat peanut oil in a wok over moderate heat. Add the chilies, ginger, and garlic. Stir constantly for 2 minutes. (It will sizzle, so be careful.) Add the sesame oil and soy sauce, and cook for 2 more minutes. Remove from the heat, cool slightly, and strain.

Kilauea Oysters

(Serves 4)

I developed this recipe for some friends who loved the idea of eating oysters but couldn't stand the raw food part of the equation. The bacon gives the baked oysters a smoked flavor. You really should try this one. Serve it with chili pepper water, or just enjoy it alone.

> *2 pounds rock or kosher salt*
> *6 thick slices bacon, diced*
> *2 cloves fresh garlic, minced*
> *¼ cup minced green bell pepper*
> *¼ cup minced red bell pepper*
> *12 oysters on the half shell*

Preheat the oven to 425°F. Make a bed of rock salt in an ovenproof baking dish. Place in the oven and heat for 15 minutes.

Meanwhile, sauté the bacon in a dry skillet until crisp. Remove the bacon to drain on paper towels; pour off all but 2 tablespoons of bacon fat. Sauté the garlic and bell peppers for 5 minutes or until peppers are tender. Combine the bacon with the bell pepper mixture.

Arrange the oysters in their shells in the bed of hot salt, pushing shells down slightly to keep them from tipping. Cover each oyster with some of the bacon-pepper mixture. Return to the oven and bake for 7 minutes. Serve immediately.

 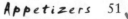

Breaded Oysters with Wasabi Cocktail Sauce

(Serves 4)

*U*sing Pacific or Japanese oysters from the West Coast makes this appetizer perfect for people who aren't crazy about oysters. Their mild flavor fades a little more when they're breaded, and the wasabi sauce provides a spicy punch. Pick any kind of oyster. The recipe works with them all.

> *12 oysters, shucked*
> *⅓ cup all-purpose flour*
> *Salt and pepper to taste*
> *2 eggs*
> *1½ cups panko (Japanese-style crispy bread crumbs) or*
>   *fine dry bread crumbs*
> *2 cups or more vegetable oil*
> *Wasabi Cocktail Sauce (see recipe on page 53)*

Drain the oysters of their liquid and lay them on paper towels to dry. Mix the flour, salt, and pepper in a shallow bowl. Beat the eggs in another shallow bowl and put the bread crumbs in a third bowl.

Coat the oysters with flour, shaking off excess, then dip them in beaten egg and roll them in bread crumbs. Let stand on a rack until all are coated. Meanwhile, heat 2½ to 3 inches of oil in a wok or deep, heavy pot over medium-high heat until it registers 365°F on a deep-fry thermometer.

Fry the oysters a few at a time for 2 or 3 minutes or until golden brown; drain on paper towels. Allow the oil to return to 365°F before adding a new batch. Serve hot with wasabi cocktail sauce.

Wasabi Cocktail Sauce

(Makes ¾ cup)

1½ tablespoons wasabi paste (Japanese horseradish)
2 teaspoons water
2 teaspoons soy sauce
½ cup ketchup
Salt and pepper to taste

Mix all ingredients.

Salads

*T*he growers who give us Hawai'i's incomparable vegetables and fruits are really an underappreciated group of people. They have done a tremendous job in making diversified tropical agriculture a quality industry in the Islands.

I remember when I first talked to farmer Ben of Kohala and he asked, "How many sugar peas do you use?"

I said, "Well, I can use close to a hundred pounds a week."

He said, "Oh, only a hundred pounds? That's all?"

"Yes."

"Oh, we can grow that."

Well, Ben wasn't used to growing sugar peas, and halfway through the crop I got a call. Ben said, "Ho, man, it's hard work, you know. Picking is a killer. It's never ending. Every second they're blooming and we have to pick."

It's true, you can't let the peas grow too big because they get tough. But Ben steadily supplies my Kona restaurant with one hundred pounds of tender pods each week.

Traditionally, Hawaiians didn't have the luxury of eating meals in courses. All foods, mainly starches and protein, were eaten simultaneously. Greens, like laulau (taro leaves), were usually mixed in and cooked with meat dishes (fish, chicken, or wild boar). Salads were introduced much later, when Europeans arrived.

Today in Hawai'i, like everywhere else in the United States, salads are served either as entrees or as side dishes.

I throw everything I can think of into my entree salads. I layer them, toss them, or arrange them. To me a bed of lettuce, no matter how exotic, seems empty, like a dark house when nobody's home. It's just waiting for something to brighten it up. So I'll sauté mahimahi that's been encrusted with macadamia nuts or lemon pepper, or I'll poach, charbroil, marinate, or grill fish, chicken, or tofu—anything to dress up the greens and turn the salad into a meal. I've even added somen noodles for an Asian flare—and, to be a little festive, I've used flour tortillas deep-fried into the shape of a salad bowl.

The side salads are just as much fun—portobello mushrooms, tropical fruit slaw, Pacific seafood pasta, or shrimp-stuffed avocado.

Make several of these entree and side salads to get the hang of the seasoning style and flavor blending, then get daring. Don't be timid. Just let it rip. You'll discover you can create some of the most colorful and tantalizing salad sensations ever.

Lasagne-Style Hibachi Tofu Salad

(Serves 2)

came up with this as a different way to serve tofu. It's unique, but simple, and people really enjoy it. Stacking it seemed like something interesting to do, and the marinade gives it a lot of flavor. This is a fun salad that has nothing to do with lasagne, other than using tofu in a lasagne-like layered fashion.

1 package firm tofu
Tofu Marinade (see recipe on page 58)
5 tablespoons olive oil
½ cup julienned zucchini
½ cup julienned carrot
½ cup julienned red bell pepper
½ cup julienned yellow bell pepper
½ cup bean sprouts
½ cup sliced shiitake mushrooms
Salt and pepper to taste
1 to 2 cups mixed greens
Wasabi Vinaigrette (see recipe on pages 58–59)
    (optional)
Sam Choy's Original Asian Creamy Dressing
    (see recipe on page 59) (optional)

Garnish:

Ginger Pesto (see recipe on page 59)

Drain tofu, and slice the whole block lengthwise into 3 equal sections, then soak in the tofu marinade for 1 to 2 hours. Prepare coals in hibachi.

 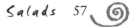

In a wok or sauté pan, heat 4 tablespoons of the olive oil until very hot but not smoking. Add vegetables, bean sprouts, and mushrooms, and stir-fry for 2 to 3 minutes, just until wilted. Season with salt and pepper. Add the greens, cook another minute, and remove quickly from the wok.

Remove tofu from the marinade, cook on the hibachi over hot coals for about 2 to 3 minutes on each side, then remove from the heat.

Place a small amount of stir-fried vegetables on a salad plate, put 1 slice of tofu on top of the vegetables, then a layer of vegetables on the tofu, and drizzle with either the wasabi vinaigrette or the Asian creamy dressing, or both. Continue alternating tofu, vegetables, and dressing until you finish with a layer of vegetables on top.

Garnish with ginger pesto.

Tofu Marinade

(Makes 2½ cups)

2 cloves fresh garlic, minced
1½ cups soy sauce
1 cup granulated sugar
¼ cup peeled and minced fresh ginger
2 tablespoons thinly sliced green onion
1 tablespoon chopped fresh cilantro
1 teaspoon sesame oil
⅛ teaspoon white pepper

Combine all ingredients.

Wasabi Vinaigrette

(Makes 3 cups)

2 cups orange juice, freshly squeezed
2 tablespoons sesame seeds
3 tablespoons granulated sugar
½ cup light salad oil

3 tablespoons vinegar
2 tablespoons soy sauce
2 tablespoons wasabi paste (Japanese horseradish)
Salt to taste

Mix all ingredients together and blend well.

Sam Choy's Original Asian Creamy Dressing

(Makes 4 cups)

3 cups mayonnaise
½ cup soy sauce
¾ cup granulated sugar
¼ teaspoon white pepper
1½ tablespoons black goma (black sesame seeds)
1 tablespoon sesame oil
2 tablespoons water (to adjust thickness)

Whisk all ingredients together until well blended. If it's too thick, you can whisk in a little water, a few drops at a time, until you get the consistency you like.

Ginger Pesto

(Makes ¾ cup)

½ cup light olive oil
½ teaspoon salt
¼ cup peeled and minced fresh ginger
¼ cup minced green onions
¼ cup lightly packed minced fresh cilantro
⅛ teaspoon white pepper

In a small saucepan, heat the oil, add the salt, and cook for 2 to 3 minutes. Cool. Stir in ginger, green onions, cilantro, and white pepper.

 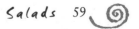

Asian Macadamia Chicken Salad with Fried Noodles

(Serves 4)

Take a piece of chicken, marinate it, fry it, then serve it with fried noodles on mixed salad greens, and you'll have a surprisingly elegant, simple-to-prepare, very satisfying salad. You can serve this with your choice of dressing. I especially like the Sweet-and-Sour Cucumber Vinaigrette (see page 39).

4 boneless chicken breast halves (skin left on), 8 ounces each
Asian Chicken Marinade (see recipe on page 61)
2 cups oil, for deep-frying
1-ounce package rice noodles
12 wonton wrappers
1 medium head iceberg lettuce, shredded
2 cups won bok (Chinese cabbage) or napa cabbage, finely chopped
1 cup bean sprouts
1 cup thin julienned red bell pepper
1 cup thin julienned yellow bell pepper
½ cup thinly sliced (diagonally) green onions
1 medium carrot, grated
6 radishes, thinly sliced
1 cup whole macadamia nuts
Sweet-and-Sour Cucumber Vinaigrette (see recipe on page 39) (optional)

Garnish:
1 head leaf lettuce, leaves separated, for salad bed
4 sprigs cilantro, coarsely chopped

Cover the chicken with the marinade, and refrigerate for 1 to 2 hours.

Heat the oil in a wok until hot but not smoking (350°F on a deep-fry thermometer). Drop in the rice noodles and remove as soon as they puff up. (Don't brown them.) Drain on paper towels and break into bite-sized pieces when cool. Set aside.

Cut the wonton wrappers into strips and deep-fry them until golden brown in the same oil you used for the noodles. Drain on paper towels and set aside.

As soon as everything else is done, and the iceberg lettuce and other vegetables are sliced, chopped, and refrigerated, you can cook the chicken. Fry breasts (skins on) in 2 tablespoons of oil until they are golden brown. Start on high heat, then finish on medium. After you turn the heat down, you can baste the chicken with marinade. Continue basting, using about ½ cup of marinade in all, until the liquid is absorbed and chicken is nicely browned. When done, let cool to room temperature and cut into strips.

Toss shredded lettuce, cabbage, bean sprouts, and remaining vegetables together with the chicken and bite-sized pieces of rice noodles in a mixing bowl. Add half the macadamia nuts and half the fried wonton strips, and toss with the salad, reserving remaining nuts and wonton strips for garnish.

Arrange a bed of your favorite leaf lettuce on individual salad plates. Use ¼ of the remaining macadamia nuts, ¼ of the remaining wonton strips, and a sprig of cilantro to garnish each salad.

Asian Chicken Marinade

(Makes 2¾ cups)

¼ cup cornstarch
1 tablespoon brown sugar
1 cup soy sauce
1 cup salad oil
¼ cup mirin (Japanese sweet rice wine)
1 teaspoon sesame oil
¼ cup minced fresh cilantro
2 tablespoons minced fresh garlic
2 tablespoons peeled and minced fresh ginger
1 teaspoon salt
½ teaspoon white pepper
2 tablespoons thinly sliced green onion

Blend the cornstarch and brown sugar and set aside. Mix together all other marinade ingredients. Slowly add the cornstarch mixture to the marinade, whisking constantly to prevent lumps.

Sunshine Salad with Broiled Garlic Chicken Breast

(Serves 1)

In Asia, people like the dark meat of the chicken better than the white; they consider it more moist and flavorful. In America, people seem to like the white meat better. To me, chicken breast can be kind of dry and boring, so I like to come up with ways to make it more interesting. I find that marinating it in garlic gives it a lot of flavor and seals in the juices.

> 1 boneless chicken breast half, about 8 ounces (with or without skin)
> Garlic Chicken Marinade (see recipe on page 63)
> 1 navel orange, peeled and segmented
> 1 medium tangerine, peeled and segmented
> ½ fresh papaya, diced
> ½ cup diced fresh mango or fresh pineapple
> 1 or 2 handfuls of mixed greens
> Sam Choy's Original Asian Creamy Dressing (see recipe on page 59)

> *Garnish:*
> A few edible flowers

Place the chicken in the marinade, cover, and refrigerate for 1 day. Mix the fruits together and chill.

In a mixing bowl, toss the salad greens and fruit with enough creamy dressing to coat them.

Grill or broil the chicken breast, slice into strips, and place them—while still warm—on top of the salad, skin side up.

Garnish with edible nasturtiums and orchids, other edible flowers, or a colorful garnish of your choice.

Garlic Chicken Marinade

(Makes 1 cup)

1 tablespoon minced fresh garlic
½ teaspoon salt
3 tablespoons sweet vermouth
3 tablespoons olive oil
1 teaspoon cracked peppercorns
1 teaspoon chopped fresh cilantro
1 tablespoon thinly sliced green onion

Mix all ingredients.

"Wow the Neighbors" Seafood Salad

(Serves 8)

*T*his recipe is loaded—shrimp, the kitchen sink. There is no way this is a side salad. It's a full-sized *meal*. I'll guarantee that when you take this to a gathering with the neighbors or friends, your generosity will shine through. They'll look in the salad bowl, and say, "Wow!" That's always the reaction I get with this dish. It's just sharing and caring, Hawai'i style.

Poaching Liquid (see recipe on page 65)
10 to 12 extra-large shrimp (21 to 25 count), peeled and deveined
10 ounces opah (moonfish) fillets, cubed
½ pound scallops
12 green-tip mussels, well scrubbed and debearded
½ pound fusilli (spiral pasta)
2 tablespoons olive oil
1 cup chopped radicchio
1 cup oyster mushrooms, cut in half
½ cup fresh shiitake mushrooms, sliced
½ cup julienned red bell pepper
½ cup julienned yellow bell pepper
½ cup chopped fresh basil leaves
4 ounces smoked Pacific salmon, cut into 1-inch cubes
¼ teaspoon minced fresh dill
Dill Vinaigrette (see recipe on page 66)

Prepare the poaching liquid and bring to a boil in a large saucepan. Add the shrimp and return liquid to a boil; then remove shrimp with a slotted spoon to a plate.

Return the liquid to a boil and add the opah, scallops, and mussels. As soon as the mussel shells open, remove the pot from the heat and transfer the seafood to the plate with shrimp; cool.

Cook the fusilli according to package directions, drain, and toss with olive oil. In a large bowl, combine the radicchio, mushrooms, julienned peppers, basil, smoked salmon, and dill. Add the fusilli and seafood. Toss lightly with the vinaigrette. Chill until serving time.

Note: To prepare live mussels, soak them in a full sink of cold water. Periodically agitate the water. (Live mussels open and close to breathe. Any mussels that don't eventually close are dead, and should be discarded.) Scrub, debeard the mussels, and wash in several changes of cold water until the water runs clear.

Poaching Liquid
(Makes 4½ cups)

3 cups water
1 cup white wine
1 cup diced celery
¼ cup diced onion
¼ cup diced carrot
Juice of 1 large orange
1½ teaspoons salt
¼ teaspoon cracked pepper
1 whole bay leaf
1 sprig fresh dill
Pinch of thyme

In a stockpot, combine all ingredients.

Dill Vinaigrette

(Makes 1¼ cups)

¼ cup mirin (Japanese sweet rice wine)
¼ cup fresh dill
2 tablespoons granulated sugar
1½ tablespoons sweet onion
2 garlic cloves
¾ cup olive oil
Salt and white pepper to taste

Machine process all the ingredients except the oil. With the food processor or blender running, add oil in a slow steady stream until the dressing is thickened. Salt and pepper to taste.

New Wave Marinated 'Ahi Salad

(Serves 1)

I call this type of dish a wok salad. It combines Chinese stir-fry cooking with fresh lettuces and greens, and provides an interesting contrast in tastes and textures—chilled greens, cold noodles, and warm fish. You can make it low-cal by omitting the deep-fried tortilla and the oil used in the marinade, and by using a low-fat dressing.

1 'ahi (yellowfin tuna) fillet, 6-ounces, about ½ inch thick,
  cut crosswise into thirds
New Wave Marinade (see recipe on page 68)
2 to 3 ounces Japanese soba noodles, or somen
1 flour tortilla

1 tablespoon olive oil for searing fish, or enough to
    coat bottom of pan
Salad greens, a handful or two
Sam Choy's Original Asian Creamy Dressing (see
    recipe on page 59) (optional)

Garnish:
Carrot, beet, and radish curls, or grated carrots and zucchini
1 or 2 sprigs of cilantro
Sprinkle of black goma (black sesame seeds), chopped
    macadamia nuts, or chopped walnuts
3 cucumber slices
3 tomato slices

Place the fish in the marinade for 5 minutes or less, then remove and set aside.

Cook the soba noodles according to package directions, rinse well in cold water, and drain. Take the 2 tablespoons of marinade you set aside and mix with noodles. Chill noodles in the refrigerator for 20 to 30 minutes.

Have everything ready to go before you cook the 'ahi, so that the fish will be hot when you serve it. Also, wait until the last minute before placing the greens and noodles on the tortilla, or it will become soggy.

Sear the marinated 'ahi over high heat on a flat griddle, or in a sauté pan in olive oil for about 1 minute on each side. (You want the fish to remain raw in the middle.)

Deep-fry the flour tortilla to golden brown and place on a salad plate. Arrange 1 to 2 handfuls of your favorite greens broken into bite-sized pieces (I like using a variety of colored lettuces) on top of the tortilla. Place the cold soba noodles on top of the greens, then arrange warm fish on top of that.

Put your vegetable curls or grated vegetable garnish on top of the fish, add a sprig of cilantro, and sprinkle with black goma or chopped nuts.

Place the slices of cucumber and tomato around the edge of the plate and serve with your favorite dressing. I prefer using my Asian creamy dressing with this salad.

New Wave Marinade

(Makes 1 cup)

½ cup soy sauce
¼ cup light salad oil
2 tablespoons mirin (Japanese sweet rice wine)
¼ teaspoon sesame oil
1½ teaspoons minced fresh cilantro
2 tablespoons thinly sliced green onion
1 tablespoon minced fresh garlic
1 tablespoon peeled and minced fresh ginger
½ teaspoon salt
¼ teaspoon white pepper
1½ teaspoons brown sugar
½ teaspoon Chinese five-spice powder
1 tablespoon black goma (black sesame seeds)
1 pinch dried red pepper flakes, or 1 fresh hot chili pepper, minced

Combine all ingredients and blend well. Before marinating fish, remove 2 tablespoons of marinade (or more, to taste), and set aside to use later on noodles.

Lemon-Pepper Mahimahi Salad

(Serves 1)

This recipe gives you an opportunity to use something that's out there on the store shelf and blend it with indigenous fish to produce a real idiot-proof, world-class dish that doesn't take all day to prepare.

> *3 mahimahi (dolphinfish) fillets, 2 ounces each*
> *Lemon-pepper seasoning*
> *1 small package bean thread noodles*
> *Asian Salad Sauce (see recipe on page 70)*
> *1 or 2 handfuls assorted salad greens*
> *2 tablespoons olive oil*
> *Wasabi Vinaigrette (see recipe on pages*
> *58–59) (optional)*
>
> *Garnish:*
> *1 or 2 sprigs fresh basil*
> *1 tablespoon finely sliced green onion*

Lightly sprinkle the fish with lemon-pepper seasoning and set aside while preparing the rest of the salad. (You want to cook the fish after everything else is ready, so you can serve it hot.)

Place the bean threads in boiling water and cook until soft, about 5 minutes. Place in a sieve, rinse with cold water, and drain. Place on a cutting board and cut into 1-inch lengths. Mix 2 to 3 tablespoons of the Asian salad sauce with about 3 ounces of the cooked bean-thread noodles, then chill, or let remain at room temperature, whichever you prefer.

Toss salad greens with ½ cup of the Asian salad sauce.

In a frying pan, heat 2 tablespoons of olive oil over medium high heat. Quickly sear the fish just until rare or medium rare. For a low-fat variation, broil the fish, but don't overcook.

Place the salad greens in a bowl, then layer with the bean threads and top with the fish. Garnish with basil sprigs and green onion.

You may find you don't need dressing (the Asian salad sauce tossed with the lettuce and noodles makes it very tasty), though I like to serve the wasabi vinaigrette with it because of the nice flavor contrasts.

Asian Salad Sauce

(Makes 1¼ cups)

½ cup salad oil
½ cup soy sauce
1 teaspoon sesame oil
2 tablespoons mirin (Japanese sweet rice wine)
1 tablespoon minced fresh garlic
1 tablespoon peeled and minced fresh ginger
½ teaspoon salt
¼ teaspoon white pepper
1½ teaspoons brown sugar

Combine all ingredients and blend well.

Macadamia Nut-Crusted Ono Caesar Salad

(Serves 4)

Caesar salad can be a meal all by itself—particularly when topped with a crisp hot fish fillet.

4 Macadamia Nut-Crusted Ono fillets (see recipe on page 71)
Caesar Salad Dressing (see recipe on page 72)
2 medium heads romaine lettuce, washed, dried, and torn
¼ cup freshly grated Parmesan cheese
Freshly ground black pepper to taste

Garnish:

Croutons

Prepare the fish fillets and the Caesar salad dressing. Toss the romaine with some of the dressing and divide equally among 4 salad plates. Place 1 fillet atop the salad on each plate, sprinkle with Parmesan and black pepper, and garnish with croutons.

Macadamia Nut–Crusted Ono

(Makes 4 fillets)

4 ono (wahoo) fillets, 6 ounces each

2 tablespoons light olive oil

1 teaspoon peeled and minced fresh ginger

1 teaspoon minced fresh garlic

Salt and pepper to taste

½ cup panko (Japanese-style crispy bread crumbs) or fine dry bread crumbs

4 tablespoons (½ stick) butter, at room temperature

½ cup chopped macadamia nuts

½ teaspoon minced fresh basil

½ teaspoon minced fresh dill

½ teaspoon minced fresh thyme

½ teaspoon paprika

Marinate the fillets for 1 hour in the olive oil, ginger, garlic, salt, and pepper. Preheat the oven to 375°F. Combine the bread crumbs, butter, macadamia nuts, herbs, and paprika; blend well. Press the marinated fish into the bread crumb mixture and bake for 8 to 10 minutes.

Caesar Salad Dressing

(Makes 2½ cups)

1 egg yolk
1 tablespoon Dijon mustard
1 teaspoon fresh lemon juice
2 cloves fresh garlic, minced
1 tablespoon minced anchovies
Dash of Tabasco
2 teaspoons Worcestershire sauce
2 tablespoons red wine vinegar
2 tablespoons grated Parmesan cheese
¼ cup water
Salt and pepper to taste
1½ cups light salad oil

Whisk the egg yolk. Stir in the remaining ingredients, except the oil, and blend well. Slowly drizzle in the oil, whisking constantly, until oil is incorporated and dressing is creamy. This may also be done in a blender or food processor. (The secret is to add the oil slowly so it incorporates completely.)

Poached Snapper Salad with Honey-Lime Vinaigrette
(Serves 1)

This recipe works very well with any deep-sea fish. I chose 'opakapaka (pink snapper) for this recipe, but you can use mahimahi (dolphinfish), ono (wahoo), red snapper, or salmon. Although their flavors are slightly different, these fish retain their shape and texture when poached. The Honey-Lime Vinaigrette is both sweet and tart, and adds a wonderful taste to this dish.

Poaching Liquid (see recipe on page 74)
1 to 2 handfuls assorted salad greens
½ cup diced fresh tomato
2 tablespoons diced sweet onion
2 tablespoons thinly sliced green onion
Pinch of salt
1 'opakapaka (pink snapper) fillet, 6 to 7 ounces
Honey-Lime Vinaigrette (see recipe on page 74)

Garnishes:
3 tomato slices
3 orange slices
1 sprig fresh dill

Bring the poaching liquid to a boil in a large skillet, then lower the heat to a simmer. Place the salad greens on a plate.

Combine the diced tomato, sweet onion, green onion, and salt. Blend well and place the mixture on the salad greens.

Submerge the fish completely in the simmering liquid, cover, and cook gently at a low simmer for 5 to 8 minutes, maximum, for a single 6- to 7-ounce fillet. Increase the cooking time slightly for large portions, but don't overcook. Prepare honey-lime vinaigrette.

Remove the fish with a spatula and place on the tomato-onion mixture. Garnish around the edges with tomato and orange slices, top with a sprig of fresh dill, and serve with honey-lime vinaigrette.

Poaching Liquid

(Makes 3½ cups)

2 cups water
1 cup white wine
½ cup diced carrots
½ cup diced onions
½ cup diced celery
Juice of ½ fresh lemon
½ teaspoon salt
½ teaspoon cracked pepper
1 whole bay leaf

Combine all ingredients.

Honey-Lime Vinaigrette

(Makes ¼ cup)

2 tablespoons honey
1 tablespoon vinegar
Juice of 1 medium lime
1 teaspoon lime zest
1 tablespoon chopped fresh parsley
1½ tablespoons light salad oil
Salt and white pepper to taste

Whisk ingredients together until well blended.

Hawaiian Barbecued Shrimp Salad with Papaya-Pineapple Marmalade

(Serves 4)

This is one of my all-time most popular recipes. It's very easy to make. You can't get much simpler than fresh whole shrimp (shells on), marinated, then cooked quickly on the hibachi. Throw the shrimp on some salad greens and marinated soba noodles and, man, you've got a winner. I like to use my Asian Creamy Dressing (page 59) with this salad, but you can use the dressing of your choice.

1 pound jumbo shrimp (16 to 20 count)
Shrimp Barbecue Marinade (see recipe on page 76)
4 flour tortillas
1 package Japanese somen noodles, 8 to 12 ounces
1 medium head iceberg lettuce, julienned
1 cup bean sprouts
1 carrot, grated
2 radishes, thinly sliced
2 cups finely chopped won bok (Chinese cabbage) or napa cabbage
½ cup diagonally sliced long strips green onions
Papaya-Pineapple Marmalade (see recipe on page 76)

Garnish:
4 to 8 wedges fresh pineapple
4 to 8 wedges fresh papaya
4 to 8 sprigs cilantro

Rinse the shrimp. Cut the top shell, but not all the way through because you're going to leave the shell on for a festive look. Peel the shells from the shrimp like a fan, leaving shell and tail attached at the tail end. Devein the shrimp. Prepare shrimp barbecue marinade. Remove 4 tablespoons of the marinade and set aside to mix with the noodles. Marinate the shrimp for 30 minutes.

Deep-fry the flour tortillas and drain them on paper towels. Set aside. Cook the noodles according to package directions; rinse, drain, and mix with 4 tablespoons of shrimp barbecue marinade; then place in the refrigerator until chilled, about 20 to 30 minutes.

In a large bowl, combine the lettuce, bean sprouts, carrot, radishes, won bok (napa cabbage), and green onions, and mix well.

Prepare papaya-pineapple marmalade; set aside.

When everything is ready, place the shrimp on the barbecue or under the broiler, and cook for 3 to 5 minutes, turning once.

Build each salad by first placing a deep-fried tortilla on a plate, adding a couple handfuls of colorful salad mix, then chilled somen noodles; then divide the shrimp into 4 servings and place on top. Garnish with a sprig or two of cilantro.

Place the wedges of pineapple and papaya around the edge of the plate, alternating with dollops of papaya-pineapple marmalade.

Shrimp Barbecue Marinade
(Makes 1¼ cups)

⅓ cup salad oil

2 tablespoons soy sauce

2 tablespoons chopped fresh cilantro

1 teaspoon peeled and minced fresh ginger

2 tablespoons minced fresh garlic

1½ teaspoons granulated sugar

¼ teaspoon red chili pepper flakes, or 1 fresh hot chili pepper, seeded and chopped

1 teaspoon sesame oil

Blend all the ingredients.

Papaya-Pineapple Marmalade
(Makes 1 cup)

½ cup diced papaya

½ cup diced pineapple

3 tablespoons granulated sugar

In a small saucepan, cook the fruit and sugar over medium-low heat for 20 minutes. Serve warm or cold.

Spicy Soy Shrimp Salad
(Serves 4)

To make this a little more fancy, you can serve it in a deep-fried flour tortilla basket instead of using the tortilla wedges. Topped with butterflied shrimp, tomato wedges, and cucumber slices, and garnished with cilantro leaves, it's a beautiful dish either way.

20 jumbo shrimp (16 to 20 count), butterflied, with shells on
Spicy Soy Marinade (see recipe on page 78)
1 package somen noodles, cooked according to package
  directions and drained
3 drops sesame oil
2 tablespoons vegetable oil
1 pound tossed mixed greens
Sam Choy's Original Asian Creamy Dressing (see recipe
  on page 59)

Garnish:
12 tomato wedges
12 cucumber slices
Four 6-inch flour tortillas, each cut into 8 wedges and deep-fried
Cilantro leaves

Marinate the shrimp in the spicy soy marinade for ½ hour. Toss cooked somen noodles with 3 drops of sesame oil.

Heat the oil in a wok. Drain shrimp. Stir-fry the marinated shrimp for 1 minute. Remove from the heat.

Divide the greens among four large plates; top with the somen and shrimp.

Prepare Asian dressing. Arrange 3 tomato wedges and 3 cucumber slices on each plate. Sprinkle with crispy flour tortilla wedges and garnish with cilantro leaves. Serve with Asian creamy dressing.

Spicy Soy Marinade

(Makes ¼ cup)

¼ cup soy sauce
1 teaspoon chopped fresh garlic
1 teaspoon chopped fresh cilantro
1 teaspoon Chinese garlic chili sauce
1 teaspoon chopped green onion
1 tablespoon granulated sugar
1 tablespoon sesame oil
1 teaspoon sesame seeds, roasted

Mix all ingredients.

Gingered Scallops with Colorful Soba Noodles

(Serves 6)

This soba salad has beautiful vegetable colors—spinach, carrots, zucchini, red bell pepper—with scallops marinated, then poached in ginger stock. It's a meal, it's an experience, it's amazing.

1½ pounds scallops
Spicy Ginger Marinade *(see recipe on page 79)*
2 teaspoons canola oil
Soba Salad *(see recipe on page 80)*

Marinate the scallops in the spicy ginger marinade for 30 minutes.

In a skillet, heat the oil over medium heat and sauté the scallops for 1½ minutes on each side; do not overcook. Pour scallops and their juices right over the soba salad.

Spicy Ginger Marinade

(Makes ½ cup)

1½ tablespoons dry white wine

1½ tablespoons orange juice

1 tablespoon peeled and minced fresh ginger

1 tablespoon minced red bell pepper, or 1 hot red chili pepper, seeded and minced

1 tablespoon minced yellow bell pepper

1 tablespoon chopped fresh basil

1 tablespoon minced fresh cilantro

½ teaspoon granulated sugar

Salt and white pepper to taste

Combine all the ingredients.

Soba Salad

(Makes about 6 cups)

½ pound soba (Japanese thin buckwheat noodles)
12 fresh spinach leaves, chopped
½ cup julienned carrots
½ cup julienned red bell pepper
½ cup julienned zucchini
12 fresh basil leaves, minced
1 tablespoon minced fresh cilantro
1 tablespoon soy sauce
1 tablespoon olive oil
1 teaspoon sesame oil
1 teaspoon minced fresh garlic

Cook the soba according to package directions; drain. In a large mixing bowl, combine soba with remaining ingredients. Toss until well combined.

Pacific Seafood Pasta Salad

(Serves 8)

Poaching is a wonderful way to prepare fish. It's a low-fat technique that gently cooks the meat without compromising its flavor. Serve my Pacific seafood pasta salad as a cool summer lunch entree, or as your potluck contribution to a block party. I've heard enough praise for this exotically tasty dish that I can guarantee you rave reviews.

½ pound extra-large shrimp (21 to 25 count)
1 mahimahi (dolphinfish) fillet, 10 ounces
Poaching Liquid (see recipe on page 82)
½ pound scallops
12 green-tip mussels, scrubbed and debearded
½ pound linguini
2 tablespoons olive oil
4 ounces smoked 'ahi (yellowfin tuna), cut into 1-inch cubes
    (optional)
½ cup chopped fresh basil leaves
1 cup chopped radicchio
1 cup oyster mushrooms, cut in half
½ teaspoon salt
¼ teaspoon black pepper
⅛ teaspoon chopped fresh dill or thyme
Basil Vinaigrette Dressing (see recipe on page 82)

Rinse the shrimp, remove shells, and devein. Cut the mahimahi fillets into 1-inch cubes.

Bring the poaching liquid to a boil in a stockpot. Add the shrimp and return liquid to a boil; then remove the shrimp to a plate. Return the poaching liquid to a full boil and add the mahimahi, scallops, and mussels. Remove the stockpot from the heat and let stand 1 minute; drain. Set the seafood aside.

Cook the linguini according to package directions. Drain and toss with olive oil.

In a large bowl, combine the linguini, seafood, smoked 'ahi, basil, radicchio, mushrooms, salt, black pepper, and dill or thyme; toss lightly. Chill until ready to serve.

Before serving, toss lightly with basil vinaigrette dressing.

Poaching Liquid

(Makes 4½ cups)

3 cups water
1 cup white wine
1 cup diced celery
¼ cup diced onion
¼ cup diced carrot
Juice of 1 large orange
1½ teaspoons salt
¼ teaspoon cracked pepper
1 sprig fresh dill
Pinch of dried thyme

In a stockpot, combine all the ingredients.

Basil Vinaigrette Dressing

(Makes 1⅛ cups)

¼ cup red wine vinegar
2 tablespoons granulated sugar
½ cup fresh basil leaves
2 shallots
2 cloves fresh garlic, peeled
1 teaspoon black pepper
¼ teaspoon salt
¾ cup salad oil

In a blender or food processor combine all ingredients except the oil. Blend until smooth. With the machine running, add the oil in a slow, steady stream.

Lu'au-Style Spinach Salad with Ginger Pesto Sauce

(Serves 1)

This recipe was inspired by traditional salads that are meals in themselves. Poached or pan-fried scallops combine nicely with the delicate flavor of spinach and are spiced up with ginger pesto. This salad has all sorts of textures and flavors, giving every bite an exciting taste.

6 sea scallops (16 to 20 count)
Ginger Pesto Sauce (see recipe on page 84)
2 tablespoons olive oil
6 ounces fresh spinach, cleaned and chopped
¼ red bell pepper, sliced
2 mushrooms, sliced
1 ounce Parmesan cheese, grated
Salt and pepper to taste

Garnish:
Lettuce leaves

Prepare ginger pesto sauce. Set aside 2 tablespoons. Marinate the scallops in remaining ginger pesto sauce for 20 to 30 minutes, maximum.

After removing scallops from marinade, sear them quickly in 2 tablespoons of hot oil in a wok on high heat until medium rare: 3 minutes, maximum—don't overcook. In a mixing bowl, toss the scallops together with the spinach, red bell pepper, mushrooms, Parmesan cheese, and reserved ginger pesto sauce. Season with salt and pepper to taste.

Arrange the scallop mixture on a bed of leaf lettuce, or top with your favorite garnish.

Ginger Pesto Sauce

(Makes 1½ cups)

½ cup olive oil
½ teaspoon salt
¼ cup peeled and minced fresh ginger
¼ cup minced green onions
¼ cup lightly packed minced fresh cilantro
⅛ teaspoon white pepper

Heat the oil in a small saucepan, add the salt, and cook for 2 to 3 minutes. Cool. Stir in the remaining ingredients and blend well.

Shrimp-Stuffed Avocado with Mango-Onion Dressing

(Serves 4)

The old folks in the Islands call avocados "pears" and "alligator pears." We grow very large variety on the rainy slopes of our mountain ranges and in the deep green valleys. Hawai'i avocados are buttery smooth, without the stringy texture of avocados grown in other parts of the world. I recommend getting large pears to maximize this superb salad, but any good avocados will do.

2 medium avocados
12 ounces small to medium shrimp, cooked and shelled
1 cup diced bell peppers (assorted colors)
2 tablespoons diced black olives
1 tablespoon minced fresh dill
Salt and pepper to taste
Mango-Onion Dressing (see recipe on page 86)

Garnish:
Lettuce leaves
Dill sprigs

Cut the avocados in half lengthwise; peel. Leave the pits in the center until you're ready to stuff them.

Combine the shrimp, bell peppers, olives, dill, salt, and pepper; toss lightly. Spoon the mixture into the avocado halves. Arrange lettuce on a platter or on individual plates and top with the stuffed avocados. Prepare the mango-onion dressing. Garnish with dill sprigs.

Serve with mango-onion dressing.

Mango-Onion Dressing

(Makes 2¼ cups)

1 small mango, peeled and cut into chunks
½ small sweet onion, cubed
1 tablespoon granulated sugar
¼ cup red wine vinegar
1 cup light salad oil
Salt and pepper to taste

In a food processor or blender, combine the mango, onion, sugar, and red wine vinegar. Blend until smooth. With the machine running, add the oil in a slow steady stream. Season with salt and pepper to taste.

Wok-Fried Red Lettuce and Red Oak Salad with Ginger Slivers, Garlic, and Fried Shrimp

(Serves 4)

The slightly wilted lettuces blend deliciously into this dish, adding an interesting texture—half salad, half soup. The furikake and black goma add an Asian flavor, while the tequila-marinated shrimp push it over the top. Wilted salads are very popular. Just be sure to cut or chop your greens into pieces that are easy to handle. I like to cut them into 1½-inch-thick strips. They are big enough to allow the texture to come through and small enough to manage with a fork.

1 tablespoon vegetable oil
1 head red leaf lettuce, cut up
1 head red oak leaf lettuce, cut up

1 tablespoon peeled and slivered fresh ginger

1 tablespoon minced fresh garlic

Salt to taste

¼ cup chicken stock

1 tablespoon furikake (dried seaweed flakes and sesame seeds)

1 tablespoon black goma (black sesame seeds)

1 tablespoon minced green onion

Batterless Deep-Fried Shrimp (see recipe below)

Heat the oil in a wok until it just begins to smoke. Add the lettuces, ginger, garlic, and salt, then the chicken stock. Stir-fry about 1 minute, until the lettuce wilts. Transfer to a bowl. Sprinkle with furikake, black goma, and green onion, and top with the deep-fried shrimp.

Batterless Deep-Fried Shrimp

(Serves 4)

Vegetable oil for deep-frying

*1 pound extra-large shrimp (21 to 25 count), shelled
     and deveined*

2 tablespoons tequila

½ teaspoon salt

1 teaspoon minced fresh garlic

1 teaspoon granulated sugar

¼ cup soy sauce

Heat 2½ to 3 inches of oil in a wok over medium-high heat until it registers 365°F on a deep-fry thermometer. Place the shrimp in a bowl, sprinkle with tequila and salt, and toss. Let marinate for 10 to 15 minutes, tossing occasionally. Drain off excess liquid. Fry the shrimp, 4 or 5 at a time, for 3 to 4 minutes. Transfer shrimp to a saucepan; when all are cooked, add the garlic, sugar, and soy sauce and simmer for 2 to 3 minutes. Remove the shrimp.

Baby Romaine Lettuce with Honey-Ginger Scallops and Shrimp

(Serves 4 to 6)

Bay scallops are mild and sweet, and are considered the best-tasting scallop. These tiny shellfish add a delicate but powerful flavor to the salad. To serve them up right, stir-fry them quickly and toss on a bed of crisp baby romaine lettuce.

8 ounces small to medium shrimp, shelled and deveined
8 ounces bay scallops
2 tablespoons honey
Juice of 1 lime
Ginger Pesto Sauce (see recipe on page 84)
Salt and pepper to taste
4 heads baby romaine lettuce
1 tablespoon vegetable oil

Marinate the shrimp and scallops in a mixture of honey, lime juice, 1 tablespoon of ginger pesto, salt, and pepper for about 5 minutes.

Meanwhile, make a bed of the romaine leaves in a salad bowl and drizzle with ginger pesto.

Heat the oil in a wok until smoking, then add the shrimp and scallops. Cook over medium-high heat about 1 minute on each side, or until just done.

Scatter the shrimp and scallops over the greens and serve at once.

Bella Mushroom Salad

(Serves 8)

I have served portobello mushrooms in sandwiches, salads, and soups, and I'm always amazed: people ask if there is meat in the dish. This mushroom has a dense, meaty texture, and, if broiled, tastes like a tender filet mignon. Toss together Italian lettuces, beefy portobellos, and colorful "bells" with a fat-free plum-tomato dressing, and *bella, bella, bella*. I don't even look Italian.

> *1 large red bell pepper*
> *Tomato Dressing (see recipe on page 90)*
> *4 large portobello mushrooms (each 6 inches in diameter), stems discarded*
> *Olive oil*
> *Salt and freshly ground black pepper to taste*
> *1 bunch arugula, torn into bite-sized pieces (about 2 cups)*
> *¼ head lollo rossa (red curly) or preferred lettuce, torn into bite-sized pieces*

> *Garnish:*
> *Grated cheese of your choice*

Roast the bell pepper directly on a gas flame or as close under a broiler as possible, turning frequently until charred all over. Put immediately into a plastic bag to steam for 5 minutes. Slip the skin off and use a small sharp knife to remove the stem, seeds, and ribs. If desired, rinse and pat dry. Slice into thin strips.

Prepare the tomato dressing and set aside.

Arrange the mushrooms on a baking sheet; brush all over with oil and season with salt and pepper. Broil, gill sides down, for 2 minutes or until tender and toasty brown on top. Cut into large chunks; keep warm.

In a large bowl, toss the arugula and lettuce with tomato dressing. Mound the dressed greens on 4 large plates. Scatter pepper strips and mushroom chunks over the top. Sprinkle with cheese.

Tomato Dressing

(Makes 1 to 1½ cups)

½ pound plum tomatoes, blanched, peeled, and seeded
1 clove fresh garlic, minced
1½ tablespoons freshly squeezed orange juice
1½ teaspoons rice vinegar
1 teaspoon soy sauce
1 tablespoon chopped fresh mint

Use food processor or blender to purée the tomatoes and garlic; pour the purée into a small bowl. Stir in the remaining ingredients.

O'ahu-Style Potato Salad

(Serves 8)

We've got all different things in this salad—crab, uncooked corn kernels that add a little crunchiness. Whew, 'ono (delicious). It's great to take to the beach or to a tailgate party. We've had this potato salad with barbecued chicken in the parking lot at Aloha Stadium before the Hula Bowl.

2 pounds new red boiling potatoes
2 cups crabmeat, picked over well
⅓ cup shelled, cooked small shrimp
4 hard-boiled eggs, chopped
1 cup fresh corn kernels
½ cup pitted medium black olives
¼ cup sliced water chestnuts
1½ cups cleaned and chopped fresh spinach
½ cup minced sweet onion

½ cup minced celery
½ cup grated carrots
2½ cups mayonnaise
Salt and pepper to taste

Cook the potatoes in lightly salted boiling water until fork-tender. Cool, peel if desired, then cut into eighths.

In a large mixing bowl, toss the potatoes with the remaining ingredients lightly to combine. Adjust seasoning with salt and pepper if necessary.

'Ahi Salad with Creamy Peanut Dressing

(Serves 4)

On one of my trips I got to taste the incredible Thai peanut dressings. I came home and put together this recipe. It's a little bit Thai, a little bit Chinese, and a lot wild, with the won bok and red cabbage, bean sprouts, and mushrooms. All the more reason to try it.

2 cups shredded won bok (Chinese cabbage) or napa cabbage
1 cup shredded red cabbage
1½ cups sliced fresh mushrooms
1½ cups fresh bean sprouts
¾ cup slivered radishes
½ cup chopped green onions
1 large tomato, cut into 12 wedges
Creamy Peanut Dressing (see recipe on page 92)
½ pound 'ahi (yellowfin tuna) (see page 11)

Garnish:
Green onions
Fresh cilantro, minced
Peanuts, finely chopped

In a large mixing bowl, toss together the won bok, red cabbage, mushrooms, bean sprouts, radishes, green onions, and tomatoes. Place the mixture on a serving platter. Prepare peanut dressing and set aside. Cut the 'ahi into 1-inch cubes and sear over high heat on a flat griddle or in a sauté pan lightly coated with olive oil. Cook for only about 1 minute on each side. Top the salad mixture with the seared 'ahi. Garnish with green onions, cilantro, and chopped peanuts. Serve with peanut dressing on the side.

Creamy Peanut Dressing

(Makes 1½ cups)

½ cup warm water
½ cup creamy peanut butter
1½ tablespoons rice vinegar
2 tablespoons soy sauce
¼ cup granulated sugar
½ teaspoon salt
1 clove fresh garlic, crushed
¼ cup salad oil
1½ teaspoons hot Asian chili paste (sambal oelek)
2 tablespoons minced fresh cilantro

Mix water and peanut butter in a small bowl until smooth. Add the remaining dressing ingredients and mix well. Let stand at room temperature at least 30 minutes.

Easy Fruit Salad for the Beach

(Serves 4 to 6)

Prepare this salad before you leave the house. Cut the fruit and mix the dressing. Keep them separate until you're ready to eat, then mix them together in a large bowl, and have at it. After swimming in salty ocean water all day, you'll find the sweet taste of melon, papaya, and pineapple is really refreshing.

½ honeydew melon, sliced into ½-inch chunks
½ cantaloupe, sliced into ½-inch chunks
1 papaya, sliced into ½-inch chunks
1 pineapple, sliced into ½-inch chunks
6 strawberries
½ bunch of grapes

Dressing:
2 tablespoons sour cream
2 tablespoons mayonnaise
Salt and pepper to taste
1 tablespoon Papaya-Pineapple Marmalade (see recipe
    on pages 76–77)

Mix the fruits together just before serving. Combine the dressing ingredients and serve with the fruit salad.

Hilo Tropical Fruit Slaw

(Serves 8)

Just about every type of fresh fruit grown in Hawai'i can be purchased at the Hilo Open Market. I go there often. I created this slaw recipe with the market in mind, using fruit I bought there. This is an ideal side salad to serve with broiled chicken breasts.

1 papaya, seeded, peeled, and thinly sliced
1 cup peeled and thinly sliced pineapple
1 medium mango, peeled and thinly sliced
1 star fruit, ribs trimmed, thinly sliced, and seeded
1 kiwi fruit, peeled and thinly sliced
6 strawberries, hulled and quartered
½ cup whole cape gooseberries (ground cherries)
1 banana, sliced
Fruit Slaw Dressing (see recipe below)
1 medium head radicchio, leaves separated

In a large salad bowl, combine the fruit and fold in the prepared fruit slaw dressing. Serve on radicchio leaves.

Fruit Slaw Dressing

(Makes ¾ cup)

1 ripe papaya, seeded and peeled
½ cup plain yogurt
2 tablespoons honey
¼ teaspoon salt
¼ teaspoon white pepper

Place all ingredients in a food processor or blender and process for 30 seconds.

Soups and Stews

While I prepared for a chef demonstration in Boston, my good friend Kevin Meeker (chef/restaurateur of Philadelphia Fish & Co. in Philadelphia) invited me to dinner. I offered to cook. I had ulterior motives.

It was well below zero outside. The air was crackling cold; it had a sound of shivering in it even though there wasn't any wind. It was hard to breathe, and when I exhaled, my breath seemed to turn to little ice crystals and fall to the ground. I never knew it could get so cold. All I could think of was getting warm with Portuguese bean soup!

When Kevin's family and their friends started asking, "What are we going to cook for dinner?" I said, "I tell you what. Because it's freezing cold, I'll make a pot of soup." They said, "What kind of soup?" I said, "I call it Da Wife's Bean Soup. It's a family favorite and my wife's specialty." They said, "Oh, Boston has a lot of Portuguese people." I said, "No, no, no, this soup is Hawaiian-style, Island-style, my wife's style."

Bean soup on the mainland is a thick pottage with beans cooked until very soft and sometimes puréed, whereas Hawaiian-style Portuguese bean soup is really stewlike, with a thin tomato-based broth, whole beans, and chunks of spicy Portuguese sausage.

So pretty soon I had the ham hocks boiling with a little garlic, some onions, and celery. Just letting it boil. Making the meat real soft.

I thought, "Yeah, perfect. I'm all warm and toasty in their big kitchen, doing what I love. Pretty soon we'll eat some hot, hot soup."

I took the ham hocks out, deboned them all, chopped up the meat, and let the soup keep on bubbling. I sliced and fried some spicy Italian sausage (they didn't have any Portuguese sausage), and set that aside. Then I added the tomato purée, checked the seasoning, and added more vegetables—potatoes, celery, carrots, onions.

People started coming into the kitchen sniffing at the soup aromas and saying, "Aaaahhh."

I tossed in a little cilantro, some salt and pepper, and the spicy Italian sausage, and two hours and five minutes later we were sitting down and having a big cauldron of some of the best Portuguese soup ever. Hooooo, I tell you what, they licked the bowls!

Maui Fisherman's Soup

(Serves 4)

Here's a hearty soup. A good soup. Originated by men of the sea who knew how best to serve up their catch.

6 cups chicken stock

2 large stalks lemongrass, tough outer leaves discarded, lower stalk trimmed to 12 inches and angle-cut into 2-inch pieces

3 large slices unpeeled fresh ginger, about 2 ounces

1 can (14 ounces) unsweetened coconut milk

1 tablespoon chili-tamarind paste

¼ cup fresh lemon juice

¼ cup packed brown sugar

¼ cup Thai fish sauce

8 fresh New Zealand green-tip mussels, scrubbed and debearded (see Note on page 65)

8 medium-sized scallops

8 medium shrimp, shelled, deveined, and butterflied

5 small fresh Thai chilies or hot chili peppers, stemmed and lightly crushed

Garnish:

Sprigs of fresh cilantro

Put the stock, lemongrass, and ginger in a soup pot. Gradually bring to a boil over medium-high heat. Boil for 1 minute. Stir in the coconut milk and return to a boil. Add the chili-tamarind paste, lemon juice, brown sugar, and fish sauce. Stir until the chili-tamarind paste and brown sugar are dissolved and blended. Reduce the heat and simmer gently while you prepare the mussels.

Return the soup to a boil. Add the mussels, scallops, and shrimp. Do not stir.

Bring back to a boil for about 1 minute. Float the Thai chilies on top, and turn off the heat.

Remove the mussels, and let cool slightly. Gently pry the mussels open, breaking them apart at the hinge ends. Discard the upper shells, reserving the mussels on their half shells. Return mussels to soup.

Ladle the soup into a tureen or individual serving bowls. Place a sprig or two of cilantro over each serving.

Cool Summer Night Cioppino

(Serves 8)

Cool summer nights call for a seafood cioppino. Eating this soup is like net fishing: you dip the net in, and heaven knows what you're going to bring up. You can use any white fish that has firm meat. I prefer ono (wahoo). Use whatever is available in your area. Serve with fresh homemade bread.

2½ cups fat-free chicken stock
2 cups clam juice
¼ cup olive oil
1 tablespoon minced fresh garlic
1 sweet onion, thinly sliced
1 cup chopped celery
1 cup julienned red bell pepper
1 large fresh tomato, diced
1¼ pounds firm white fish, cut into 1-inch cubes
1 pound extra-large shrimp (21 to 25 count), shelled and deveined
¼ pound clams, shells scrubbed and rinsed, or scrubbed and debearded mussels (see Note on page 65)
1 cup white wine
1 cup chopped fresh basil

1 hot chili pepper, seeded and chopped, or ¼ teaspoon
    red chili pepper flakes
Pinch of saffron
1 spiny lobster (1 pound), cleaned and cut in half, or
    1 pound frozen rock lobster tails, thawed
Salt and pepper to taste

Combine the chicken stock and clam juice in a large pot; bring to a boil.

In another large pot, heat the oil and sauté the garlic, onion, celery, bell pepper, and tomato for 2 to 3 minutes. Toss in the fish, shrimp, and clams or mussels. Add the wine and cook for 2 minutes more. Add the hot stock, basil, chili pepper, saffron, and lobster. Adjust seasoning with salt and pepper. Cook 8 minutes, or until the lobster is done.

Wok-Seared Jumbo Shrimp in Lemongrass Broth

(Serves 4)

You know on those "north wind" days, when it's really cold outside, try making this fragrant soup. The aroma alone will make you feel warm inside.

¼ cup peanut oil
12 jumbo shrimp (16 to 20 count), shelled and deveined
1 cup sugar snap peas, cut in half lengthwise
1 cup sliced carrots
1 cup fresh straw mushrooms
1 cup sliced fresh water chestnuts
Lemongrass Broth (see recipe on page 100)

Heat the oil in a wok and sear the shrimp over high heat, turning once. Remove the shrimp from the wok and set aside. Drain off the excess oil, add sugar snap peas, carrots, straw mushrooms, and water chestnuts, and stir-fry for 30 seconds.

Add the lemongrass broth and simmer for 45 seconds. Return the shrimp to the pan and simmer for 45 more seconds. Divide among 4 bowls, arranging shrimp on top. Serve immediately.

Lemongrass Broth

(Makes 3 cups)

1 tablespoon peanut oil
1 fresh hot chili pepper, chopped
2 stalks lemongrass, diagonally cut
1 clove fresh garlic, chopped
1 tablespoon peeled and chopped fresh ginger
1 kaffir lime leaf (optional)
1 sprig fresh tarragon (optional)
3 cups chicken stock

In a hot wok, heat the peanut oil and stir-fry the chili pepper, lemongrass, garlic, ginger, lime leaf, and tarragon for 1 minute. Add the chicken stock. Let simmer for 10 to 15 minutes.

Quick and "Tastes Good" Barley Soup

(Serves 8)

The secret to making an incredible soup is to pay attention. Every now and then you need to stir it, adjust the temperature, check the seasoning and flavor. The slightest scorching will tinge the taste.

1¼ cups pearl barley, rinsed and drained
2 tablespoons olive oil
½ cup coarsely chopped onion
⅓ cup finely chopped prosciutto (2 ounces)

1 tablespoon coarsely chopped cilantro

1 teaspoon minced fresh rosemary

1 medium potato, peeled and cut into ½-inch dice

1 large carrot, cut into ½-inch dice

1 can (14½ ounces) chicken stock

Salt and freshly ground pepper to taste

2 to 3 tablespoons freshly grated Parmesan cheese

Place the barley in a large pot and add water to a point 3 inches above barley. Bring to a boil, then simmer partially covered for 1 hour.

Meanwhile, in a small skillet, heat the oil and sauté the onion for 3 minutes. Add the prosciutto and cook for 2 to 3 minutes, stirring occasionally. Add the cilantro and rosemary; cook 1 minute.

Add the prosciutto mixture, potato, carrot, chicken stock, salt, and pepper to the cooked barley; add a little water if soup is too thick. Cook on low heat, stirring occasionally, for 30 minutes or until the potatoes and carrots are tender. Stir in grated Parmesan cheese just before serving.

 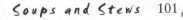

Da Wife's Bean Soup

(Serves 8)

At family gatherings, it's the wife's soup or mine. My soup always has leftovers, her soup's always gone. I think we eat more to make her feel better—just kidding. Serve with freshly baked bread.

2 cups dried beans—kidney, pinto, or small red
2 smoked ham hocks, or ham shanks
3 cups chicken stock
1 cup chopped fresh cilantro
6 cups water
1 Portuguese sausage (10 ounces), or Italian sausage
2 cups diced potatoes
2 cups diced carrots
1½ cups diced onions
½ cup diced celery
2 cups tomato purée
Salt and pepper to taste

Soak the beans in water overnight. Drain.

In a stockpot, combine the soaked beans, ham hocks, chicken stock, cilantro, and water. Bring to a boil, then simmer until meat and beans are tender, about 1½ to 2 hours. Remove the ham hocks and set aside to cool.

When cool enough to touch, extract the meat from the ham hocks, discarding the skin and bones. Shred the meat and return to the stockpot. Slice and fry the Portuguese sausage and blot with paper towels. Add the sausage to the stockpot along with the potatoes, carrots, onions, celery, and tomato purée. Cook until the potatoes are tender. Season with salt and pepper.

Ula'ino Watercress Soup

(Serves 6)

One of the most beautiful spots in the world is a little waterfall near the Ula'ino stream just outside of Hana, Maui. Across the stream and up the beach is a place the locals call Blue Pool. Water pours down a moss wall into a teal-green plunge pool. The walls of the cliff are covered with watercress with thick, spicy stems and radish-hot leaves.

6 ounces boneless chicken
6 ounces lean boneless pork
3½ cups chicken stock
¼ cup sliced green onions
1-inch piece fresh ginger, peeled and crushed
½ teaspoon salt
Pinch of white pepper
1 bunch watercress, cut into 2-inch lengths

Remove skin from the chicken. Cut the chicken and pork into thin strips. In a stockpot bring the chicken stock to a boil; add the pork, chicken, green onions, and ginger. Reduce the heat and simmer for 3 minutes. Season with salt and white pepper. Add the watercress and cook for 3 more minutes. Serve hot.

My Dad's Ong Choy and Pork Soup

(Serves 6 to 8)

One of the exciting things about growing up in my family was playing outside and then coming in and smelling that unforgettable aroma of my dad's soup simmering on the stove. It's delicious, and very simple to make. It's a great soup when you don't have much time to spend in the kitchen.

¼ pound lean boneless pork
8 cups chicken stock
One ¾ x ¾- inch piece fresh ginger
¼ cup julienned celery
1 bunch ong choy (New Zealand spinach), washed and cut into
*   2-inch sections*
2 cups sliced shiitake mushrooms
¼ cup julienned scallions or green onions
¼ cup shrimp, shelled and deveined
Salt and white pepper

Cut the pork into slivers. Bring the chicken stock to a boil in a soup pot and add the ginger, pork, and celery. Reduce heat and simmer, covered, for 10 to 15 minutes. Add the ong choy, mushrooms, scallions, and shrimp, and cook about 3 minutes. Adjust seasoning with salt and white pepper to taste. Remove ginger before serving.

Cold Papaya, Mango, and Cape Gooseberry Bisque

(Serves 4 to 6)

I like to take overripe papaya, mango, and berries, and blend them into a beautiful fruit bisque. It's a great way to utilize fruits that are too ripe, and it's also a way to use fruit that you have frozen. You can freeze any fruit. It's just not very appealing after it comes out of the freezer, so here is a way to use it that makes it look and taste great.

1 pound mangoes
1½ pounds papayas
2 cups fresh cape gooseberries (ground cherries)
2 cups pineapple juice, or enough to cover fruit
1 large piece peeled fresh ginger
½ cinnamon stick
¼ teaspoon allspice powder
3 to 4 black peppercorns
½ cup honey
1 cup cornstarch mixed with ½ cup water, for thickening, as needed
Lemon juice to taste

Garnish:
Sour cream
Toasted macadamia nuts, chopped

Peel, seed, and chop the mangoes and papayas. Husk the cape gooseberries and leave them whole. Place the fruit in a saucepan, cover with pineapple juice, add the spices and honey, and simmer until the fruit is tender. Discard the cinnamon stick. Purée the mixture in a blender until very smooth. Strain, if desired.

Return the soup to the saucepan and bring to a simmer. If necessary, thicken by adding cornstarch mixture a little at a time to the simmering soup, stirring constantly until desired consistency is reached. Adjust the flavor with lemon juice.

Chill thoroughly. Just before serving, garnish each portion with a dollop of sour cream and a sprinkling of toasted macadamia nuts.

Big Island Avocado Bisque

(Serves 3 to 6)

Many backyards in Kona, Hawai'i, have avocado trees, and a lot of avocados hit the ground and either get eaten by wild pigs or turn into compost. I'm always experimenting with new ways to use this tasty and very nutritious fruit so it doesn't go to waste. This delicious and unique bisque is just one result of that experimentation.

2 or 3 large ripe avocados, peeled and pitted
¾ cup lime juice
Salt and pepper to taste
2 cups chicken stock
3 cups heavy cream
2 tablespoons minced fresh cilantro

Optional Garnish:
Cooked small shrimp

Place the peeled avocados in a large mixing bowl with the lime juice and whip with a wire whisk until smooth and creamy. Season with salt and pepper. Slowly add the chicken stock, stirring to blend, then add the heavy cream. Fold in the cilantro. Chill. Be sure this soup is very cold before serving.

Optional: Garnish the top of each cup of soup with chilled cooked small shrimp.

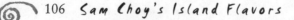

Seafood Cream of Broccoli Soup

(Serves 4)

This is a hearty, stick-to-the-ribs soup for those cold rainy-season nights when you wish you had a fireplace. There's no garnish or fanfare needed; just bring it to the table. It makes a basic, very satisfying, earthy meal.

¾ cup ono (wahoo), cubed
½ cup diced shrimp
½ cup crabmeat, picked over, or diced imitation crabmeat
8 cups chicken stock
1 medium onion, diced
¾ cup diced celery
1 teaspoon minced fresh garlic
6 tablespoons butter
4 cups chopped broccoli, stems and florets
½ cup all-purpose flour
1 cup heavy cream
Salt and pepper to taste

In a pot, cook the seafood—ono, shrimp, and crabmeat—in chicken stock for 4 to 5 minutes. Separate the seafood from the broth and set aside.

In a soup pot, sauté the onion, celery, and garlic in butter until onion is translucent. Add the broccoli and cook until broccoli is soft. Stir in the flour and mix well. Stir in the reserved broth slowly, blend well, and simmer for 25 minutes. Add the cream, then salt and pepper to taste. Simmer for 15 more minutes. Purée and strain. Fold in cooked seafood, and serve hot.

Creamy Macadamia Nut Soup

(Serves 6)

In 1994, when I was invited to go pick macadamia nuts for the first time after living on the Big Island for five years, I quickly found out how hard, and how backbreaking, it is to go and harvest those little buggers. It's worth it, though. Every bite lightens you up. I don't mean in weight, but in spirit. When you eat them it's like being a kid in a candy store—you just want to eat more and more, and you get all excited about it. This soup catches some of that excitement.

2½ cups macadamia nuts
¾ cup minced onions
1 quart chicken stock
6 tablespoons butter
6 tablespoons all-purpose flour
4 cups heavy cream
Salt and white pepper to taste

Garnish:
6 teaspoons chopped fresh parsley

Coarsely chop the macadamia nuts and place in a saucepan (reserve a small amount for garnish). Add the onions and chicken stock. Bring to a boil, reduce the heat, and simmer for about 15 minutes.

In a large pan, melt the butter and stir in the flour. Cook, stirring with a wooden spatula, over high heat for 2 minutes—do not brown.

Gradually add the simmering stock mixture to the flour mixture, stirring until thickened. Add the cream and bring to a simmer over medium-low heat. Let cook for 3 to 4 minutes. Add salt and pepper to taste. Garnish with chopped parsley and sprinkle with the reserved chopped macadamia nuts.

Best Crabmeat Soup with Taro

(Serves 8)

Taro is really good when it's sweet and fresh, then poached and folded into crabmeat soup with coconut milk, spinach, and sweet onions. If you can't get taro in your area, you can use potatoes. The flavor will be very different, but it'll be a great soup anyway.

4 tablespoons (½ stick) butter
2 cups diced onions
2 tablespoons all-purpose flour
2 cups heavy cream
1½ cups chicken stock
2 cups coconut milk
3 cups fresh spinach, washed, stemmed, and chopped
1½ cups crabmeat, picked over well
1½ cups cooked and diced taro or potatoes (see Note)
Salt and white pepper to taste

In a large pot, melt the butter and sauté the onion until translucent. Add the flour and blend well. Slowly stir in the cream and add the chicken stock; simmer 5 minutes, stirring frequently. Stir in the coconut milk, spinach, crabmeat, and taro; cook 3 minutes, stirring frequently. Season with salt and white pepper.

Note: Be sure to cook the taro thoroughly. Uncooked taro enzymes cause a scratchy sensation in your throat.

Sam Choy's South Point Chowder

(Serves 8)

Places like South Point on the Big Island, Nihoa on Kaua'i, and the windward coasts of every island harbor an abundance of fish, but the rough seas and turbulent weather are too treacherous for most people. You have to know what you're doing out there. That's where you find the real fishermen. I live on the Big Island, so most of the fish I use in my kitchen are from South Point.

1 pound firm white fish of your choice (wahoo, snapper, or tuna)
¼ pound shrimp
¼ pound scallops
6 strips bacon, diced
1 onion, minced
3 stalks celery, minced
1 potato, peeled and diced
1 sweet potato, peeled and diced
2 cups Fish Stock (see recipe on page 111)
8 New Zealand green-tip mussels, soaked, cleaned, drained, and
*   debearded (see Note on page 65)*
Salt and white pepper to taste
Pinch of fresh thyme
½ cup canned cream-style corn
½ cup fresh corn kernels
2 cups heavy cream

Garnish:
2 tablespoons chopped parsley

Cube the fish. Shell and devein the shrimp. Set the seafood aside.

In a heavy stockpot, fry the bacon with the onion and celery until the onion is translucent. Add the potatoes and fish stock. Bring to a boil, cover, and simmer until potatoes are cooked. Add fish, prepared mussels, shrimp, scallops, salt, pepper, and thyme. Cover and simmer until fish is firm and opaque.

Remove the mussels and remove the upper shells. Return mussels to the soup.

Add the cream-style corn and corn kernels. Stir in the heavy cream and heat thoroughly but don't boil. Garnish with parsley.

Fish Stock

(Makes 2 cups)

2½ *pounds fish bones, rinsed*
1 *cup white wine*
4 *stalks celery, chopped*
1 *carrot, chopped*
1 *onion, chopped*
1 *tablespoon peeled and minced fresh ginger*
2 *whole bay leaves*
1½ *teaspoons salt*
½ *teaspoon white pepper*

Place the fish bones in a large pot. Add the white wine, vegetables, ginger, bay leaves, salt, pepper, and enough water to cover the bones. Bring to a boil. Reduce the heat and simmer for 25 minutes. Strain. Fish stock should be used when fresh.

Beef Lu'au Stew

(Serves 12)

This is always an interesting dish. It calls for lu'au (taro leaves). You can substitute fresh spinach, which does not need precooking. A lot of the old-timers will toss a hot chili pepper into the stew while it's cooking to spice it up.

> *2 pounds lu'au (young taro leaves), or spinach leaves*
> *5 cups water*
> *2 tablespoons rock or kosher salt*
> *½ teaspoon baking soda*
> *1 tablespoon canola oil*
> *2 pounds beef brisket cut into 2-inch cubes, or meaty short ribs*
> *1 cup chopped onions*
> *3 cups beef stock*
> *Salt and pepper to taste.*

Rinse the lu'au and trim off the stems and thick veins. Bring 3 cups of water, 1 tablespoon of rock salt, and the baking soda to a boil in a stockpot. Add the lu'au, then cook, partially covered, for 30 minutes. Drain, and squeeze out excess liquid.

In another pot, heat the oil and brown the beef. Add the onions and sauté until translucent. Add the beef stock, remaining 2 cups of water, and 1 tablespoon of salt. Cook, partially covered, until the meat is fork-tender, 1½ to 2 hours. Add the cooked lu'au or raw spinach leaves and simmer 30 minutes more.

Adjust seasoning with salt and pepper.

Variation: For pork lu'au stew, use country-style pork spareribs and chicken stock in place of the beef and beef stock.

Local Boy Beef Stew

(Serves 6)

One of my secrets for making a thick, rich stew is that I use mochiko (Japanese glutinous rice flour) diluted with a little water for thickening. This stew is best the next day, after all the flavors have had a chance to blend.

4 pounds boneless chuck roast, cut into 1-inch cubes
Salt and pepper to taste
About ½ cup all-purpose flour
½ cup salad oil
2 cloves fresh garlic, crushed
1 small onion, minced
½ cup chopped celery leaves
5 cups beef stock
2 cups chicken stock
1½ cups tomato paste
3 medium carrots, peeled and chunked
4 potatoes, peeled and chunked
2 medium onions, peeled and chunked
4 stalks celery, chunked
Enough mochiko (Japanese glutinous rice flour) and water to thicken

Sprinkle the beef with salt and pepper, then dust with flour. Heat the oil in a heavy-lidded pot and brown the meat with the garlic, onion, and celery leaves for about 10 minutes on medium or medium-low heat. Keep stirring to avoid burning.

Drain off the oil. Add the beef stock, chicken stock, and tomato paste to the pot. Bring to a boil, then reduce to a simmer. Cover and let cook for about 1 hour, or until the beef is tender.

Add the carrots and potatoes and cook 5 minutes. Add the onion and celery chunks, and cook for 10 minutes more. Adjust thickness with mochiko and water, combining about 1 tablespoon of mochiko with 1 tablespoon of water and adding to the simmering stew a little at a time until you get the right consistency. Taste for seasoning and add salt and pepper if needed.

Island Seafood Stew

(Serves 6)

This recipe is great when you don't have a lot of one thing for a meal, but have a little of many different things. It's the same basic idea as cioppino or bouillabaisse, but uses different ingredients and seasonings, so you get a very exotic taste.

1½ pounds opah (moonfish), 'opakapaka (pink snapper),
   mahimahi (dolphinfish), or firm white fish of your choice
½ pound extra-large shrimp (21 to 25 count)
½ pound clams or mussels
3 cups clam juice
3½ cups chicken stock
1 cup white wine
Juice of 1 lemon
2 tablespoons tomato paste
½ cup olive oil
1 large onion, diced
1 cup thinly sliced celery
1 cup diced carrots
½ cup cubed sweet potatoes, parboiled 5 to 6 minutes
½ cup cubed taro, or potatoes, parboiled 5 to 6 minutes
1 tablespoon minced fresh garlic
1 medium tomato, minced
¼ teaspoon red chili pepper flakes, or 1 hot chili pepper, chopped
1 cup chopped fresh basil
Pinch of saffron
½ cup chopped fresh cilantro

Cut the fish into 1-inch cubes. Shell and devein the shrimp. Scrub the clams, or scrub and debeard the mussels (see Note on page 65).

In a large pot, combine the clam juice, chicken stock, white wine, lemon juice, and tomato paste, and bring to a boil. Add the shrimp and return to a boil. Remove the shrimp and set aside.

Return the stock to a boil and add the fish and clams or mussels. Remove the pot from the heat and let stand 2 minutes. Remove the seafood from the stock and set aside.

In a skillet, heat the olive oil and sauté the onion, celery, carrots, parboiled sweet potatoes and taro or potatoes, and garlic for 2 minutes. Add this mixture to the stock, along with the remaining ingredients. Return the pot to the heat and simmer for 15 minutes. Stir in the reserved seafood. Serve hot.

Shellfish

Just outside of Hukilau Bay and off to the right, the water gets really deep. You can tell by the color—baby-blue means it's shallow, and when it turns cobalt you know that's where the shelf drops away and the ocean plunges to black.

Anyway, just before the water takes on a deepening blue tinge, a little sea mount pops straight up, out of nowhere, all crusted over with coral. There's great fishing out there: all kinds of reef fish, and underneath there are little shelves and pukas (holes) packed with lobster. It's just antennas, legs, and claws everywhere, kind of scary.

I was in my early teens when my dad first took me out there. We went lobster fishing, and had to wear work gloves to protect our hands from the spiny shells. We'd just pluck up enough bugs—we called them bugs—for dinner. But that was Hukilau in those days. Good fish, plenty of lobster. We also picked up crabs from the shallows around the point, and 'opihi (limpets) from the surf-washed lava rock of Goat Island. We fished and swam and fished. It was like heaven: blue water, blue sky, white clouds, and white sand.

Today, most of the shellfish that folks eat in Hawai'i is shipped in, either fresh or fresh frozen. A few aquafarmers have taken on the difficult task of raising shellfish here. It's a fledgling industry, and we all support the aquafarms. Shellfish is a major part of our local cooking. As usual, we've combined ethnic flavors here for a uniquely Island taste.

You can use just about any cooking style when working with shellfish. The flavors blend well in stir-fry, cioppino, au gratin, or curry with coconut milk. Shellfish can be poached, grilled, baked, or steamed. The versatility is astonishing. They're also good in combinations: shrimp and clams, lobster and crab, oysters and abalone.

You should be able to find most of the shellfish used in this section—crabmeat, lobster, mollusks, scallops, shrimp, and calamari—in the fresh fish or freezer compartments of your local supermarket. Use them in these recipes and you'll have a "local" Hawaiian experience in your very own dining room.

Calamari Stir-Fry

(Serves 4)

This is one of the fastest and easiest stir-fries you can make, and one of the tastiest. Calamari is also a most economical seafood. If you plan to serve this to guests, and you want to wow them, you can prepare all the ingredients ahead of time, then stir-fry everything in a portable wok right at the table. This adds a lot of show, and will have your guests oohing and aahing.

12 medium-sized fresh calamari (squid)
Calamari Marinade (see recipe on page 120)
2 tablespoons olive oil
1 tablespoon butter
4 cups of your 5 favorite stir-fry vegetables, julienned
Teriyaki Glaze (see recipe on page 25)

Clean the calamari (or have your fishmonger do this for you) and cut them into ½-inch rings. Marinate in the calamari marinade for 1 hour.

Heat the oil and butter in a large pan or wok and stir-fry the calamari real quick—a minute, or maybe a minute and a half. You just want to sizzle it. Remove calamari from the pan. Stir-fry the vegetables for 2 to 3 minutes. Add the teriyaki glaze, then fold in the calamari. You can serve it with hot rice as a full meal or just by itself as an appetizer.

Calamari Marinade

(Makes about 2¼ cups)

1 cup soy sauce
1 cup salad oil
¼ cup mirin (Japanese sweet rice wine)
1 teaspoon sesame oil
¼ cup minced fresh cilantro
2 tablespoons minced fresh garlic
2 tablespoons peeled and minced fresh ginger
1 teaspoon salt
½ teaspoon white pepper
2 tablespoons thinly sliced green onion
¼ cup cornstarch
1 tablespoon brown sugar

Combine all ingredients and stir until cornstarch is dissolved.

Steamer Clams with Ginger Pesto Butter

(Serves 4)

Steamer clams are a small, East Coast soft-shell variety that has a thin, brittle shell. They are named appropriately, as they're most delicious when steamed or served in a stew. This dish boasts a fine blend of Asian flavors, crowned with spicy Ginger Pesto Butter.

24 steamer clams
1 medium onion, thinly sliced
½ teaspoon chopped fresh garlic

3 cups chicken stock
1 cup julienned fresh shiitake mushrooms
2 cups julienned mustard cabbage
1 tablespoon chopped green onion
Salt and pepper to taste
4 tablespoons Ginger Pesto Butter (see recipe below)

Garnish:
4 sprigs fresh cilantro leaves

Rinse the clams thoroughly in several changes of water.

Place clams, onion, garlic, and chicken stock in a small pot over medium heat. Cook for one minute. Add all vegetables and cook for 2 to 3 minutes. Salt and pepper to taste, then remove from stove.

Divide the clams among 4 serving bowls. Dollop each serving with 1 tablespoon of the ginger pesto butter. Garnish with cilantro leaves, and serve immediately.

Ginger Pesto Butter

(Makes 2¼ cups)

¼ cup peeled and minced fresh ginger
1 clove fresh garlic, minced
¼ cup chopped fresh cilantro
½ cup chopped green onions
1 cup light olive oil
½ cup butter, softened
Salt and pepper to taste

Mix all ingredients in a blender, then cream into softened butter.

Ginger Clams with Black Bean Sauce

(Serves 4)

*J*ust try this simple dish once and you'll be hooked. Use any kind of clams—cherrystones from the Pacific Northwest, Manila clams, or New Zealand clams. This goes great with hot steamed rice.

½ tablespoon dau see (salted fermented black beans)
36 fresh clams in shells
2 tablespoons peanut oil
½ cup ground pork
½ cup peeled and julienned fresh ginger
2 cloves fresh garlic, minced
½ teaspoon minced hot chili pepper, or red chili pepper flakes
1½ cups chicken stock
¼ cup sherry
¼ cup chopped green onions
2 tablespoons soy sauce
1 tablespoon oyster sauce
1 teaspoon granulated sugar
1½ tablespoons cornstarch mixed with 3 tablespoons water

Garnish:
½ cup chopped fresh cilantro

Soak black beans in water for 30 minutes, drain, then rinse, and mash into a paste. Scrub the clams thoroughly until free of all mud and grit. Rinse under cold running water. In a wok, heat the oil over medium-high heat and add the pork, ginger, garlic, and chili pepper; stir-fry 3 to 4 minutes. Add the clams, chicken stock, dau see paste, sherry, green onions, soy sauce, oyster sauce, and sugar. Bring to a boil, reduce the heat, then simmer covered until clams open. Remove the clams from the wok and place in a bowl.

Mix the cornstarch and cold water; add to the wok mixture and stir for 1 minute to thicken sauce. Return the clams to the wok.

Serve in a large bowl, and garnish with cilantro.

Tomato Crab

(Serves 6)

You've heard of the traditional Chinese stir-fry dish, tomato beef. Well, this is "tomato crab." It's simple, good, easy, and different, and it teams perfectly with hot cooked rice.

1 large frozen Dungeness crab

2 tablespoons canola oil

4 ripe, fresh tomatoes, cut into wedges

1 cup sliced assorted vegetables (onions, celery, bell peppers, and mushrooms)

1 tablespoon chopped fresh garlic

2 tablespoons soy sauce

2 tablespoons oyster sauce

1 teaspoon tomato paste

1 cup chicken stock

To prepare the crab, cut off the eyes and mouth, remove the gills and then the top shell. Cut the body into 4 to 6 pieces, leaving a leg on each piece.

In a wok or heavy skillet, heat the oil and stir-fry the crab for 1 minute. Add the tomatoes, mixed vegetables, and garlic, and toss until coated with oil. Combine the soy sauce, oyster sauce, tomato paste, and chicken stock and stir in. Cover and cook over medium high heat until vegetables are just tender, 2 to 3 minutes.

Island-Style Lobster Boil with Chili Peppers & Other Things

(Serves 1)

I use elemental ingredients in this basic recipe: rock salt, hot chili peppers, and, in my opinion, "the King of Seafood"—lobster. I call these "clean" ingredients—foods that require very little to bring their natural flavors to the forefront. This recipe is easy to make, takes almost no time, and best of all, it tastes wonderful!

Pinch of Hawaiian (rock) or kosher salt
1 or 2 fresh chili peppers, crushed
1 fresh lemon, cut into quarters
1 tablespoon chopped fresh cilantro
1 tablespoon cracked peppercorns
2 tablespoons white wine
3 cups water
1 live lobster
1 cooked carrot, chopped
1 cooked onion, chopped
1 cooked celery stalk, chopped
½ cup drawn butter (optional)

Combine salt, chili peppers, lemon, cilantro, peppercorns, white wine, and water in a large wok or kettle. Bring to a boil. Add the lobster and cover. Cook about 9 to 12 minutes or until the shell turns bright red. Reserve ½ cup of liquid.

Cut the lobster down the center. Serve with the cooked carrot, onion, and celery. Drizzle some reserved cooking liquid or drawn butter over the top.

Ginger, Ginger Steamed Mussels

(Serves 6)

Here's a light broth packed with a heavy ginger flavor. There's never enough ginger. Try adding just one chili pepper to the broth. Whew, I like this one—especially with garlic bread.

6 pounds mussels (see Note on page 65)

2 cups light clam broth

1 cup dry white wine

2 tablespoons peeled and minced fresh ginger

2 tablespoons minced shallots

2 tablespoons chopped fresh parsley

2 tablespoons butter

1 tablespoon chopped fresh garlic

Salt and pepper to taste

1 cup seeded and diced tomatoes

¼ cup minced combination green onion and cilantro

Under cold running water, scrub the mussel shells and pull off the beards, or filaments. In a large pot, combine the clam broth, wine, ginger, shallots, parsley, butter, garlic, salt, and pepper. Bring to a boil. Add the mussels. Cover and return to a boil. Cook about 10 minutes, until the mussel shells open. (Discard any that refuse to open.) Transfer the mussels with shells to a serving platter.

Boil the liquid to reduce by half. Stir in the tomatoes, green onion, and cilantro. Adjust seasoning with salt and pepper. Pour the sauce over the mussels and serve.

Fried Oysters with Spicy, Vine-Ripened Tomato Relish

(Serves 4)

Furikake is a Japanese condiment made of seaweed and sesame seeds. There are many different types on the market, some with dried ground shrimp, fish, and other shellfish and seasonings. Furikake gives the rémoulade in this recipe an interesting seaweed flavor. I wanted to use ogo in the tomato relish, but the furikake supplied the seaweed zing.

24 large oysters, shucked (reserve bottom shells for presentation)
1 cup all-purpose flour
Salt and pepper to taste
3 whole eggs, beaten
3 cups panko (Japanese-style bread crumbs), or fine bread crumbs
2 or more cups vegetable oil, for deep-frying
Spicy, Vine-Ripened Tomato Relish (see recipe on page 127)
Hijimi Rémoulade (see recipe on page 127)

Garnish:
Furikake (dried seaweed flakes and sesame seeds)
2 cups rock salt (for oyster bed)

Drain the oysters of their liquid and lay them on paper towels to dry. Mix the flour, salt, and pepper in a shallow bowl. Beat the eggs in another shallow bowl and put the bread crumbs in a third bowl.

Coat the oysters with flour, shaking off excess, then dip them in beaten egg and roll them in bread crumbs. Let stand on a rack until all are coated. Meanwhile, heat 2½ to 3 inches of oil in a wok or deep, heavy pot over medium-high heat until it registers 365°F on a deep-fry thermometer.

Fry the oysters a few at a time for 2 or 3 minutes or until golden brown; drain on paper towels. As the oysters are fried, place them in a 200°F oven to keep warm until all are cooked. Allow the oil to return to 365°F before adding a new batch.

Meanwhile, prepare a bed of rock salt on a large platter and arrange the oyster half-shells on the salt, making small indentations to prevent tipping. Spoon a little tomato relish into each shell.

Place the fried oysters over the tomato relish and sprinkle with furikake. Serve immediately, with hijimi rémoulade on the side.

Spicy, Vine-Ripened Tomato Relish

(Makes 1½ cups)

3 large vine-ripened tomatoes, diced small
1 medium sweet onion, diced small
½ cup thinly sliced green onions
1 hot chili pepper, minced
½ cup minced yellow bell pepper
1 teaspoon minced fresh garlic
Sea or rock salt to taste
Juice of 2 fresh limes
½ cup light salad oil

Mix all ingredients together.

Hijimi Rémoulade

(Makes 1¼ cups)

1 cup mayonnaise
1 teaspoon hijimi (a spicy, Japanese pepper sprinkle)
1 teaspoon chopped fresh garlic
1 tablespoon chopped green onion
1 teaspoon furikake (Japanese condiment of dried seaweed flakes and sesame seeds)
1 teaspoon lemon juice
2 tablespoons water

Blend all ingredients. Serve at room temperature.

Stir-Fried U-10 Shrimp and Fresh Asparagus

(Serves 4)

Shrimp and asparagus are two of my favorite foods. Together, they make up my one-two punch—jumbo U-10 (under 10 count) shrimp, with tender-crisp asparagus, flavored with dau see, ginger, sesame oil, garlic, onions, and brown sugar. It's a winner. Serve these giant shrimp over steamed rice or noodles.

1 pound fresh asparagus

1 tablespoon dau see (salted fermented black beans), soaked in water for 30 minutes then drained

2 tablespoons minced green onion

1 clove fresh garlic, minced

½ teaspoon peeled and minced fresh ginger

1 tablespoon soy sauce

½ teaspoon sesame oil

½ teaspoon brown sugar

2 teaspoons cornstarch

2 teaspoons cold water

1 tablespoon canola oil

12 U-10 shrimp (under 10 count), shelled and deveined

½ cup chicken stock

Trim the tough white ends from the asparagus and cut the stalks into ½-inch diagonal slices. Mash the black beans with the green onion, garlic, and ginger; stir in the soy sauce, sesame oil, and brown sugar. Mix the cornstarch and cold water in a separate bowl; set aside.

In a wok, heat 2 teaspoons of the oil and stir-fry the shrimp for 2 minutes, or until they are firm and opaque; remove to a plate. Heat the remaining 1 teaspoon oil and stir-fry the asparagus until just tender. Stir in the black bean mixture and the shrimp. Add the stock and heat quickly. Add the cornstarch mixture and stir until the sauce is thickened and clear.

Smoked Shrimp with Mango Salsa

(Serves 4)

Kiawe (mesquite) bushes grow along the hot, sandy beaches on the leeward coasts of all of the Hawaiian Islands. The thorns are a nuisance, but the wood chips add a glorious flavor to smoked dishes. This recipe's different—and challenging—preparation technique gives juicy shrimp the mouth-watering accents of smoking and pineapple.

1½ pounds large shrimp (26 to 35 count), shelled and deveined
Salt and pepper to taste
1 tablespoon minced fresh garlic
1 teaspoon brown sugar
2 pieces pineapple rind (outer peel)
Mango Salsa (see recipe on page 130)

Season the shrimp with salt, pepper, garlic, and brown sugar. In a heavy baking pan, spread kiawe chips and pineapple rind. Put a rack in the pan. Place the pan directly on a stove burner over high heat. When the chips start to smoke, place the shrimp on the rack and seal the pan tightly with foil. Reduce the heat to low, and cook the shrimp until done, 10 to 15 minutes. Be sure to watch closely for possible flare-ups.

Serve with mango salsa.

Mango Salsa

(Makes 3 cups)

2 cups chopped fresh mango
½ cup chopped red onion
½ cup chopped fresh basil
¼ cup chopped red bell pepper
2 tablespoons chopped fresh cilantro
2 tablespoons granulated sugar
1 hot chili pepper, seeded and minced
½ teaspoon powdered cumin
Salt and pepper to taste

Combine all ingredients; blend well.

Nihoa Shrimp Kabobs

(Serves 4)

Catching deep-sea shrimp in Hawai'i is getting tougher and tougher, because you have to go way down deep and drag the bottom, which wipes out all the shrimp. It's so cold and dark down in the deep ocean that it takes years and years for the shrimp to reproduce and make a comeback. Because of that, most shrimp served in Hawai'i's restaurants today have been raised on aquaculture farms. Some still come from places like Nihoa on the north coast of the island of Moloka'i, though. A few people can taste the difference, but most can't.

Barbecue Shrimp Marinade (see recipe on page 131)
24 jumbo shrimp (16 to 20 count), shelled and deveined
Oil to coat grill
Nihoa Dipping Sauce (see recipe on page 132)

Heat coals in a hibachi and prepare the barbecue shrimp marinade.

Thread the shrimp on bamboo skewers and marinate in the mixture for 45 minutes to 1 hour.

Wipe oil on the grill rack to prevent sticking.

Grill the shrimp kabobs about 1½ minutes per side. Shrimp are done when they turn pink all over. Don't overcook. Serve with Nihoa dipping sauce—one of my favorites.

Barbecue Shrimp Marinade
(Makes 2½ cups)

1 cup salad oil

1 cup soy sauce

2 teaspoons sesame oil

¼ cup mirin (Japanese sweet rice wine)

2 tablespoons minced fresh garlic

2 tablespoons peeled and minced fresh ginger

½ teaspoon salt

½ teaspoon white pepper

1 tablespoon brown sugar

½ teaspoon minced hot chili pepper

1 teaspoon minced fresh cilantro

Mix all the ingredients.

Nihoa Dipping Sauce

(Makes about ¼ cup)

1 teaspoon granulated sugar
1 teaspoon minced fresh cilantro
2 teaspoons hoisin sauce
2 tablespoons Chinese garlic chili sauce
¼ cup ketchup

Blend all ingredients and stir until sugar is dissolved.

Garlic Shrimp with Spinach, Red Peppers, and Oyster Mushrooms

(Serves 4)

Definitely the best of the best: Not only is this an elegant dish, but the flavor blends are as rich as the colors. The juice from the shrimp goes into the oyster mushrooms, along with the garlic and spinach. Add the piquance of the chili pepper and you've got fireworks.

3 large red bell peppers
8 tablespoons olive oil
12 ounces oyster mushrooms, sliced
3 bunches fresh spinach, preferably left whole, rinsed well and dried
Salt and pepper to taste
6 large cloves fresh garlic, minced
1 tablespoon finely chopped hot chili pepper
1¼ pounds large shrimp (26 to 35 count), peeled and deveined
2 tablespoons chopped fresh cilantro

Char the bell peppers over a gas flame or under a broiler until the skin on all sides is blackened. Place the peppers in a plastic bag for 10 minutes; then remove the skin, cores, and seeds. Quarter the peppers and arrange on a platter.

In a large, heavy skillet, heat 4 tablespoons of the oil over medium heat, and sauté the mushrooms and spinach until tender, about 6 to 8 minutes. Season with salt and pepper. Arrange on the platter with the bell peppers.

In the same skillet, heat the remaining 4 tablespoons of oil over medium-high heat. Sauté the garlic, chili pepper, shrimp, and salt and pepper to taste until the shrimp turn pink and opaque, about 2 to 4 minutes. Fold in the cilantro and arrange the shrimp over the peppers, mushrooms, and spinach.

Ginger-Boiled Fresh Shrimp with My Dad's Favorite Dipping Sauce

(Serves 1 to 2)

This dish is best when you use the freshest shrimp, right out of the ocean. You poach them by dropping them into boiling ginger broth, then take them out the moment they turn pink. The dip brings out the sweetness of the shrimp. The fresher the shrimp, the sweeter they taste.

Poaching Liquid (see recipe on page 134)
1 pound jumbo shrimp (16 to 20 count), rinsed, with shells
    left on
My Dad's Favorite Dipping Sauce (see recipe on page 134)

Bring the poaching liquid to a boil. Add the shrimp. As soon as it starts to boil again, remove the shrimp. Don't overcook. Shrimp are cooked before they curl up, so remove them promptly. Serve with the dipping sauce.

Poaching Liquid

(Makes 6 cups)

4 cups water
1 medium finger peeled fresh ginger, crushed
½ cup chopped fresh cilantro
2 cups white wine
1 cup mixture of diced carrots, onion, and celery

Mix all ingredients together in a saucepan.

My Dad's Favorite Dipping Sauce

(Makes ¾ cup)

½ cup soy sauce
2 teaspoons granulated sugar
1 teaspoon salad oil
½ teaspoon sesame oil
1 teaspoon minced fresh cilantro
1 hot red chili pepper (optional)

Bring the soy sauce and the sugar to a boil. Remove from the heat and pour into a dip bowl. Heat the oils, then pour into soy sauce mixture. Fold in the cilantro. If you like it spicy, you can throw in a whole red chili pepper when you heat the oils.

Baked Coconut Shrimp 'Anaeho'omalu Bay

(Serves 4)

We were camping at 'Anaeho'omalu Bay, north of Kailua-Kona on the Big Island of Hawai'i, and I created this in a baking pan over a hibachi. It was a *hit*! These things don't happen by planning.

1 pound jumbo shrimp (16 to 20 count)
2 tablespoons olive oil
1 tablespoon soy sauce
1 tablespoon peeled and minced fresh ginger
2 teaspoons minced fresh herbs (combination of basil,
*   dill, and/or thyme)*
1 clove fresh garlic, minced
Coconut Shrimp Filling (see recipe on page 136)

Preheat the oven to 350°F.

Shell and devein the shrimp, leaving the tails on. To butterfly shrimp, slice the underside almost through but without cutting them in half, then spread and flatten. In a mixing bowl, combine the olive oil, soy sauce, ginger, fresh herbs, and garlic; marinate the butterflied shrimp in this mixture for 20 to 30 minutes.

Press 1 teaspoon or more of coconut shrimp filling into each shrimp. Place the shrimp, stuffing side up, on a lightly greased baking sheet. Bake until shrimp are pink and stuffing is lightly browned, about 10 to 12 minutes. Serve hot.

Coconut Shrimp Filling

(Makes about 1 cup)

8 tablespoons (1 stick) butter, softened
¼ cup fine dry bread crumbs
¼ cup grated or thinly sliced fresh coconut
2 tablespoons freshly grated Parmesan cheese
½ teaspoon paprika
Salt and pepper to taste

Combine all the ingredients and mix thoroughly.

Braised Colossal Shrimp with Black Bean Sauce

(Serves 4)

In my opinion, black beans bring out the best in fresh seafood. They add a salty and fermented wild gusto to the taste of the dish. The flavor is catching on. Some chefs have begun to serve a black bean butter sauce with their seafood dishes.

1 to 2 tablespoons dau see (salted fermented black beans)
1 clove fresh garlic
1 tablespoon cornstarch mixed with 2 tablespoons water
    for thickening
3 tablespoons canola oil
½ teaspoon salt
2 pounds colossal shrimp (10 to 15 count), shelled and deveined
1 cup chicken stock
½ cup julienned onion
½ cup julienned green bell pepper
1 teaspoon soy sauce
Dash of black pepper

Soak the black beans for 30 minutes in warm water, rinse, and drain. Mash the garlic. Mix the cornstarch and cold water; set aside.

In a wok, heat the oil over medium-high heat. Stir-fry the black beans, garlic, and salt for a few seconds to heat through. Add the shrimp and brown lightly. Stir in the stock, heat quickly, and simmer 3 to 4 minutes. Add the onion and bell pepper and simmer, covered, for 2 minutes, or until tender. Stir in the soy sauce and pepper. Add the cornstarch mixture and cook for 1 minute, or until thickened.

Paradise Shrimp Scampi with Dill Cream Sauce over Linguini

(Serves 4)

Scampi is usually shrimp in butter and garlic sauce. My version uses cream with dill. It's a whole different experience. This makes a delicious meal with garlic bread and salad.

2 pounds jumbo shrimp (16 to 20 count), shelled and deveined
Paradise Marinade (see recipe on page 139)
1 cup all-purpose flour, or enough to dust shrimp
2 tablespoons olive oil
2 tablespoons butter
1 tablespoon minced fresh garlic
1½ pounds linguine, cooked and drained
1 tablespoon soy sauce
5 cups heavy cream, or as needed
2 tablespoons minced fresh dill
Salt and pepper to taste
5 tablespoons grated Parmesan cheese

Mix the shrimp with the paradise marinade so that all are thoroughly coated; let stand for 15 to 20 minutes.

Dust the shrimp with flour, shaking off excess. Heat the olive oil in a large skillet and sear the shrimp quickly over medium-high heat, about 1 minute on each side. Remove from the heat and set aside (shrimp will be raw on the inside).

Melt the butter in a large saucepan and sauté the garlic over medium-low heat until fragrant but not brown, about 2 minutes. Set aside.

Cook the linguini according to package directions, drain, and transfer to the saucepan with the garlic butter. Add the soy sauce and cream; bring to a rolling simmer. Continue simmering until thick, about 3 to 4 minutes. You need to keep your eye on it. If the pasta absorbs a lot of the cream, you may need to add a little more. If you add more cream, continue to cook until reduced to a nice thick consistency. Add the shrimp and dill, and adjust seasoning with salt and pepper. Cook for another minute, until shrimp is done, then fold in the grated Parmesan cheese.

Serve in pasta bowls.

Paradise Marinade

(Makes 2 tablespoons)

1 tablespoon minced fresh garlic
1 tablespoon olive oil
Salt and pepper to taste

Mix all ingredients.

Baked Scallops au Gratin with Fresh Asparagus

(Serves 6)

*T*his recipe gives you the feeling of being creative, yet it's simple. Layer the ingredients right in your dishes, sprinkle the tops with Parmesan, pop them into the oven, and they are done.

1½ pounds sea scallops, 10 to 20 per pound
1 cup dry white wine
¼ cup chopped green onions
1 tablespoon chopped fresh dill
½ teaspoon salt
4 tablespoons (½ stick) butter
2 tablespoons all-purpose flour
½ cup heavy cream
Salt and white pepper to taste
24 fresh asparagus spears, trimmed and blanched
1 tablespoon fine dry bread crumbs
¼ cup Parmesan cheese, freshly grated

Cut the scallops in half, or into bite-sized pieces.
In a medium saucepan, simmer together the wine, green onions, dill, and salt

for 2 to 3 minutes. Add the scallops and simmer covered for 1½ to 2 minutes; remove the scallops to a bowl. Boil the wine mixture until reduced to ½ cup liquid.

In a saucepan, cook 2 tablespoons of the butter with the flour for 2 minutes. Gradually stir in the hot wine mixture and heavy cream. Adjust the seasoning with salt and white pepper. Stir in the scallops.

In 6 mini casserole dishes, layer in order: asparagus side by side lengthwise along the bottom of the dish (halved if necessary to fit in one layer), a layer of scallops, and then a sprinkling of bread crumbs and Parmesan cheese.

Melt the remaining 2 tablespoons of butter and drizzle over the mini casseroles. Broil casseroles until bubbling hot and lightly browned. Serve immediately.

Stir-Fried Curried Scallops

(Serves 6)

Curry and scallops are like ginger pesto and chicken—another great marriage of flavors. Tasting the purity of the scallop is the most important thing. Serve these over freshly cooked rice.

2 teaspoons cornstarch
½ teaspoon granulated sugar
Salt and pepper to taste
2 to 3 tablespoons cold water
2 to 3 tablespoons curry powder
1 medium onion, diced
1 pound sea or bay scallops
½ cup chicken stock

Blend the cornstarch, sugar, salt, pepper, and cold water.

In a dry wok over low heat, stir-fry the curry powder and onion for 2 minutes, or until the curry odor is pungent. Increase the heat to medium and stir-fry the scallops briefly to coat with curry. Stir in the stock and cook, covered, for 2 minutes, or until they are opaque, stirring once or twice. Stir in the cornstarch paste to thicken sauce.

Serve immediately.

Seared Ginger Scallops with Tomato-Chanterelle Lomi

(Serves 4)

The contrast of the deep red tomatoes and brown mushrooms with the white scallops on top laced with the chopped green onion makes this a spectacular dish. The Hawaiian word lomi means to toss, mix, or massage. I call the Tomato-Chanterelle a lomi because the ingredients are quickly mixed into a chunky salsa-style condiment. Serve with rice.

Tomato-Chanterelle Lomi (see recipe on page 142)
¼ cup all-purpose flour
Salt and pepper to taste
1½ teaspoons sesame seeds
1 teaspoon powdered ginger
20 sea scallops
2 tablespoons light olive oil

Garnish:
2 tablespoons chopped green onion

Make the tomato-chanterelle lomi and set aside.

Mix the flour with the salt, pepper, sesame seeds, and powdered ginger in a shallow bowl. Roll the scallops in the flour mixture. In a large sauté pan, sear scallops in oil over high heat for about 1 minute on each side or until they just turn opaque (cut one open to test). Do not overcook.

Spoon some of the tomato-chanterelle mixture on a plate, top with a portion of scallops, and sprinkle with green onion. Serve right away.

Tomato-Chanterelle Lomi

(Makes ¾ cup)

2 tablespoons light olive oil
1 cup sliced fresh chanterelle mushrooms
½ cup sliced sweet onion
1 teaspoon peeled and chopped fresh ginger
½ cup chopped green onions
2 medium tomatoes, diced
3 tablespoons soy sauce
2 tablespoons chicken stock
1 teaspoon Dijon mustard
1 tablespoon rice wine vinegar
2 tablespoons sesame oil
Salt and pepper

Heat the olive oil in a wok. Stir-fry the chanterelles, sliced onion, and ginger for 1 minute. Add the rest of the ingredients, and salt and pepper to taste. Cook for 1 to 2 minutes and keep warm.

My Kids' Favorite Seafood Lasagne

(Serves 12 to 20)

If you give my kids a choice, they'll say lasagne every night, whether it's with tomato sauce and cheese, or vegetables, or seafood. When I make seafood lasagne, they get the most excited. They like the big chunks of fish, shrimp, and scallops in cream sauce with all that pasta and cheese. Man, that sounds so good I think I'll go make some right now.

1 pound lasagne noodles
Salad oil
Poaching Liquid (see recipe on page 144)
2 cups broccoli florets
2 cups 2-inch zucchini chunks
1 pound scallops
1 pound shrimp, shelled and deveined
1 pound fresh mahimahi fillets, sliced ¼ inch thick
1 pound salmon fillets, sliced ¼ inch thick
Cheese Filling (see recipe on page 145)
White Sauce (see recipe on page 145)
4 ounces Parmesan cheese, freshly grated
1 pound mozzarella cheese, grated

Cook the lasagne noodles according to package directions. Rinse well and drain. Mix the noodles gently with enough oil to keep them from sticking together. Set aside.

Bring the poaching liquid to a boil and drop in the broccoli florets and zucchini. Blanch them for about 30 seconds, then remove. (To stop the cooking process and maintain the crispness of the vegetables, plunge them into an ice water bath immediately after removing from poaching liquid. They will chill, but you're going to heat them up again.) Julienne the zucchini and set aside with the broccoli. Poach the seafood and fish for 2 minutes, then remove from poaching water. (Again, to stop the cooking process, plunge seafood into an ice bath.) Cut seafood into bite-sized pieces and set aside.

Prepare the cheese filling and the white sauce.

Preheat the oven to 350°F.

Grease a large baking dish and spread a thin layer of white sauce on the bottom. Build the lasagne by alternating layers of noodles, cheese filling, seafood, white sauce, mozzarella, and Parmesan cheese. Reserve all the blanched vegetables and some of the shrimp until the very end.

For the top layer, proceed as for the other layers, then finish with a layer of vegetables and shrimp. Cover with remaining cream sauce, mozzarella, and Parmesan.

Bake at 350°F for 30 minutes. Remove from oven and let stand for 10 minutes before serving.

Poaching Liquid

(Makes 7 cups)

1 teaspoon peeled and minced fresh ginger

4 cups water

2 cups white wine

1 cup diced carrots

1 cup diced celery

1 cup diced onions

Juice of 1 lemon

1 teaspoon salt

½ teaspoon cracked pepper

Combine all ingredients.

Cheese Filling

(Makes 2½ cups)

4 eggs
1 pound ricotta cheese
Salt and pepper to taste
2 tablespoons minced fresh dill
2 tablespoons minced fresh parsley

Beat the eggs and blend well with the ricotta; stir in the salt, pepper, dill, and parsley.

White Sauce

(Makes 4 cups)

¼ cup minced onion
2 tablespoons minced fresh garlic
8 tablespoons (1 stick) butter
6 tablespoons all-purpose flour
1 quart milk
Salt and pepper to taste

First, sauté the onion and garlic in 2 tablespoons of butter for about 5 minutes and set aside. Melt the remaining 6 tablespoons of butter in a saucepan. Add flour and cook over low heat for 10 minutes, stirring constantly—don't brown.

Heat the milk until just before it boils, then pour over the butter-flour mixture and stir vigorously with a whisk until smooth. Add the onion and garlic and simmer, uncovered, over low heat for 15 minutes. Adjust seasoning with salt and pepper.

Fish

Kailua-Kona, my home on the Big Island of Hawai'i, is ideal for deep-sea fishing. The water is usually flat because it lies in the wind shadow of two huge volcanoes—Mauna Kea and Mauna Loa.

My favorite fishing nowadays is deep-sea. From the art of the lures to the thrill of a fast sport-fishing boat, to the excitement of reeling in a fighting marlin, it's the best.

I've learned how important lures are. For good reason the lure makers are proud of their craft. They listen to fishing stories and note the colors that attract certain fish, or how the trailing ends produce a streak of irresistible foam.

'Ahi go after purple, blue, and silver, and smaller beads on the lure. Marlin like purple and black. "But you know, Sam," says a friend who owns a tackle shop, "the lures catch the fisherman before they catch the fish." You go into the store and pick lures that look pretty. They catch your eye. You buy.

The ones you keep are the ones that work. The best lures won't help, though, unless you know the tricks to finding the fish. You have to check currents and tides, the water temperature. You scan the horizon for "bird piles," which are sea birds stacked up over schools of bait fish. That's where the big fish are feeding.

You go and troll with the birds. And if you're lucky there's a strike. You know when you've got a big one: the reel spins with that great sound, half scream, half song.

Then it's Chinese fire drill, everyone scrambling to help land the monster. Whoever's in the fighting chair is assisted in whatever way, someone hand-lining the fish, others shouting encouragement. There's nothing like landing a marlin, or a quick-darting mahimahi. Fishing for the biggest fish in the Pacific is the greatest thrill a fisherman could hope for.

When I cook my catch, I imagine the whole difficult process of finding and bringing in the fish. I want to make sure not to steal the show, but to let the snapper or tuna fillet be the main attraction. You want to taste the sweetness of the meat, not the spices or gravy. My secrets for success in preparing fish are to buy it fresh, never overcook it, and don't let other ingredients dominate its delicate flavor. Use a dainty hand with the seasonings, and remember: showcase the fish.

Steamed Mahimahi Laulau

Crab-and-Shrimp Stuffed Shiitake Mushrooms
with Mango Béarnaise Sauce

Paniolo Chicken Fajitas

Sam Choy's World Famous
Fried Marlin Poke

Poached Snapper Salad with
Honey-Lime Vinaigrette

"Wow the Neighbors"
Seafood Salad

Maui Fisherman's Soup

Sam's Amazing No-Fat
Fish and Vegetables

Stuffed 'Ahi with Hana
Butter and Papaya Coulis

Stir-Fried U-10 Shrimp and Fresh Asparagus

Macadamia Nut Chicken Breasts
with Tropical Marmalade

Stir-Fried Chicken with
Sweet Peppers
and Onions

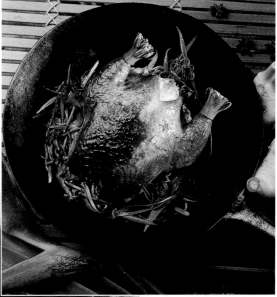

Spicy Braised Chicken
with Ginger

Chicken Hekka

Sam Choy's Award-Winning
Roast Duck

Hawaiian Barbecued
Tri-Tip Steak

Hilo Tropical Fruit Slaw

Sesame-Ginger
Snap Peas

Black Goma Asparagus

Ginger-Pineapple Sherbet

Mango-Guava
Sorbet

Haupia
Profiteroles

Minaka's MacNut Brownie

Macadamia Nut Pie

Tropical Drinks

Stuffed 'Ahi with Hana Butter and Papaya Coulis

(Serves 4)

This dish is a tropical version of Chicken Kiev, with seasoned butter inside a big chunk of 'ahi. Bake it, then cut open the tender fish fillet and watch the butter ooze out.

    4 'ahi (yellowfin tuna) fillets, 6 ounces each
    Hana Butter Log (see recipe below)
    All-purpose flour
    2 egg whites, lightly beaten
    ¾ cup sesame seeds, toasted in dry skillet
    2 tablespoons canola oil
    Papaya Coulis (see recipe on page 150)

Preheat the oven to 350°F.

For each serving, roll a fish fillet around a section of Hana butter log. Coat the rolled fillet with flour, dip in egg white, and coat with sesame seeds.

In a skillet, heat the oil over medium heat and sear the fish until lightly browned. Place on a baking sheet and bake for 5 to 6 minutes.

Spoon some papaya coulis onto individual plates and top with fillets.

Hana Butter Log

(Makes ¼ cup)

    4 tablespoons (½ stick) butter, softened
    1 tablespoon minced fresh cilantro
    Salt and coarsely ground pepper to taste
    Pinch red chili pepper flakes

Blend all ingredients and shape into a log ½-inch in diameter. Freeze until firm. Cut into 4 sections.

Papaya Coulis

(Makes 2 cups)

1 ripe papaya, seeded and peeled
1 tablespoon white vinegar
1 tablespoon granulated sugar
¼ cup finely chopped fresh cilantro

Dice enough papaya to make ½ cup.

In a food processor or blender, process the remaining papaya to make a purée. In a small saucepan, combine the papaya purée, vinegar, and sugar; cook for 5 minutes. Stir in the diced papaya and cilantro.

Simmered Shoyu-Sugar Butterfish
with Vegetables

(Serves 4)

Butterfish (black cod) is an oily fish that falls apart easily. When you simmer or poach it in a sugar-shoyu mixture and add vegetables, it's like nichime (Japanese stew). It's a very popular dish in my restaurants in Japan. Serve with hot sticky rice. 'Onolicious!

1 pound butterfish (black cod), mackerel, or sea bass

2½ tablespoons granulated sugar

⅓ cup soy sauce

1 tablespoon water

½ cup julienned carrot

½ cup julienned celery

*½ bunch fresh watercress, leaves separated and stems
    cut into 1½-inch lengths*

4 green onions, cut into 1-inch lengths

1 block (20 ounces) firm tofu, drained and cubed

Spray the fish for up to 5 seconds with nonstick vegetable-oil cooking spray. In a large skillet over medium heat, sauté the butterfish for about 1 minute on each side; remove to a plate.

Mix the sugar, soy sauce, and water. Put half of this mixture into the skillet along with the carrots and celery; cook for 6 to 8 minutes. Push the carrots and celery to one side and return the butterfish to the skillet. Pour the remaining soy sauce mixture over the fish and vegetables; cook, covered, for 5 minutes. Add watercress stems, and cook for 1 minute. Then top with onions, tofu, and watercress leaves; cook 2 minutes. Do not overcook.

Pan-Fried Catfish with Sam's Sweet & Sour Sauce

(Serves 2)

This recipe is dedicated to those people who are starting to raise catfish in Wai'anae, Waimanalo, and Waimea on O'ahu, and up the Hilo side. The hard work and diligence of our aquafarmers have given us a fresh source of very tasty catfish right here in the Islands.

2 catfish fillets, 4 ounces each
Pinch of salt
Pinch of pepper
All-purpose flour
2 tablespoons canola oil
1 tablespoon peeled and minced fresh ginger
1 tablespoon minced fresh garlic
1 cup assorted sliced vegetables, such as bell peppers, tomatoes, carrots, onion, and broccoli florets
½ cup Sam's Sweet & Sour Sauce (see recipe on page 153)
1 tablespoon hot prepared mustard

Garnish:
1 tablespoon chopped green onion

Season the fillets with salt and pepper, then dust with flour. Heat the oil in a frying pan over medium-high heat, and cook the fish for about 3 minutes on each side. Remove fish to a warm platter.

Add the ginger, garlic, and vegetables to the pan; toss and cook for about 2 minutes. Add the sweet and sour sauce and mustard; cook, stirring for 1 minute, or until the mixture is heated through. Pour the sweet-and-sour vegetable mixture over the fish.

Garnish with chopped green onions.

Sam's Sweet & Sour Sauce

(Makes 2½ to 3 cups)

2 tablespoons cornstarch mixed with 1½ tablespoons water
    for thickening
1 cup granulated sugar
½ cup ketchup
½ cup vinegar
½ cup water
¼ cup orange marmalade
2 tablespoons pineapple juice
2 teaspoons soy sauce
1½ teaspoons peeled and minced fresh ginger
1 teaspoon minced fresh garlic
¼ teaspoon hot pepper sauce

Blend the cornstarch and water; set aside. In a saucepan, combine the remaining ingredients. Bring to a boil, and add the cornstarch mixture. Reduce the heat and simmer, stirring frequently, until thickened.

Blackened Snapper with Tropical Salsa

(Serves 2)

I love experimenting with cultural elements that have never appeared together—like combining hot Cajun spices with the sweet, tropical flavors of mango, pineapple, and papaya. Then I throw in a touch of Choy, and away you go. I prefer using a snapper for this dish, but swordfish will do. Remember, though, swordfish won't be as moist.

> *2 tablespoons soy sauce*
> *2 tablespoons honey*
> *1 8-ounce ehu (orange snapper) fillet, or substitute any*
> *   other snapper.*
> *Blackening Mix (see recipe on page 155)*
> *Tropical Salsa (see recipe on page 155)*
> *2 tablespoons canola oil*

Mix the soy sauce and honey and coat the fish with this mixture. Roll the fish in blackening mix.

In a heavy skillet, heat the oil until it starts to smoke. Lower the fish carefully into the hot oil to prevent splashing. Cook about 3 minutes on each side, depending on the thickness of the fish. Serve with tropical salsa.

Blackening Mix

(Makes about ¼ cup)

1 tablespoon paprika
1 tablespoon cayenne pepper
1 teaspoon ground black pepper
1 teaspoon garlic salt
1 teaspoon salt
1 teaspoon powdered oregano
1 teaspoon crumbled dried thyme

Combine all ingredients.

Tropical Salsa

(Makes 2 cups)

½ cup diced fresh mango
½ cup diced fresh papaya
½ cup diced fresh pineapple
¼ cup diced red bell pepper
2 tablespoons chopped fresh cilantro
1 teaspoon granulated sugar
1 teaspoon vinegar

Combine all ingredients and refrigerate until served.

Cilantro Salmon Steaks

(Serves 6)

Kamano is the Hawaiian name given to any freshwater fish that is not indigenous to the Islands. The name kamano was first given to the rainbow trout that were introduced into streams on Kaua'i. Salmon were later brought in and given the name kamano as well. But neither the rainbow trout nor the hardy Pacific Northwest Coast salmon were able to establish themselves in the Islands. Today, they are shipped to Hawai'i frozen.

½ cup rosé wine
1 tablespoon minced fresh cilantro
2 tablespoons minced onion
1 teaspoon chopped fresh garlic
½ cup light olive oil
Salt and pepper to taste
6 kamano (salmon) steaks, each 1 to 2 inches thick

Garnish:
2 vine-ripened tomatoes, cut into wedges
1 sweet onion, cut into wedges
Italian dressing of your choice
Chopped cilantro

Combine the wine, cilantro, onion, garlic, olive oil, salt, and pepper. Pour the mixture over the salmon in a shallow glass pan. (The amounts of seasoning in the marinade can be increased to your taste. Use more marinade if necessary to cover the salmon steaks.)

Refrigerate for 1 hour, turning the salmon once. Drain well.

Preheat the broiler and position the oven rack as close as possible to the heat source. Broil the steaks 3 to 6 minutes, or until browned on top. Turn and broil other sides for 3 to 5 minutes more, depending on thickness, until fish is almost opaque in center (it will continue cooking when removed from the heat).

Top with tomato and sweet onion wedges, drizzled with your favorite Italian dressing. Garnish with a sprinkling of chopped cilantro.

Baked Teriyaki Mahimahi

(Serves 10)

Pair a favorite fish with a favorite Island cooking style for an easy, irresistible oven-baked dish.

⅔ cup soy sauce

6 tablespoons packed brown sugar

¼ cup sake (yellowish, slightly sweet Japanese rice wine)

2 tablespoons orange juice, or ½ small orange, juiced

1 tablespoon canola oil

1½-inch piece fresh ginger, peeled and crushed

1 tablespoon chopped green onion

1 teaspoon white miso (fermented soybean paste)

2 cloves fresh garlic, minced

4 pounds mahimahi (dolphinfish), cut into 4-ounce pieces

Garnish:
Shredded cabbage or sautéed fresh vegetables

Combine all ingredients except the mahimahi in a large bowl. Add the mahimahi and marinate for 4 to 6 hours in the refrigerator.

Preheat the oven to 350°F. Pour off the marinade and arrange the mahimahi in one layer in a greased baking pan. Place in the oven and bake uncovered for 10 to 15 minutes, until the fish just turns opaque.

Present on a platter of shredded cabbage or sautéed fresh vegetables of your choice.

Crunchy Hale'iwa Mahimahi

(Serves 2)

The word *crunchy* in the title is used to describe the vegetables, not the fish. It's the very quickly stir-fried sugar snap peas, onion, carrots, and zucchini that give this recipe its name. The fish is unreal 'ono-'ono. Eat in good health.

1 tablespoon chopped fresh cilantro
Salt and pepper to taste
1 tablespoon brown sugar
1 tablespoon minced fresh garlic
1 tablespoon peeled and minced fresh ginger
4 mahimahi (dolphinfish) fillets, 3 ounces each
2 tablespoons butter
1 tablespoon vegetable oil
1 sweet onion, cut into julienne
½ cup julienned carrots
½ cup julienned zucchini
1½ cups sugar snap peas or snow peas
1 tablespoon soy sauce
1 tablespoon oyster sauce

Blend the cilantro, salt, pepper, brown sugar, garlic, and ginger in a shallow bowl. Press into the mahimahi fillets to coat, and let stand for about 5 minutes. Meanwhile, heat the butter in a heavy skillet. Cook the mahimahi fillets for about 2 minutes on each side.

In a separate skillet or a wok, heat the oil and stir-fry the onion for 30 seconds over medium-high heat. Add the carrots, zucchini, and sugar snap peas, and stir-fry for 2 more minutes. Add the soy sauce and oyster sauce to the pan and cook for 1 minute longer. Remove from heat, and place around the mahimahi.

Place the fillets on a serving plate and arrange the vegetables around the fish. Serve hot.

Crusted Mahimahi with Coconut Cream Spinach Sauce

(Serves 4)

This dish came from taking a traditional local cooking method that was used on festive occasions, and shaking it up to bring it to the everyday household. I think I've made it simple enough for folks to use it at home. I like to crust just one side of the fish because it makes for a nice contrast in textures—crisp on one side and moist on the other.

> *Sesame-MacNut Crust (see recipe on page 160)*
> *Coconut Cream Spinach Sauce (see recipe on page 160)*
> *4 mahimahi (dolphinfish) fillets, 6 ounces each*
> *Salt and pepper to taste*
> *3 tablespoons all-purpose flour, for dusting*
> *2 eggs, lightly beaten*
> *1 tablespoon olive oil*
> *3 tablespoons butter*

Prepare the sesame-macnut crust and the coconut cream spinach sauce. Set aside.

Lightly season the fish with salt and pepper, and dust with flour. Dip just one side of a floured mahimahi fillet in the beaten egg, let excess egg drip off, then dip into the crust mixture and firmly press onto fish. Continue with remaining fillets.

In a large frying pan, heat the oil and butter. Make sure it's hot before adding the fish. Place the fish with the crust side down and cook until golden brown, about 1½ minutes (keep a close eye on it—macadamia nuts tend to brown very quickly). Turn and cook the other side for about 1½ minutes. Remove from the pan to a platter and cover with foil to keep warm.

Serve the fish crust side up on stir-fried mixed vegetables, or on pasta, or garlic mashed potatoes, with coconut cream spinach sauce around the edge. Don't pour sauce over the crust—it will become soggy.

Sesame-MacNut Crust

(Makes 1¼ cups)

½ cup finely chopped macadamia nuts
¼ cup sesame seeds, toasted
½ cup panko (Japanese-style crispy bread crumbs) or fine dry bread
    crumbs

Mix the ingredients well.

Coconut Cream Spinach Sauce

(Makes 5¼ cups)

3 tablespoons butter
2 cups chopped fresh spinach
1 medium onion, minced
1 cup heavy cream
2 cups canned unsweetened coconut milk
2 tablespoons cornstarch mixed with 1½ tablespoons water,
    if needed for thickening
Salt and pepper to taste

In a saucepan, melt the butter, add the spinach and onion, and cook while stirring for 4 or 5 minutes, until onion becomes translucent. Add the heavy cream. Bring to a boil, reduce the heat, and simmer for 1 to 2 minutes. Add the coconut milk. Cook for another 2 minutes. If the sauce is thin, add some cornstarch mixture and cook for another minute. Adjust seasoning with salt and pepper. Set aside and keep warm.

Steamed Mahimahi Laulau

(Serves 4)

Laulau is a traditional Hawaiian dish. The old folks wrapped pork, fish, beef, or chicken in ti leaves, tied off the tops, and put them in an earth oven called an imu. This recipe calls for ti leaves, but if you can't get ti leaves, you can use corn husks or aluminum foil. I guess the upside of foil is that you don't have to use a string to tie off the bundles.

2 cups julienned carrots
2 cups julienned zucchini
1 cup sliced shiitake mushrooms
Herb Sauce (see recipe on page 162)
8 ti leaves (or substitute corn husks, banana leaves, or aluminum
    foil cut into 12 × 18-inch lengths)
12 fresh mahimahi (dolphinfish) fillets, 2 ounces each
Salt and pepper to taste

Mix the carrots and zucchini together and divide into 4 equal portions. Divide the mushrooms into 4 portions.

Prepare the herb sauce and set aside.

Remove the hard ribs from the ti leaves to make them flexible, or cook the leaves on high in the microwave for 1 minute to soften.

To build each laulau, first make a cross on a work surface by laying 1 ti leaf, corn husk, banana leaf, or strip of foil over another at right angles. Sprinkle vegetable mix in the center, then lay a mahimahi fillet on top of the vegetables. Spread a thin layer of herb sauce on the fish, and sprinkle with more vegetables. Place another fillet on top, spread with sauce, sprinkle with vegetables. Finish with a third fillet that is topped with sauce, vegetable mix, and a sprinkle of mushrooms. Season with salt and pepper to taste.

Gather up the ti leaves (or aluminum foil) to make a purse around the fish, and tie tightly with string just above bundle. Repeat for all four portions, using a fourth of the vegetables and three mahimahi fillets for each laulau.

Arrange the packages in a bamboo steamer and steam for 8 to 10 minutes.

Herb Sauce

(Makes 1½ cups)

1½ cups mayonnaise
1 tablespoon soy sauce
1 tablespoon fresh dill, chopped

Mix ingredients together, and set aside.

Red Snapper with Tropical Herb Salsa

(Serves 4)

I created this as a layered meal. I think it's fun to build dishes like this one—one level after another of delicious flavors—but it's not necessary to present it this way. If you prefer, just place each prepared fillet on a separate plate and top with salsa. But if you want to be daring, layer the ingredients into a tower and cut it into quarters. Either way, it's 'ono (delicious).

12 onaga (red snapper) fillets, 2½ ounces each
¼ cup all-purpose flour
¼ cup vegetable oil
Tropical Herb Salsa (see recipe on page 163)

Dust the fish with flour. Heat the oil in a large skillet. Place the fish in hot oil and cook about 3 minutes on each side, being careful not to overcook. Build each plate by alternately layering salsa and onaga, starting and ending with the salsa, and serving three pieces of onaga per plate.

Tropical Herb Salsa

(Makes 2 to 2½ cups)

1 tomato, with the seeds, diced
1 papaya, diced
1 red bell pepper, diced
½ cup diced strawberries
1 medium red onion, diced
½ cup diced pineapple
Juice of 1 lemon
½ cup light olive oil
Salt and pepper to taste
1 bunch fresh cilantro, chopped
1 tablespoon peeled and minced fresh ginger

Combine all ingredients and mix well.

Stir-Fried Ono and Hawaiian Hot Peppers

(Serves 4)

Stir-frying is an Asian method of cooking that quickly blends the flavors of food by allowing it to simmer in its own juices. Stir-fry the pieces of fresh ono real quick. Add a little stock, then throw in some hot peppers, and *zing*—you're an instant hero. Serve this over hot rice.

1½ pounds ono (wahoo)
1 egg white, lightly beaten
1 tablespoon sherry
1 teaspoon cornstarch
3 tablespoons canola oil
1 clove fresh garlic, minced
¼ teaspoon peeled and minced fresh ginger
1 green bell pepper, diced
½ cup bean sprouts
1 or 2 Hawaiian or red hot chili peppers, minced
1 tablespoon soy sauce
1 teaspoon granulated sugar
½ teaspoon salt

Cut the ono into medium chunks, about 1 by 1½ inches. In a shallow bowl, combine the egg white, sherry, and cornstarch. Add the ono and toss to coat.

In a wok, heat 1½ tablespoons of the oil over medium-high heat and cook the garlic and ginger for 30 seconds. Add the ono and stir-fry for 2 minutes, or until the fish starts to brown; remove to a plate.

In the same wok, heat the remaining 1½ tablespoons of oil. Stir-fry the bell pepper, bean sprouts, and chilies for 2 or 3 minutes. Return the ono to the wok, along with the soy sauce, sugar, and salt. Stir-fry for 2 to 4 minutes. Serve immediately.

Opah Macadamia Nori with Dill Cream Sauce

(Serves 4)

I know that the name "opah" sounds like a Hawaiian word, but it's not. It's the French name (from West Africa) for moonfish. Be creative using Japanese nori—it's not only for sushi; you can also wrap fish with it.

8 opah (moonfish) fillets, about 3 ounces each

¼ cup olive oil

1 tablespoon minced fresh herbs (combination of basil, dill, thyme, and/or rosemary)

Salt and black pepper to taste

All-purpose flour

3 eggs, beaten

1 cup finely chopped macadamia nuts

4 sheets nori (seasoned dried seaweed used for sushi)

2 tablespoons canola oil

Dill Cream Sauce (see recipe on page 166)

Marinate the fish for 1 hour in a combination of olive oil, fresh herbs, salt, and pepper. Dust the marinated fillets with flour and dip in beaten egg, then in macadamia nuts. Cut the nori into 8 strips, each 1 by 4 inches wide. Wrap 1 nori strip around the midsection of each fillet.

In a skillet, heat the oil and sauté the wrapped fillets until golden brown on both sides. On individual plates, lace some of the dill cream sauce and top with the macadamia nori fillets.

Dill Cream Sauce

(Makes about 1 cup)

1 tablespoon minced shallots
1 tablespoon butter
½ cup white wine
2 cups heavy cream
1 tablespoon minced fresh dill
Salt and pepper to taste

In a small saucepan, sauté shallots in the butter until translucent, about 3 minutes. Add the wine and simmer for 8 minutes. Add the heavy cream, bring to a boil, and reduce by half. Stir in the dill and season with salt and pepper.

Baked Whole Snapper with Coconut Milk

(Serves 6)

I wrap the fish in ti leaves before baking, to keep it moist. You can use corn husks or plain aluminum foil. I remember doing this on my television cooking show, and many people called to thank me for that recipe.

6 ti leaves (substitute banana leaves, corn husks, or aluminum foil)
3-pound whole 'opakapaka (pink snapper)
1½ tablespoons kosher or rock salt
1 tablespoon peeled and minced fresh ginger
½ cup mayonnaise
1½ cups coconut milk
1 sweet onion, diced

Preheat the oven to 350°F. Rinse the ti leaves, and strip the back of the leaf ribs so leaves become flexible.

Scale and clean the whole 'opakapaka and cut 3 or 4 crosswise slashes in each side. Sprinkle salt and ginger on the fish and spread mayonnaise over its surface. Place the fish on ti leaves, arranged on a large piece of foil. Pour coconut milk and sprinkle onions over the fish. Wrap the fish in ti leaves, then seal in foil.

Place the wrapped fish on a baking sheet. Bake for 25 to 30 minutes, depending on the thickness of the fish. Remove fish bundle from the oven. Unwrap the foil and discard. Place the ti leaf–wrapped fish on a serving platter.

Ginger Pesto-Crusted Snapper with Coconut Cream Sauce

(Serves 4)

This recipe works well with just about any type of fish. I prefer snappers because of their mild flavor and moist texture. But I've used swordfish, sea bass, trout—even salmon. The Coconut Cream Sauce and Ginger Pesto Sauce blend well with the fish, and the flavor combinations are just melt-in-your-mouth great.

> 8 fresh 'opakapaka (pink snapper) fillets, 3-ounce pieces
> Ginger Pesto Sauce (see recipe on page 84)
> 1 tablespoon oil, for frying
> Coconut Cream Sauce (see recipe on page 168)

Marinate the 'opakapaka for 1 to 2 minutes in 1½ cups of cooled ginger pesto sauce. Place the fillets in a heated skillet and cook for 1½ to 2 minutes on each side over medium-high heat.

Pour 2 ounces of coconut cream sauce on each of 4 serving plates. Arrange 2 pieces of fish on each plate and drizzle with reserved ½ cup of ginger pesto sauce.

Coconut Cream Sauce

(Makes about 3 to 3½ cups)

3 tablespoons butter
1 medium round onion, minced
1 cup heavy cream
2 cups canned unsweetened coconut milk
2 tablespoons cornstarch mixed with 1½ tablespoons water,
    if needed for thickening
Salt and pepper to taste

Heat the butter in a saucepan. Add the onion and cook 4 to 5 minutes, until translucent. Add the heavy cream. Bring to a boil, reduce the heat, and simmer for 1 to 2 minutes. Add the coconut milk and cook for another 2 minutes. If the sauce seems thin, add the cornstarch mixture and boil for 1 minute or until thickened. Adjust seasoning with salt and pepper.

Sautéed Snapper with Spinach Coconut Lu'au Sauce

(Serves 4)

Here's a takeoff on a traditional Hawaiian dish called squid lu'au. Take the squid out of that recipe, make a thinner sauce, and add it to 'opakapaka, an excellent flaky fish. The combination is just right—really, really 'ono.

4 'opakapaka (pink snapper) fillets, 6 ounces each
1 teaspoon peeled and minced fresh ginger
1 teaspoon minced fresh garlic
½ teaspoon salt
¼ teaspoon white pepper
¼ cup all-purpose flour

2 tablespoons butter

1 tablespoon olive oil

Spinach Coconut Lu'au Sauce (see recipe below)

Season the fillets with ginger, garlic, salt, and pepper. Dredge in flour. In a large heavy skillet, heat the butter and oil. Sauté fish just until lightly browned on both sides and opaque in the center. Do not overcook.

Transfer the fish to a warm serving platter. Serve with spinach coconut lu'au sauce.

Spinach Coconut Lu'au Sauce

(Makes 10 servings, 1 ounce each)

3 tablespoons minced sweet onion

½ teaspoon peeled and minced fresh ginger

2 tablespoons butter

1 cup heavy cream

½ cup cooked and chopped fresh spinach

¼ cup coconut milk

Salt, pepper, and sugar to taste

In a small saucepan, sauté the onion and ginger in the butter for 3 minutes or until the onion is translucent. Add the heavy cream, bring to a boil, and reduce by half. Stir in the spinach and coconut milk, and cook for 2 minutes. Season to taste with salt, pepper, and a pinch of sugar.

Poached Salmon with Spicy Fruit Salsa

(Serves 4)

Seasoning is important, but you have to make sure you don't overdo it. Most of my recipes call for "salt and pepper to taste." Everyone has a different tolerance level for seasoning, and I want to leave it up to the cook. I'm known for blending small amounts of various spices in interesting ways, so that the seasoning enhances, rather than overpowers the food. I never use MSG—it's not necessary. The proper use of seasoning is to guide and balance the natural flavors of the food.

Spicy Fruit Salsa (see recipe on page 171)
Poaching Liquid (see recipe on page 171)
8 kamano (salmon) fillets, 3 ounces each

Garnish:

Sprigs of fresh herb of your choice (dill, mint, cilantro, and so on)

Prepare the spicy fruit salsa and set aside.

Bring the poaching liquid to a boil in a skillet. Reduce the heat to medium and lay the fillets in a single layer in the liquid. Cover the pan and cook for about 3 to 4 minutes, depending on thickness of fillets. As soon as the salmon turns opaque in the middle, it's done.

Divide the spicy fruit salsa into 4 portions. On each plate spread the salsa into a pool. Top with 2 fish fillets and add a dollop of salsa on top of the fish.

Garnish with a sprig of fresh herb.

Spicy Fruit Salsa

(Makes 3 to 3½ cups)

1 cup diced mangoes or lychee, or seasonal tropical fruit
1 cup diced papaya
1 cup diced pineapple
½ cup chopped fresh cilantro
¼ cup diced red bell pepper
¼ cup diced tomatoes
1 teaspoon ground cumin
½ teaspoon hot red pepper flakes
Salt and pepper to taste

Blend together all ingredients, and let stand at room temperature for 30 minutes.

Poaching Liquid

(Makes 6 to 6½ cups)

4 cups water
½ cup chopped fresh cilantro
2 cups white wine
1 cup mixture of diced carrots, onion, and celery
Juice of 1 lemon
1 teaspoon salt
½ teaspoon cracked pepper

Mix all ingredients and bring to a boil.

Seared Albacore Tuna with Coconut-Ginger Sauce

(Serves 4)

Albacore is also known by its Japanese name, tombo 'ahi. The names are sometimes a little confusing. There are so many different kinds of tuna that are known as 'ahi. Once marinated, the albacore tuna steaks are perfect for searing. I added a coconut-ginger sauce for a touch of sweetness.

> 4 albacore tuna steaks, 6 ounces each and ¾ inch thick
> Seafood Marinade (see recipe below)
> 2 tablespoons vegetable oil
> Coconut-Ginger Sauce (see recipe on page 173)

Marinate the tuna steaks in the seafood marinade for 10 minutes.

Heat the oil in a frying pan over high heat. Sear the steaks for 2 minutes on each side. They should be medium rare. Serve hot with warm coconut-ginger sauce.

Seafood Marinade

(Makes 1½ cups)

> 1 cup soy sauce
> 1 tablespoon oyster sauce
> 1 tablespoon sesame oil
> ½ cup packed brown sugar
> 1 tablespoon chopped fresh cilantro
> 1 teaspoon red chili pepper flakes
> 1 teaspoon minced fresh garlic
> ¼ teaspoon Chinese five-spice powder

Mix all ingredients and stir until sugar is dissolved.

Coconut-Ginger Sauce

(Makes 1½ cups)

1 cup coconut milk
¼ cup granulated sugar
1 tablespoon peeled and minced fresh ginger
1½ tablespoons cornstarch mixed with 3 tablespoons water for
  thickening
Salt and pepper to taste

In a saucepan, combine the coconut milk, sugar, and ginger. Bring to a boil. Mix the cornstarch and water together; whisk into the sauce and boil for 1 minute to thicken. Add salt and pepper to taste.

Kona Cuisine Seafood Brochettes

(Serves 8)

These elegant, succulent brochettes feature the best elements of Kona—fresh seafood and luscious fruit. I chose hapu'upu'u (sea bass) for this recipe, but you can substitute any firm, mild-tasting fish, such as a snapper (onaga, or red snapper; 'opakapaka, or pink snapper; uku, or gray snapper) or halibut.

8 slices lean bacon
1½ pounds hapu'upu'u (sea bass), thick steaks or fillets
¼ whole fresh pineapple, peeled
1 medium mango, peeled
1 medium bell pepper, seeded
16 sea or bay scallops
6 tablespoons olive oil
6 tablespoons orange juice
1 teaspoon minced fresh basil
Salt and pepper to taste

Bring a large pot of water to a boil and blanch the bacon for 3 to 5 seconds to make it easier to handle.

Cut the fish, pineapple, and mango into 1-inch cubes; cut the bell pepper into 1-inch squares. Wrap a piece of bacon around each scallop. On skewers, alternately thread the seafood, fresh fruit, and bell pepper. Do not crowd.

Mix the olive oil and orange juice; marinate brochettes in the mixture on a large platter for 30 minutes.

Preheat the broiler or a gas-fired grill, or prepare a charcoal fire. Just before grilling, dust the brochettes with basil, salt, and pepper. Barbecue, basting occasionally with marinade and turning as each side browns, about 10 to 12 minutes, or until fish is opaque.

Sam's Amazing No-Fat Steamed Fish and Vegetables

(Serves 1)

I'm always trying to come up with recipes that cut calories without cutting taste. This dish of steamed fish and vegetables, seasoned with fresh herbs, is as delicious as food can be without added fat. You may serve it hot, on a bed of hot rice or noodles, or cold. Drizzle the dish with a little soy sauce if you choose.

2 pieces of uku (gray snapper) or salmon

2 broccoli florets

2 cauliflower florets

4 stalks asparagus

2 shiitake mushrooms

½ red bell pepper, sliced

Salt and pepper to taste

1 medium ginger finger, peeled and cut into very fine shreds

Sprig of fresh dill

1 tablespoon soy sauce (optional)

Arrange the fish and vegetables in a bamboo steamer basket, or on a plate in an impromptu steamer (a pot in which you've placed a bowl upside down with a plate on top).

Season with salt and pepper and sprinkle with ginger. Lay a sprig of dill on top of the fish, and steam for 6 to 8 minutes, or until the fish is opaque and the vegetables are tender but still crisp.

Poultry

Chicken, turkey, game hens, and duck play a major, succulent role in local cooking. Poultry has a delicate texture and a flavor that blends well with many of our ethnic spices. There are just a few handling rules to remember. You never want to freeze, thaw, refreeze, and thaw again. That's dangerous. Bacteria have an opportunity to grow when you do this. The methods of thawing are also very important. I like to thaw poultry in the refrigerator. But let's be honest—there are times you have to rush, and you bring the bird out and leave it covered on the counter. Just make sure you cook your poultry until the internal temperature measures at least 165°F to kill all the bacteria.

Poultry is a healthful food if you remove the skin and fat. It's a versatile meat that works great with any type of cooking technique. People always ask me how I make my roasted birds taste so good. It's all in the basting mixture. I use about 1 tablespoon of oil, 1 tablespoon honey, and ½ teaspoon soy sauce, and then baste (or glaze) the meat toward the end of the roasting. Honey is the magic ingredient. It makes the bird golden brown and brings out the characteristic sweetness of the meat.

Among all the birds, chicken is the most available and the easiest to prepare. I like to semi-bone it to make a big pot of stew or stir-fry it with spicy peppers. It's great on the hibachi: the chicken juices quickly pick up the grill flavor. I sometimes take hibachi-grilled chicken, slice it up, and toss it onto a salad.

Most of the recipes in this section are for chicken, but I've included my famous Sam's Special "Big-O" Thanksgiving Turkey, an incredible low-fat feast; Sam Choy's Award-Winning Roast Duck, a bow to my Chinese heritage; and my spicy Island-Style Barbecued Cornish Game Hens, a perennial crowd pleaser.

Just remember: like anything else, if you overcook the birds, they toughen up, lose their flavor, and taste like chewy cardboard. Not a very good dish to serve guests. So trust me. Follow the recipes with care, and these golden birds will turn to golden feasts in your very own kitchen.

Roasted Chicken with Macadamia Nut Stuffing

(Serves 2 to 4)

This is a variation on a dish my mom made for Sunday dinners. Mom used walnuts, sometimes almonds in the stuffing. I like the rich taste of macadamia nuts. I stuff the chicken, put it in a roasting pan, and slip it into the oven before the football game starts. By half-time, the house is filled with a wonderful aroma, and the chicken is ready to eat.

Salt and pepper to taste
1 tablespoon vegetable oil
1 whole 3- to 4-pound whole chicken, rinsed and patted dry
Pinch of paprika
Macadamia Nut Stuffing (see recipe on page 180)

Preheat the oven to 350°F.

Rub salt, pepper, and oil all over the chicken. Set aside.

Prepare the macadamia nut stuffing and loosely stuff the body and neck cavities. Sew or skewer the openings. Place the chicken in a shallow roasting pan and sprinkle with paprika.

Roast in the preheated oven for about 1 hour, until the chicken is done. There's no need to baste. You can make gravy with the pan drippings if you like.

 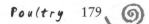

Macadamia Nut Stuffing

(Makes 3½ to 4 cups)

½ cup minced onion

6 slices bacon, chopped

1 stalk celery, minced

1 medium apple, with peel on, chopped

½ cup sliced fresh mushrooms

4 tablespoons (½ stick) butter

½ cup hot chicken stock

1 tablespoon chopped parsley

1 teaspoon poultry seasoning

12 ounces dry croutons

1 cup macadamia nuts, coarsely chopped, or nut halves

Salt and pepper to taste

In a large pot, sauté the onion, bacon, celery, apple, and mushrooms in the butter until the onion is translucent. Add the chicken stock and bring to a boil. Reduce heat to a simmer. Add the parsley and poultry seasoning. Cook for 2 minutes. Add croutons and nuts. Mix well. If the croutons absorb all the liquid and seem too dry, you can add a little more broth or butter. Let cool, then stuff chicken.

Spicy Braised Chicken with Ginger

(Serves 4)

Star anise is reddish brown and shaped like an irregular, eight-pointed star. In fact, its Chinese name means eight points. This spice's strong licorice-like aroma adds an extra kick to this dish.

2 tablespoons olive oil

2 tablespoons sesame oil

1 whole fryer chicken, rinsed and patted dry

¼ cup soy sauce

¼ cup sherry

Six ¼-inch slices peeled fresh ginger, bruised

2 green onions, cut in 2-inch pieces

3 whole star anise

1 tablespoon Szechuan (wild pepper) peppercorns

1½ tablespoons granulated sugar

Garnish:

4 sprigs fresh cilantro

In a large, heavy pan, heat the olive oil and sesame oil. Brown the whole chicken on all sides. Add the soy sauce, sherry, ginger, green onions, star anise, and peppercorns. Bring to a boil, reduce the heat, cover, and simmer on very low heat for 40 minutes or until almost done, turning once or twice for even cooking.

Add the sugar and simmer covered for 5 more minutes. Cool slightly, then cut the chicken in serving-size pieces. Garnish with cilantro.

Braised Ginger-Honey Chicken

(Serves 6)

I got hooked on cooking with ginger while helping my dad in the kitchen. When he cooked with fresh ginger, it was either *bang!* with the big cleaver, smashing the root into flat splinters, or chop, chop, chop, mince, mince, mince into diced little pieces. Either way, the oils that were locked in its fibers were released, and you could taste the peppery scent in the air even before Dad added it to the dish. This ginger chicken should be served with steamed rice.

¼ cup canola oil
3-inch piece peeled fresh ginger, minced
1 green onion, cut into ½-inch pieces
1 whole, 3- to 4-pound chicken, rinsed and patted dry
½ cup sherry
2 tablespoons honey
½ cup fat-free chicken stock
2 tablespoons soy sauce
1 teaspoon salt
8 sprigs fresh cilantro

In a heavy wok or pan, heat the oil over medium-high heat and stir-fry the ginger and green onion for a few minutes. Brown the chicken on all sides, about 6 to 8 minutes; drain off excess oil.

Combine the remaining ingredients except the cilantro and pour slowly over the chicken. Bring to a boil, reduce the heat, then simmer, covered, for 40 minutes or until done, basting frequently, and turning occasionally.

Use a cleaver to chop chicken, bones and all, in 2-inch pieces.

Quick and Easy Shoyu Chicken

(Serves 6)

Marinating food in a soy sauce–sugar mixture is a basic, and very traditional, Japanese method of curing meat. Japanese immigrants came to the Islands to work on the sugar plantations, and brought with them their culinary secrets. They shared their food with the many other cultures that immigrated to the plantation camps, and each group of workers contributed their own version of the teriyaki-style dishes. Shoyu chicken is now considered an Island classic.

Tailgate Teri Sauce (see recipe on page 184)
1 tablespoon minced fresh cilantro
½ teaspoon Chinese five-spice powder
2 pounds chicken thighs, skinned and boned
1 tablespoon cornstarch
2 tablespoons water

Garnish:
Green onions, chopped
Bean sprouts

In a medium saucepan, combine the teri sauce, cilantro, and five-spice powder. Bring to a boil, add the chicken, then simmer 20 minutes or until tender. Remove the chicken from the sauce; set aside and tent with foil to keep warm. Measure the sauce and return 1 cup to the pan.

Blend the cornstarch and water. Bring the 1 cup of sauce to a boil and stir in the cornstarch to thicken into a glaze. Brush the chicken pieces with the glaze. Garnish with green onions and bean sprouts.

Tailgate Teri Sauce

(Makes 2 cups)

1 cup soy sauce
Juice of 1 medium orange
½ cup mirin (Japanese sweet rice wine)
½ cup water
¼ cup packed brown sugar
1½ teaspoons minced fresh garlic
1½ teaspoons peeled and minced fresh ginger

Combine all ingredients and blend well.

Breast of Chicken with Shiitake Sherried Butter Sauce

(Serves 6)

One of my restaurant distributors offered me some very fine chicken breasts at a great price. I couldn't pass up the offer, so I took them. There I was, stuck with cases and cases of the stuff. Isn't it interesting how life presents you with opportunities to be creative? I took the chicken breasts, some shiitake mushrooms, some sherry, and butter, and created a dish that got rave reviews from my customers. Best of all, *it's easy to make.*

Shiitake Sherried Butter Sauce (see recipe on page 185)
6 boneless skinless chicken breast halves, 5 ounces each
Salt and pepper to taste

Prepare the shiitake sherried butter sauce.
Season both sides of the chicken breasts with salt and pepper. Spray with non-

stick vegetable oil cooking spray, then grill over high heat, turning once or twice, for about 4 minutes on each side, until firm but still moist.

Slice the cooked chicken across the grain into ½-inch pieces and top with the shiitake sherried butter sauce.

Shiitake Sherried Butter Sauce

(Makes 2 cups)

2 tablespoons butter
1 tablespoon chopped onion
1 clove fresh garlic, minced
¾ pound fresh shiitake mushrooms, sliced into strips
1 teaspoon chopped fresh cilantro
Salt and pepper to taste
½ cup sherry
2 sticks (½ pound) butter, softened

In a sauté pan, heat the 2 tablespoons butter and sauté the onion and garlic until the onion is translucent; do not let garlic brown. Add shiitake mushrooms and cilantro; lightly sauté. Season with salt and pepper. Add sherry to deglaze the pan, and simmer until the liquid reduces by half. Whisk in the ½ pound of butter, a little at a time, until combined well. Adjust the seasoning, and keep sauce warm until needed.

Hibachi Chicken Breasts

(Serves 3 to 6)

This recipe goes great with stir-fried vegetables and steamed rice, or with the chicken cut into julienne and tossed with mixed greens and served with one of my signature salad dressings. But my favorite way is on a whole wheat bun with mayonnaise, lettuce, tomatoes, and onions. *Mmmmmmmmmm!*

> *6 chicken breast halves*
> *Hot Hibachi Marinade (see recipe below)*

Prepare and light coals in a hibachi. Marinate the chicken breasts in hot hibachi marinade for 30 minutes.

Grill over coals, turning every 2 to 3 minutes, for a total cooking time of 8 to 10 minutes. If you prefer, you may pan-fry the chicken breasts or broil them in the oven. The cooking time is the same.

Hot Hibachi Marinade

(Makes about 2½ cups)

1 teaspoon sesame oil
1½ cups soy sauce
2 cloves fresh garlic, minced
1 cup granulated sugar
½ cup peeled and minced fresh ginger
2 tablespoons thinly sliced green onions
1 tablespoon minced fresh cilantro
⅛ teaspoon white pepper

Blend all the ingredients thoroughly. Stir until the sugar is dissolved.

Lemon Chicken

(Serves 4)

There are a couple of Chinese dishes—beef broccoli and lemon chicken—that are staples in local Hawaiian cooking. Lemon sauce gives the chicken a wonderful sweet-and-sour flavor. Serve this alone over steamed rice, or with any other stir-fry dish. The lemon blends very well with just about anything.

2 cups water
½ cup chopped fresh cilantro
1-inch piece fresh ginger, peeled and crushed
½ teaspoon salt
6 boneless, skinless chicken breast halves
½ cup cornstarch
¼ cup all-purpose flour
Oil for deep-frying
Lemon Sauce (see recipe on page 188)

Garnish:
½ lemon, cut into thin slices
Sprig of fresh cilantro

In a large bowl, combine water, cilantro, ginger, and salt. Add the chicken and marinate for 30 minutes.

Combine the cornstarch and flour. Remove chicken from the marinade. Dredge chicken in the cornstarch mixture, shaking off the excess.

Heat 2½ to 3 inches of oil in a deep, heavy pot or wok over medium-high heat until a deep-fry thermometer registers 375°F. Fry the chicken in batches until golden brown, about 7 to 8 minutes. Remove to a paper towel-lined platter. Let cool slightly, then cut into 1-inch strips.

Arrange the chicken strips on a serving platter. Pour lemon sauce over the chicken and top with lemon slices and a sprig of cilantro.

Lemon Sauce

(Makes 1½ cups)

½ cup chicken stock
⅓ cup granulated sugar
½ cup lemon juice
2 tablespoons vinegar
1-inch piece fresh ginger, peeled and crushed
1 tablespoon cornstarch
2 tablespoons water
2 drops yellow food coloring (optional)

In a small saucepan, combine the chicken stock, sugar, lemon juice, vinegar, and ginger. Bring to a boil.

In a small bowl, blend the cornstarch and water. Stir into the chicken stock mixture. Reduce heat and simmer, stirring frequently, until thickened and translucent. Remove from heat and discard ginger. Stir in yellow food coloring if desired.

Ka'u Lime Chicken

(Serves 4)

I like using ingredients from the Big Island—like limes from the Ka'u district, located on the southern tip of the island. It's a desert terrain, covered with fresh lava, and is the least populated area in the fiftieth state. The weather is perfect for growing limes. But any limes will do when making this tart and zesty chicken dish.

1 pound boneless, skinless chicken thighs
1 tablespoon minced shallot
3 tablespoons butter
¼ cup white wine
Juice and grated zest of 1 lime
Salt and pepper to taste

Garnish:
1 lime, thinly sliced
1 tablespoon chopped macadamia nuts

In a skillet, sauté the chicken and shallot in butter for 6 to 7 minutes, until the chicken is tender. Remove the chicken to a serving plate; set aside and keep warm. Add the white wine to the skillet and boil until reduced by half. Add lime juice, and cook until the sauce thickens. Season to taste with salt and pepper. Pour the sauce over the chicken and sprinkle with lime zest. Garnish with lime slices and a sprinkling of macadamia nuts.

Macadamia Nut Chicken Breasts
with Tropical Marmalade
(Serves 6)

Macadamia nuts are not indigenous to Hawai'i. Mr. E. W. Purvis introduced macadamia trees to the Islands from Australia in 1885. Macadamia nut production increased as the sugar cane industry waned, and today macadamia nuts bolster the Big Island economy. I like to encase chicken in a macadamia nut crust. You can't beat it. The crust keeps all the moisture in and adds a rich, nutty flavor to the meat. This dish is a very popular menu item in my restaurants.

6 boneless, skinless chicken breast halves
Chicken Barbecue Marinade (see recipe on page 191)
1 cup macadamia nuts, finely chopped
¾ cup fine dry bread crumbs
½ cup all-purpose flour
3 eggs, lightly beaten
2 tablespoons oil
1 tablespoon butter
Tropical Marmalade (see recipe on page 31)

Marinate the chicken in chicken barbecue marinade for 1 hour, turning occasionally. Remove the chicken, and allow to drain.

Combine the macadamia nuts and bread crumbs. Dredge the chicken in flour, dip in beaten eggs, and coat with the macadamia nut mixture.

In a heavy skillet, heat the oil and butter over medium heat. Sauté the chicken for 6 to 8 minutes, turning once. Add a little oil if necessary, since macadamia nuts may absorb oil. Serve with tropical marmalade.

Chicken Barbecue Marinade

(Makes about ¾ cup)

½ cup soy sauce
1½ tablespoons brown sugar
1 tablespoon mirin (Japanese sweet rice wine)
1 tablespoon olive oil
1 teaspoon minced fresh garlic
1 teaspoon peeled and minced fresh ginger

Combine all ingredients.

Sweet-and-Sour Chicken Breasts with Tropical Fruits

(Serves 4)

I really like making this dish because it gives a whole new twist to sweet-and-sour sauce. Adding the fresh tropical fruit makes it different. It takes away the boredom.

4 boneless, skinless chicken breast halves, 6 to 8 ounces each
Maui Moa Marinade (see recipe on page 192)
½ cup all-purpose flour
3 tablespoons vegetable oil
1 cup diced fresh pineapple
1 cup chopped fresh papaya
1 cup chopped mangoes, or tropical fruit of your choice
Sweet-and-Sour Sauce (see recipe on page 193)

Garnish:
Green onion strips
Sprigs of fresh cilantro

Cover the chicken with the marinade and let stand for 30 minutes.

Remove the chicken from the marinade and blot off excess liquid. Dust the chicken with flour to coat. Pan-fry in 3 tablespoons of oil until golden brown, about 4 minutes per side on medium heat. Remove chicken, set aside, and tent with foil to keep warm.

Discard most of the oil in the pan, leaving about 1 tablespoon. Stir-fry the fruit for 2 minutes. Add sweet-and-sour sauce and heat through.

Arrange the chicken breasts on a serving platter, pour some sauce over them, and garnish with green onion strips and cilantro. Pass the remaining sauce separately.

Maui Moa Marinade

(Makes 1½ cups)

½ cup soy sauce

½ cup canola oil

2 tablespoons mirin (Japanese sweet rice wine)

1 tablespoon minced fresh garlic

1 tablespoon peeled and minced fresh ginger

½ teaspoon salt

¼ teaspoon white pepper

2 tablespoons cornstarch mixed with 1½ tablespoons water

1½ teaspoons brown sugar

Combine all ingredients.

Sweet-and-Sour Sauce

(Makes about 4 cups)

½ cup ketchup
½ cup vinegar
½ cup water
2 teaspoons soy sauce
1 cup granulated sugar
¼ cup orange marmalade
1½ teaspoons peeled and minced fresh ginger
1 teaspoon minced fresh garlic
¼ teaspoon hot pepper sauce
2 tablespoons pineapple juice
2 tablespoons cornstarch blended with 1½ tablespoons water

Combine all ingredients except the cornstarch and water in a medium saucepan. Bring to a boil. Add the cornstarch mixture, reduce heat, and simmer, stirring frequently, for 1 to 2 minutes or until thickened.

Stir-Fried Chicken with Sweet Peppers and Onions

(Serves 2)

*J*umping, stirring, mixing, pouring out, adding in—that's what makes wok cooking exciting. It's a good idea to have all of the elements prepared and waiting next to the wok. Things can get pretty fast and furious when the wok heats up. This is another recipe that is great over steamed rice.

> 2 chicken breast halves or 2 whole chicken legs (thighs plus drumsticks), skinned and boned
> Sam's Simple Soy Marinade (see recipe on page 195)
> 2 tablespoons canola oil
> 2 red bell peppers, julienned
> ½ onion, julienned
> 2 tablespoons oyster sauce
> ½ teaspoon salt
> Pinch of white pepper
> ¼ cup chicken stock
>
> Garnish:
> 2 sprigs fresh cilantro

Thinly slice the chicken, then cut into strips. Mix thoroughly with the marinade and let stand for 1 hour.

In a wok, heat the oil and stir-fry the chicken for 1 minute or until slightly browned; remove from pan. Stir-fry the bell peppers and onion for 1 minute. Season with oyster sauce, salt, and pepper; stir-fry 1 minute more. Return the chicken to the wok and add the stock. Cook covered for 2 or 3 minutes over medium heat.

Garnish with cilantro. Serve immediately.

Sam's Simple Soy Marinade

(Makes 1½ tablespoons)

1 tablespoon soy sauce
1 teaspoon canola oil
½ teaspoon granulated sugar

Combine all ingredients.

Christopher's Stir-Fried Chicken

(Serves 4)

One favorite dish of my younger son, Christopher, is stir-fry: stirring the chicken, adding vegetables, squirting in cornstarch. He's got well-formed, busy hands—hands are important for a chef. I like to let my kids cook. It turns messy if you don't get after them to clean up. But how else will they learn? This is another dish that is delicious over steamed rice.

2 whole boneless, skinless chicken legs (thighs plus drumsticks), thinly sliced into strips

Christopher's Chicken Marinade (see recipe on page 196)

2 teaspoons cornstarch

2 tablespoons cold water

3 tablespoons canola oil

8 ounces assorted fresh vegetables of choice (carrots, celery, onion, red bell pepper, sugar snap peas, Chinese snow peas, wing beans, etc.), julienned

1 cup chicken stock

1 tablespoon oyster sauce

Salt and pepper to taste

Coat the chicken with the marinade and let stand for 1 hour. Combine the cornstarch and cold water; set aside.

In a wok, heat 1½ tablespoons of the oil and stir-fry the chicken for 2 to 3 minutes; remove to a plate. In the same wok, heat the remaining 1½ tablespoons of oil and stir-fry the vegetables. Add the chicken stock and oyster sauce, and return chicken to the wok. Bring to a boil and adjust seasoning with salt and pepper. Stir in cornstarch mixture to thicken. Cook 1 minute more.

Christopher's Chicken Marinade

(Makes about ¼ cup)

2 tablespoons sherry
1 tablespoon soy sauce
½ teaspoon granulated sugar
2 slices (¹⁄₁₆ inch each) fresh ginger, minced
1 clove fresh garlic, minced

Combine all ingredients.

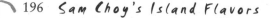

Makawao Chicken Chili

(Serves 4)

I attended a rodeo in the little town of Makawao, in Upcountry Maui on the slopes of Haleakala volcano. I'm always on the lookout for interesting food, cooked by local folks. As I walked past the vendors' tents that lined the outskirts of the fairground, I stopped. An incredible aroma was coming from a makeshift kitchen under a white tarp. The sign read, "Help our Makawao keiki." I bought a big bowl of chili and rice. It contained tender chunks of seasoned chicken, tomatoes, beans, and vegetables in a spicy sauce. I thought you might like a taste. This is best served over rice.

2 tablespoons light vegetable oil
1 pound boneless, skinless chicken thighs, cut into 1-inch chunks
1 teaspoon sea salt
1 teaspoon freshly ground pepper
1 tablespoon minced fresh garlic
½ cup diced onion
½ cup diced carrots
½ cup diced celery
2 tablespoons chili powder
1 teaspoon ground cumin
1 teaspoon oregano
½ cup canned tomatoes, chopped
¼ cup tomato paste
1 8-ounce can pinto beans
1 8-ounce can black beans

Heat the oil in a wok. Add the chicken, salt, pepper, garlic, onion, carrots, and celery, and stir-fry for about 2 minutes. Add the chili powder, cumin, and oregano. Stir in the tomatoes, tomato paste, and beans. Let cook on low heat for about 20 minutes.

Chicken Hekka

(Serves 4 to 6)

Chicken Hekka is one of those dishes that show up at every lu'au or party in the Islands. It's kind of Chinese, kind of Japanese, kind of like Hawai'i's multicultural mix. I like to eat this on a Sunday afternoon. It's light, with vegetables and noodles, and it's easy to make. You combine all the ingredients in one pot, cook it up, steam some rice, and enjoy the meal.

2½ pounds boneless, skinless chicken thighs or breasts
Hekka Marinade (see recipe on page 199)
1 can (2½ cups) sliced bamboo shoots, drained and rinsed
10 green onions, cut into 1-inch lengths
1 onion, cut into half-moon slices
1 medium carrot, julienned
1 pound shiitake mushrooms, sliced
2 stalks celery, julienned
½ pound watercress, chopped into 1-inch lengths
3 tablespoons vegetable oil
½ finger fresh ginger, peeled and crushed
Sake Sauce (see recipe on page 199)
1 bundle (2 ounces) bean thread noodles, cooked and
    cut into 1-inch lengths

Marinate the chicken for 30 minutes in hekka marinade.

Meanwhile, mix the bambo shoots, onions, carrot, mushrooms, celery, and watercress, and set aside.

Brown the chicken in 3 tablespoons oil to which you have added crushed ginger. Add all the vegetables and stir-fry for 1 minute. Add the sake sauce and bean threads and simmer on medium heat for 5 minutes. Serve at once.

Hekka Marinade

(Makes 1½ cups)

2 tablespoons cornstarch
½ cup soy sauce
½ cup vegetable oil
2 tablespoons mirin (Japanese sweet rice wine)
1 tablespoon minced fresh garlic
1 tablespoon peeled and minced fresh ginger
½ teaspoon salt
¼ teaspoon white pepper
1½ teaspoons brown sugar

Dissolve the cornstarch in the soy sauce and mix with the remaining ingredients.

Sake Sauce

(Makes 2¼ cups)

½ cup granulated sugar
¾ cup soy sauce
½ cup chicken stock
½ cup sake

Blend all ingredients.

Paniolo Chicken Fajitas

(Serves 2)

This is not one of my signature recipes, but I wanted to include it. My older son, Sam Jr., created this dish for Tommy Jean Sheldrake's surprise birthday party in California. It was a hit at the party, and it's been a pleaser ever since. Lucky kid, and I'm proud of him.

1 boneless, skinless chicken breast half, thinly sliced
Spicy Fajita Marinade (see recipe below)
1 tablespoon canola oil
1 cup assorted sliced fresh vegetables (bell peppers, broccoli, carrots)
4 flour tortillas
1 tablespoon hoisin sauce (sweet-spicy soybean sauce)
Green onions, chopped

Coat the chicken slices with the marinade and let stand for 15 minutes. In a heavy skillet, heat the oil and cook the meat for about 4 minutes. Add the vegetables, and cook for about 2 minutes more.

In a dry skillet over high heat, warm the tortillas for about 30 seconds per side. On each tortilla, spread ¼ of the hoisin sauce and top with ¼ of the meat-vegetable mixture. Sprinkle with green onions and roll up.

Spicy Fajita Marinade

(Makes ¼ cup)

2 tablespoons soy sauce
1 tablespoon peeled and minced fresh ginger
1 tablespoon minced fresh garlic
1 tablespoon chopped green onion
1 teaspoon chopped fresh cilantro

1 teaspoon red chili pepper flakes
1 teaspoon brown sugar
Salt and pepper to taste

Combine all ingredients.

Chicken Tofu with Watercress

(Serves 4 to 6)

This is very simple to make. Just be sure to wait until the end to fold in the tofu—you don't want to overcook it and have it crumble away to mush. And remember to use firm tofu. Prepare the marinade and the sauce before you do anything with the chicken, so that things are ready to go once you start cooking. This makes a great meal served straight from the skillet or wok with hot steamed rice.

Wiki-Wiki Rub (see recipe on page 202)
12 boneless, skinless chicken thighs, cut into 1-inch cubes
2 tablespoons oil
Shaka Shoyu Sauce (see recipe on page 202)
2 medium onions, cut into half-moon slices
1 bunch watercress, cut into 1-inch sections
1 block firm tofu, cubed
Salt and pepper to taste

Put the wiki-wiki rub in a mixing bowl with the chicken and stir thoroughly until all the chicken pieces are coated. Let stand for 30 minutes.

In a skillet or wok, stir-fry the chicken in the 2 tablespoons of oil over medium-high heat until it is semi-brown on all sides. Add the shoyu sauce and bring to a boil. Add the onions and watercress and cook for 2 to 3 minutes. Add the tofu, reduce the heat, and simmer for about 3 minutes, until the tofu absorbs some of the liquid. Adjust seasoning with salt and pepper.

Wiki-Wiki Rub

(Makes about ¼ cup)

4 tablespoons soy sauce
1 teaspoon minced fresh garlic
1 teaspoon brown sugar
2 tablespoons salad oil

Mix all ingredients together.

Shaka Shoyu Sauce

(Makes ¾ cup)

½ cup soy sauce
2 tablespoons mirin (Japanese sweet rice wine)
1 tablespoon minced fresh garlic
1 tablespoon peeled and minced fresh ginger
½ teaspoon salt
¼ teaspoon white pepper
1½ teaspoons brown sugar

Combine all ingredients.

Wok the Chicken with Eggplant and Hot Peppers

(Serves 2)

This dish is almost like ma-po, a popular Chinese recipe where all the ingredients are cooked together like mush. I've spiced up the eggplant and chicken with the hot peppers. It's real hot, and real good. I like this one.

2 whole chicken legs (thighs plus drumsticks), skinned and boned

1 tablespoon soy sauce

1 tablespoon sherry

1 tablespoon cornstarch

1 teaspoon granulated sugar

4 tablespoons canola oil

2 fresh chili peppers, seeded and minced

2 or 3 slices (1/16 inch each) fresh ginger, minced

1 clove fresh garlic, minced

1/4 cup chicken stock

1 medium eggplant, cut into strips

Thinly slice the chicken, then cut into strips. Combine the soy sauce, sherry, cornstarch, and sugar; toss chicken in the mixture to coat.

In a wok, heat 2 tablespoons of the oil and stir-fry the chilies until they change color; remove to a plate. Heat the remaining 2 tablespoons of oil and stir-fry the chicken 1 minute or until it loses pinkness. Stir in the ginger and garlic. Add the chicken stock and eggplant, and return the chilies to the wok. Cook, stirring, 2 to 4 minutes to heat through and blend flavors.

Serve immediately.

Sam's Special "Big-O" Thanksgiving Turkey

(Serves 6 to 8)

For as long as I can remember, after every Thanksgiving dinner two things happened—one, I'd feel like I ate myself into outer space; and two, I needed to take about a year off from eating. So that's one of the reasons I came up with the "Big-O" (meaning zero fat) turkey dinner. With this meal you feel full, yet by the next day you're ready to get back into your normal eating schedule.

1 teaspoon salt
¼ teaspoon white pepper
2 to 3 pounds boneless, skinless turkey breast
2 cups chicken stock
½ cup chopped carrots
½ cup chopped celery
½ cup chopped onion
2 tablespoons cornstarch mixed with 2 tablespoons water
   for thickening
No-Fat Mashed Potatoes (see recipe on page 205)
No-Fat Stuffing (see recipe on page 205)
Cranberry Sauce (see recipe on page 205)

Preheat the oven to 375°F. Rub salt and pepper into the turkey breast for 2 to 3 minutes, massaging the seasonings into the meat.

Pour 1 cup of chicken stock into the bottom of a roasting pan. Add the vegetables. Place the turkey in the pan and cover tightly with foil or an ovenproof lid.

Roast for 30 minutes, then reduce the heat to 350°F and cook for 20 more minutes. Remove the foil and brown for about 10 minutes. Total cooking time should be about 1 hour. Remove the turkey from the oven and cool before slicing.

Transfer the drippings and cooked vegetables to a saucepan. Add the remaining cup of stock. Bring to a boil. Stir the cornstarch mixture into the boiling broth and simmer 2 to 3 minutes. Strain and set the gravy aside.

Slice the turkey breast. Serve with no-fat mashed potatoes, no-fat stuffing, and cranberry sauce. Pass the no-fat gravy in a gravy boat.

No-Fat Mashed Potatoes

(Cooking tip)

I like to boil the potatoes with garlic and chives, which add a lot of flavor, and I use chicken broth in place of butter and milk.

No-Fat Stuffing

(Makes 4½ to 5 cups)

1 teaspoon poultry seasoning
1 cup chopped apples
1 cup chopped onions
1 cup chopped celery
2 cups chicken stock
3 cups toasted croutons (or more, for dryer stuffing)
Salt and pepper to taste

Combine all ingredients except croutons. Bring to a boil and simmer until the vegetables are soft, then fold in the croutons. Serve hot.

Cranberry Sauce

(Makes about 5 cups)

1 cup fresh pineapple juice
1 cup fresh orange juice
3 cups whole cranberries
1 whole orange, sliced, with rind

Bring all ingredients to a boil, then cook down to the consistency of jam, 25 to 30 minutes, or until reduced to the desired consistency. It tastes good as is, but if you want it sweeter, add a little sugar.

Island-Style Barbecued Cornish Game Hens

(Serves 6)

I like barbecuing Cornish game hens. It's quite easy. You have to leave the skins on to keep the meat moist, and basting is vital. But they cook up fast and are incredibly succulent. They are tasty birds, so you don't need many ingredients.

3 Cornish game hens, butterflied
Barbecue Marinade (see recipe below)

Garnish:
Chopped green onions

Marinate the hens for 1 to 2 hours in the refrigerator, turning them several times. Grill skin side down, basting occasionally with reserved marinade, for 15 minutes. Turn and continue cooking until the skin is crisp and the juices run clear, 25 to 30 minutes total.

Barbecue Marinade

(Makes ¾ cup)

½ cup orange juice
¼ cup olive oil
1 small clove fresh garlic, minced
Salt and pepper to taste

Combine all ingredients.

Sam Choy's Award-Winning Roast Duck

(Serves 4)

Roasting duck the traditional Chinese way is a lot of work, but I've found an easy way to do it that I think tastes just as good. Everyone raves about this duck. It's like a shining star on our menu. The best award we've ever won is the people's award, and this dish keeps winning it over and over again. We serve it with steamed rice.

> 1 5-pound duck
> ¾ cup soy sauce
> "Dry" Duck Marinade (see recipe below)

Rinse the duck. Remove the wings, neck flap, tail end, excess fat, and drumstick knuckles. Place in a dish and pour soy sauce over the bird. Roll the duck in the soy sauce to coat, and let it sit for about 10 minutes. Keep rolling in the soy sauce every 3 to 4 minutes.

Preheat the oven to 550°F. Place the duck, breast side up, on a rack in a large shallow roasting pan, and sprinkle thoroughly with dry marinade. Put a little marinade inside the cavity.

Roast at 550°F for 30 minutes. Reduce the heat to 325°F. Cook for 1 hour, or until a meat thermometer registers an internal temperature of 170°F to 175°F. No basting is necessary.

"Dry" Duck Marinade

(Makes 3 tablespoons)

> 1 tablespoon salt
> 1 tablespoon garlic salt
> 1 teaspoon garlic powder
> 1 teaspoon paprika
> ½ teaspoon white pepper
> 1 tablespoon whole coriander seeds

Mix all ingredients.

Beef

History has had a dramatic impact on the culinary landscape of Hawai'i. Here in the Islands, we divide our past into two distinct periods—pre-discovery and post-discovery. When Captain Cook arrived on January 18, 1778, everything changed for the Hawaiian people, including their basic foods.

In 1803, British captain George Vancouver gave the great Hawaiian chief Kamehameha a small herd of longhorn cattle from Monterey, California. Kamehameha put a kapu, or taboo, on the animals, prohibiting anyone from killing them, and the tough breed quickly multiplied and ran wild in the fields of North Kohala on the Big Island of Hawai'i.

In 1815, King Kamehameha hired John Palmer Parker, a Boston-born entrepreneur, to manage his herd, and that started the century-old dynasty of the 220,000-acre Parker Ranch. John Parker's son, Samuel, brought in Spanish and Mexican range riders to train the Hawaiians in the art of ranching. The Hawaiians called these españoles "paniolo."

The paniolo started the tradition of "hulihuli," or rotisserie cooking over an open fire. Soon Japanese, Filipino, Chinese, Caucasian, and Korean immigrants began coming to the Islands, bringing with them their favorite foods. Today, Hawaiian beef is seasoned, roasted, hibachied, braised, stewed, teriyakied, stir-fried, marinated, kal bied, and glazed.

My favorite method of beef preparation is to season it with a teriyaki marinade, and barbecue it on a hibachi. When the weather is warm, which is most of the year, folks dust off the hibachi, set it up on the back porch, and grill three or four times a week.

I went to the 1996 Pro Bowl football game and walked through the Aloha Stadium parking lot to check out what people were firing up on their hibachis. There were so many folks celebrating over grills and inviting me to join them that I almost missed the kickoff!

I've included a variety of culturally influenced beef recipes in this section to give you an idea of how these different ethnic groups have blended, like fine flavors, here in the Islands. Some of these recipes have been in my family for generations, handed down from my great-grandparents and parents, and I know I'll pass them on to my kids, because even today these dishes are able to bring people joy. I'm Hawaiian Chinese, and these recipes come from both sides of my family. My mom's mom, my tutu, was trained in England after being hand-picked to serve Hawaiian royalty. That's where some of the traditional European cookery came in. I call these recipes classics because they are timeless comfort foods. They are dishes that excited me when I was growing up. They are special to me, foods that I hold close to my heart.

Hawaiian Prime Rib au Jus

(Serves 14 to 20)

This is a traditional Western Hawaiian prime rib. The basic recipe has been in my mother's family for a long time. My grandmother said it was a dish that my great-grandmother learned from her father. That goes back a long way. I've added a few herbs, like rosemary and thyme, to spice up the meat, but it's really the garlic that sets it all off.

10 cloves fresh garlic, crushed

14-pound standing beef rib roast

2 tablespoons salt, mixed with 1 tablespoon cracked pepper and
    2 tablespoons garlic salt

2 tablespoons chopped fresh rosemary mixed with 1 teaspoon dried
    thyme

2 cups chunked carrots

2 cups chunked celery

2 cups chunked onions

1 quart chicken stock

1 quart beef stock

1 cup cornstarch mixed with ½ cup cold water

Additional salt and pepper to taste

Preheat the oven to 350°F.

Peel back the fat cover and place the crushed garlic cloves on the meat, then sprinkle with half the salt–cracked pepper–garlic salt mixture. Roll fat cover back into place, and sprinkle the top of the fat with the remaining salt mixture, the rosemary, and thyme.

Place the meat on a rack in a deep roasting pan and roast for 45 minutes. Add the chunked vegetables and beef and chicken stock to the pan, making sure the rack is high enough so liquid doesn't touch the meat. Depending on the depth of your pan, you may have to use less broth.

Continue roasting the meat until the internal temperature reaches 135°F for medium-rare. Test with a meat thermometer. Remove from the oven and let rest about half an hour.

To make gravy, remove the roast from the pan and place the pan on a burner. Skim off the fat. Bring the drippings to a boil, then add the cornstarch mixture, stirring constantly until thickened. Adjust seasonings with salt and pepper, strain, and keep warm.

Carve the meat to whatever thickness you like, and serve with gravy and all the trimmings.

Kamuela Dry-Rub Tenderloin
(Serves 2)

*T*ender beef raised in Kamuela, on the slopes of Mauna Kea on the northern part of the Big Island, is enhanced by dry spicing and fast searing. It's a big-time hit. The dry seasoning salt is also great with chicken, pork, or fish. Serve this dish with pan-fried potatoes.

> *Dry Seasoning Salt (see recipe on page 213)*
> *1 teaspoon minced fresh basil*
> *¼ teaspoon fresh thyme*
> *2 beef tenderloin fillets, 6 ounces each*
> *Cooking spray*

Sprinkle dry seasoning salt over the fillets as needed and let stand for 10 minutes.

Sprinkle the basil and thyme over the fillets, and massage into the meat. In a skillet sprayed with nonstick vegetable oil cooking spray, pan-fry the fillets over medium-high heat for 2½ minutes per side (the way I like it), or until done to your preference.

Dry Seasoning Salt

(Makes about 1 tablespoon)

1 teaspoon sea salt
1 teaspoon garlic salt
1 teaspoon paprika
½ teaspoon black pepper
¼ teaspoon onion powder

In a salt shaker, combine ingredients, and shake to blend well. Set aside.

Pulehu Rib Eye

(Serves 4 to 8)

This is one of my favorite cuts of beef—with its small tender strap on top, just the right amount of fat for flavor and tenderness, and then that tasty eye.

4 rib-eye steaks, 8 ounces each
Pulehu Beef Marinade (see recipe on page 214)
Special Teriyaki Glaze (see recipe on page 214)

Garnish:
Fried Onions (see recipe on page 215)

Marinate the steaks in the beef marinade overnight in the refrigerator.
Grill the steaks over charcoal, or broil in the oven just the way you like them. Drizzle with special teriyaki glaze and top with thin and crispy fried onions.

Pulehu Beef Marinade

(Makes 2½ to 2¾ cups)

2 cloves fresh garlic, minced
1½ cups soy sauce
1 cup granulated sugar
¼ cup peeled and minced fresh ginger
2 tablespoons thinly sliced green onion
⅛ teaspoon white pepper

Combine all the ingredients and blend well.

Special Teriyaki Glaze

(Makes 1 cup)

½ cup soy sauce
¼ cup mirin (Japanese sweet rice wine)
¼ cup water
2 tablespoons brown sugar
1 teaspoon minced fresh garlic
1 teaspoon peeled and minced fresh ginger
1 tablespoon cornstarch mixed with 2 tablespoons water

In a small saucepan, bring all the ingredients, except the cornstarch mixture, to a boil. Blend cornstarch and water. Stir into the pan. Reduce heat and simmer, stirring frequently until thickened.

Fried Onions

(Makes ½ cup)

1 medium onion
All-purpose flour, enough to dust onion slices
Oil for deep-frying

Slice the onion into paper-thin circular slices, then dust the slices with flour. Heat 2 inches of oil to 350°F in a deep heavy kettle or a wok. Drop in the onions, a handful at a time, and fry until golden brown while moving slices around with tongs so they don't stick together. Drain on paper towels.

Hawaiian Barbecued Tri-Tip Steak

(Serves 4 to 6)

The Hawaiian word for barbecue is "pulehu." Literally, it means to broil on hot embers. This is a big piece of beef, and what makes it really good is that it's crusty on the outside and nice and rare on the inside, almost like beef sashimi. It's great eating when it's hot, and it makes the best cold sandwiches the next day when the flavors have had a chance to be absorbed all the way through the meat. This dish is great for tailgate or beach parties.

½ cup kosher or sea salt
1 tablespoon minced fresh garlic
1½ teaspoons cracked peppercorns
1 tablespoon granulated sugar
2½ pounds tri-tip steak (triangular tip of the sirloin)

Light your charcoal. Rub salt, garlic, pepper, and sugar into the meat, and let stand for 30 minutes. Pulehu (broil on hot embers), turning the meat every 4 minutes. Total cooking time is about 10 to 15 minutes, depending upon the thickness of the cut.

Tailgate Teri Steaks

(Serves 4)

At one football game between the University of Hawai'i and Brigham Young University (Hawai'i's biggest WAC rival), we had live lobsters, steaks, and shrimp in the cooler. I marinated the steaks and shrimp with this recipe's Teriyaki Sauce, and put them on the hibachi. Everything was so tasty we returned to the parking lot after the game and ate some more.

4 lean New York steaks, 10 ounces each
Teriyaki Sauce (see recipe on page 217)
1 tablespoon cornstarch
1 tablespoon water

Garnish:
Pineapple wedges
Toasted coconut

Marinate the steaks in 3 cups of the teriyaki sauce for 4 to 6 hours, turning occasionally.

Remove steaks from marinade and discard marinade.

Blend the cornstarch and water. Bring the reserved marinade to a boil and stir in the cornstarch mixture to thicken. Grill or broil steaks to your desired taste, basting with thickened sauce.

Grill or broil pineapple wedges. Garnish each steak with a broiled pineapple wedge and a sprinkling of toasted coconut.

Teriyaki Sauce

(Makes 4 cups)

2 cups soy sauce
1 cup mirin (Japanese sweet rice wine)
1 cup water
½ cup packed brown sugar
1 tablespoon minced fresh garlic
1 tablespoon peeled and minced fresh ginger
2 medium oranges, sliced (optional)

Combine all ingredients, and reserve 1 cup.

Traditional Backyard Beef Teriyaki

(Serves 4 to 6)

One of the nice things about living in Hawai'i is being able to barbecue all year long. When anybody in the neighborhood puts something on the grill, the aroma makes your taste buds go wild, and you know the first chance you get you gotta fire up your own barbecue. Teriyaki is one of those things everybody does, but it's a real winner. You just can't go wrong with it.

Steak Marinade (see recipe on page 218)
2 pounds steak of your choice, thinly sliced
Special Teriyaki Glaze (see recipe on page 218)

Marinate the meat in steak marinade for 4 to 6 hours in the refrigerator.

Grill over hot coals (a hibachi seems to make the best flavor) for 2 or 3 minutes on each side, or until cooked to your taste. The meat is thin, so you don't want to overcook it. After it's done, place on a serving platter and drizzle a little of my special teriyaki glaze over the top.

Steak Marinade

(Makes 3½ cups)

3 cups soy sauce
1 cup granulated sugar
½ cup peeled and minced fresh ginger
4 cloves fresh garlic, minced
4 tablespoons thinly sliced green onions
¼ teaspoon white pepper
2 tablespoons chopped fresh cilantro
2 teaspoons sesame oil

Blend all ingredients well.

Special Teriyaki Glaze

(Makes 1 to 1¼ cups)

½ cup soy sauce
¼ cup mirin (Japanese sweet rice wine)
¼ cup water
2 tablespoons brown sugar
1 teaspoon minced fresh garlic
1 teaspoon peeled and minced fresh ginger
1 tablespoon cornstarch mixed with 2 tablespoons water

In a small saucepan, bring all ingredients except the cornstarch mixture to a boil. Blend cornstarch and water. Stir into pan. Reduce the heat and simmer for 1 or 2 minutes, stirring until thickened.

Braised Anise Beef Brisket

(Serves 6 to 8)

This dish is good either hot (served with rice), or cold (in a sandwich). The aniseed gives the brisket a slight licorice taste. It has a nice aromatic flavor and a spicy Asian flare. This is 'ono with steamed rice or served cold.

3 tablespoons soy sauce
1 teaspoon minced fresh garlic
1 teaspoon peeled and minced fresh ginger
3 pounds beef brisket
3 tablespoons vegetable oil
1 quart chicken stock, or enough to cover meat
2 tablespoons whole aniseed
1 finger fresh ginger, peeled and crushed
4 cloves fresh garlic, crushed
1½ cups granulated sugar

Rub the soy sauce, minced ginger, and minced garlic into the meat. Heat the oil in a large Dutch oven and brown the meat on both sides. Cover with chicken stock. Add the aniseed, crushed ginger, crushed garlic, and sugar. Bring to a boil, then reduce the heat and let simmer, covered, for 1½ to 2 hours, or until tender. Set aside until cooled slightly. Slice thin.

Lana'i Ranch Pot Roast

(Serves 8 to 10)

There aren't that many cows on the island of Lana'i, so when the locals do get some home-grown beef, they take special care in preparing it. When I say "special care," I don't mean they spend a lot of time slaving over the stove. They are careful with the seasoning, so that the flavor of the meat isn't lost. This is one of the easiest one-pot dinners you can fix, and with today's slow cookers it's even easier. The herbs and spices will do the rest.

Salt and pepper to taste
1½ tablespoons minced fresh garlic
1 boneless 4-pound cross rib (shoulder roast), or cut of your choice
All-purpose flour, enough for dusting beef
3 tablespoons vegetable oil
2 medium onions, chunked
2 medium carrots, chunked
2 medium potatoes, chunked
4 stalks celery, cut up
1½ quarts chicken stock, plus 1 quart beef stock, or
*   enough to cover meat*
¾ cup tomato purée
2 bay leaves
1 sprig fresh rosemary
Mochiko (Japanese glutinous rice flour) and water to make
*   thickening agent*

Preheat the oven to 350°F. Rub salt, pepper, and garlic on the meat, and set aside for a few minutes.

Flour the meat, then sear in the oil over medium heat in a Dutch oven until very well browned on all sides, about 10 minutes. Add vegetables, stocks, and tomato purée. Bring to a boil. Add bay leaves and rosemary.

Cover and bake for 1½ hours, or until fork-tender. Other cuts of meat may take longer, up to 3 or even 4 hours, depending on thickness or toughness.

Remove pot roast and vegetables from Dutch oven and arrange on serving platter.

To make gravy, strain the drippings. Bring the liquid to a boil and thicken with mochiko diluted with water. Cook and stir until you get the consistency you like.

Big Island Beef Short Ribs
(Serves 4)

Cowboys, or paniolo, are always having big outdoor cookouts on ranches throughout Hawai'i, and short ribs is one of their favorites for barbecuing. Asian groups cook ribs too, but I like the Hawaiian way: rub in the seasoned salt and let it sit a few minutes, then brown it on the coals. It doesn't get any better.

1 tablespoon kosher or rock salt
1 teaspoon cracked peppercorns
2 pounds beef short ribs
1 teaspoon minced fresh garlic
1 cup dry vermouth
1 tablespoon soy sauce

Light your charcoal. While it's getting hot, mix the salt and pepper and rub into the meat. Massage in the garlic, put the ribs in a bowl, then pour the vermouth over and drizzle with soy sauce. Let marinate 20 to 30 minutes in the vermouth-soy sauce mixture, then grill 5 to 6 minutes for rare, 6 to 8 minutes for medium-rare, or to your choice of perfection.

Stir-Fried Beef with Honaunau Snow Peas

(Serves 4)

I named this recipe after the sweet snow peas grown by farmers in the district of Honaunau on the Big Island. This is a simple dish, best served over steamed rice. The hardest part is cutting the beef and cleaning the snow peas. The cooking goes real quick. Before you know it, you're sitting down enjoying delicious tender morsels of beef and sweet snow peas. I can see you now, licking your chops. Remember, don't overcook the snow peas. They should be crisp, not limp.

1 pound lean boneless beef

2 teaspoons cornstarch

1 teaspoon granulated sugar

1 tablespoon soy sauce

1½ tablespoons sweet vermouth

1½ tablespoons water

3 tablespoons vegetable oil

½ finger fresh ginger, peeled and sliced

½ pound snow peas, ends trimmed

1 cup chicken stock

Salt and pepper to taste

1 tablespoon cornstarch mixed with 1 tablespoon of water and
 1 teaspoon of granulated sugar for thickening

Slice beef thinly against the grain. Combine the cornstarch, sugar, soy sauce, vermouth, and water, and massage into the meat for 2 or 3 minutes. Let stand 2 or 3 minutes to marinate.

Heat 1 tablespoon of oil on medium-high heat in a wok or sauté pan. Stir-fry the ginger for a minute or two. Add the snow peas and stir-fry for 1 or 2 minutes more. Remove with a slotted spoon and set aside.

Add another 2 tablespoons of oil, and stir-fry the beef over medium-high heat until it begins to brown, then add the stock and return the snow peas to the pan. Bring to a boil. Season with salt and pepper to taste. Add the cornstarch mixture, return to a boil, and stir until thickened.

Pepper Beef Stir-Fry

(Serves 4)

I love the stir-fry cooking technique. Its utilitarian simplicity and sizzling flamboyance make even the most mundane recipe exotic. In Hawai'i, when you don't have much time and you want something fresh and filling, stir-fry is the answer. Once you get the technique down, and the basic elements of the recipes, you can get creative, using ingredients from your local grocery store. This one is delicious over rice or noodles.

1 tablespoon vegetable oil

8 ounces lean boneless beef, cut into thin strips

1 small onion, julienned

1 stalk celery, halved crosswise and julienned

1 small green bell pepper, cut into ½-inch strips

1 small red bell pepper, cut into ½-inch strips

1 tablespoon minced fresh garlic

1 tablespoon peeled and minced fresh ginger

Salt and pepper to taste

¼ cup dashi or chicken stock

1 tablespoon soy sauce

1 tablespoon oyster sauce

*1 tablespoon cornstarch mixed with 1 tablespoon water
    for thickening*

Heat the oil in a wok until just smoking. Add the beef, onion, and celery. Cook and stir for about 1 minute. Add the bell peppers, garlic, ginger, salt, pepper, dashi, soy sauce, and oyster sauce, and cook about 3 minutes more, being careful not to overcook the meat. Stir in the cornstarch mixture to thicken.

Papa Choy's Tomato Beef

(Serves 6)

When I was a kid and came home from school, my dad would go to the refrigerator and take out a bunch of vegetables. He'd wash, chop, and slice them, lay them out in a pan, then take some beef, slice it thin, and marinate it. After a quick stir-fry, this delicious dish was ready to eat. It's just amazing how quick he could do it, and how good it tasted. Dad finally taught me how to make his famous Tomato Beef when I was fourteen. It's great over steamed rice.

> 1 pound round steak, flank steak, or beef of your choice
> Beef Marinade (see recipe on page 225)
> 1 tablespoon vegetable oil
> 3 medium tomatoes, cut into wedges
> 1 medium onion, sliced into half-moons
> 1 large green bell pepper, sliced into strips
> 4 green onions, cut into 1-inch lengths
> 1 stalk celery, thinly sliced on the diagonal
> Stir-Fry Sauce (see recipe on page 225)
> Salt and pepper to taste

Slice the beef into thin strips, or bite-sized pieces. Massage the marinade into the meat. Let marinate for 30 minutes.

Heat the oil in a wok or frying pan over medium-high heat. Stir-fry the beef for about 2 minutes; remove from pan and set aside. Add vegetables to the pan, and stir-fry until onion is translucent, about 3 minutes. Add stir-fry sauce to the vegetables. Cook for about 2 minutes, until it comes to a boil. Add the beef and adjust seasoning with salt and pepper.

Beef Marinade

(Makes about ¼ cup)

1 tablespoon soy sauce
1 tablespoon sherry
1 tablespoon vegetable oil
1½ teaspoons granulated sugar
1 clove fresh garlic, minced
¼ finger fresh ginger, peeled and minced

Combine all ingredients and mix well.

Stir-Fry Sauce

(Makes 1 cup)

1 cup chicken stock
1 tablespoon cornstarch
2 tablespoons soy sauce
2 teaspoons salt
2 teaspoons brown sugar
1 teaspoon oyster sauce

Combine all ingredients and mix well.

'Onolicious Teri-Glazed Meat Loaf

(Serves 6–8)

My mom makes a good meat loaf. She says, "Oh, that's Grandma's meat loaf." My grandparents weren't around when I was growing up, so I just have to listen when my mom tells all the stories. The meat loaf mixture can also be formed into meatballs. Bake meatballs at 350°F for 25 to 30 minutes, depending on size. Then simmer them for 5 minutes in Tailgate Teri Glaze. These are excellent as a pupu (appetizer).

1½ pounds lean ground beef
½ pound ground raw chicken
1½ cups fresh bread crumbs, toasted
1 can (8¼ ounces) crushed pineapple, drained well
½ cup chopped onion
½ cup chopped celery
2 eggs
¼ cup milk or heavy cream
¼ cup soy sauce
1 tablespoon peeled and minced fresh ginger
Salt and black pepper to taste
Tailgate Teri Glaze (see recipe on page 227)

Garnish:
2 tablespoons thinly sliced green onion

Preheat the oven to 350°F. Combine all ingredients except the glaze and blend lightly but well. Press into a loaf pan. Bake 50 minutes. Pour ¼ cup tailgate teri glaze over the meat loaf 5 minutes before the end of cooking time.

Slice meat loaf, sprinkle with green onion, and pass the remaining ¾ cup of glaze in a sauceboat.

Tailgate Teri Glaze

(Makes 1 cup)

1 tablespoon cornstarch
2 tablespoons water
½ cup soy sauce
Juice of ½ orange
¼ cup mirin (Japanese sweet rice wine)
¼ cup water
2 tablespoons brown sugar
¾ teaspoon minced fresh garlic
¾ teaspoon peeled and minced fresh ginger

Blend the cornstarch and water. In a small saucepan, combine the remaining ingredients and bring to a boil. Add the cornstarch mixture and stir for 1 to 2 minutes, until thickened.

Local-Style Osso Bucco with Shiitake Mushrooms

(Serves 4)

It's natural when you hear the phrase "osso bucco" automatically to think Italian, but what we're doing here is taking the osso bucco cut of veal and braising it Asian style, then adding shiitake mushrooms. This recipe blends a great cut of meat with Asian flavors without losing the delicate tastes of the veal or mushrooms.

4 meaty slices veal shank, about 1½ inches thick
Salt and pepper to taste
¼ cup all-purpose flour for dusting meat
3 tablespoons vegetable oil
4 cloves fresh garlic, crushed
¼ cup coarsely chopped carrot
½ cup coarsely chopped onion
3 tablespoons chopped fresh cilantro
1 tablespoon Chinese five-spice powder
½ cup soy sauce
Enough chicken stock to cover meat
1 cup granulated sugar
½ cup sherry
Shiitake Mushroom Sauce (see recipe on page 229)

Preheat the oven to 350°F.

Sprinkle the veal shanks with salt and pepper, dust with flour, then brown in 3 tablespoons of oil in large braising pan for 1 or 2 minutes per side. Add the garlic, carrot, onion, cilantro, five-spice powder, and soy sauce. Brown it all together for another 5 minutes.

Cover with chicken stock. Bring to a boil and add sugar and sherry. Cover with foil or an ovenproof lid, and braise in the preheated oven for 1 to 2 hours, or until tender. Strain the stock and use it to make the mushroom sauce.

Place the shanks on a serving platter and drizzle with some of the shiitake mushroom sauce. Pass the remaining sauce separately.

Shiitake Mushroom Sauce

(Makes 5 to 5½ cups)

3 tablespoons vegetable oil
½ cup julienned red and yellow bell peppers
½ cup julienned onion
¼ to ½ pound snow peas
1 cup sliced shiitake mushrooms
3 cups strained stock from braised veal
4 tablespoons cornstarch mixed with 3 tablespoons water

Heat the oil over medium-high heat in a large sauté pan or wok, and stir-fry the vegetables for 2 to 3 minutes. Add the strained stock, bring to a boil, and stir in the cornstarch mixture. Cook for 1 to 2 minutes, until the sauce is thickened and clear.

Pork and Lamb

Although pigs and sheep are not indigenous to Hawai'i, the Islanders are historically linked to these light meats.

When the first known Polynesian immigrants arrived, they brought with them their food staples: taro, coconuts, chickens, and a species of coarse-bristled pig that now runs wild in the remote rain forests on all the Hawaiian Islands.

During the nineteenth century, the New England missionaries who settled in Hawai'i brought sheep as a familiar source of food from their beloved American homeland.

Pork and lamb became favorite "specialty" meats because of their naturally sweet flavor and ability to be easily infused with robust seasonings. These meats have been smoked, salted, candied, crusted, and bathed in marinade for barbecue.

By the late 1800s, with pork and lamb as increasingly common fare on local sugar plantations, the cane workers from Asia added their seasonings to the Island mix, giving us unique sauces and marinades.

I love taking traditional Western dishes and experimenting with the flavors. I've included recipes for braised lamb shanks, barbecued ribs, and stuffed lamb chops that have a very distinctive Island flare. I love the exotic combination of garlic, ginger, and soy sauce. Watching people experience these flavors for the first time—their eyes closed, savoring the taste—really warms my heart.

I've also included a few old family favorites—pork and lamb recipes that friends request over and over again.

Handling uncooked meat is always a serious matter, especially when working with pork. Here are a few tips: (1) Pork must always be cooked to eliminate any parasites that might be present in the meat. To be extra-safe, cook it at low temperatures, around 325°F in the oven, or over medium-low heat on the stovetop or barbecue grill, until the internal temperature reaches 150°F. (2) Do not use a microwave to cook pork. This process dries out and hardens the meat very quickly. (3) If all visible fat is removed before roasting or cooking, a little fat should be added to protect the meat's tenderness and preserve the juices. All of these precautions are worth the effort. When pork is prepared correctly, it is the juiciest, most delicious meat available.

Ka'u MacNut-Crusted Roast Loin of Pork with Tropical Marmalade

(Serves 6)

If you simply season a pork loin with salt and pepper and some fresh herbs, it's going to be OK, but there's a big difference between OK and *great*! The marinade and the macadamia nut crust in this recipe are what make the difference. Marinating pork loin puts it in a different world, and the crust makes it heavenly. Add the tropical marmalade, with spicy pineapple and papaya, and you've got a real guest pleaser.

> *1 boneless pork loin, about 3 pounds*
> *Pua'a Marinade (see recipe below)*
> *Crumb Crust Mixture (see recipe on page 234)*
> *Tropical Marmalade (see recipe on page 31)*

Preheat the oven to 350°F.

Season the loin with the marinade; let stand for 20 minutes. Place on a rack in a roasting pan and roast for 45 minutes.

Ten minutes before the end of cooking time, remove the roast from the oven and coat it with the crumb crust mixture. Return to the oven and roast for the final 10 minutes.

Let stand 10 minutes before carving. Serve with tropical marmalade.

Pua'a Marinade

(Makes about 2 tablespoons)

> *1 tablespoon soy sauce*
> *1 tablespoon minced fresh garlic*
> *½ teaspoon salt*
> *½ teaspoon cracked black pepper*

Combine all ingredients.

Crumb Crust Mixture

(Makes about 4 cups)

1½ cups fine dry bread crumbs
¾ cup macadamia nuts, finely chopped
½ cup poha (cape gooseberry) jelly
8 tablespoons (1 stick) butter, softened
1 tablespoon minced fresh parsley
2 teaspoons paprika

Combine all ingredients and mix well.

'Ulupalakua Stuffed Pork Loin with Upcountry Bean Sauce

(Serves 4 to 6)

Pork loin is generally very dry because it is frequently cooked to the well-done stage, and it's hard to maintain the moisture when you have to keep it in the oven so long. What I like to do is stuff it, and the stuffing blend adds to the flavor and keeps it moist. Then to top it off, I add my upcountry bean sauce, which makes it just wonderful. This dish is best served with my Kahuku Corn Smashed Potatoes (pages 266–267).

1 boneless center-cut pork loin, about 3 pounds
'Ulupalakua Stuffing (see recipe on page 235)
Salt and pepper to taste
1 teaspoon minced fresh garlic
½ cup all-purpose flour
3 tablespoons olive oil
Upcountry Bean Sauce (see recipe on page 236)

Cut a 2-inch-wide slit lengthwise down the middle of the whole loin, being careful not to pierce the sides. Set aside while you make and cool the stuffing.

Stuff the pork loin with the cooled 'Ulupalakua stuffing. (You can truss the stuffed loin with string if you feel it's necessary to hold it together.) Any extra stuffing can be baked in a buttered casserole, covered, along with the pork. Rub the outside of the meat with salt, pepper, and minced garlic. Roll in flour and brown well in olive oil.

Roast in a 325°F oven for 40 to 45 minutes. After removing from the oven, let stand for 10 to 15 minutes to make slicing easier.

Serve with upcountry bean sauce.

'Ulupalakua Stuffing

(Makes 5 to 5½ cups)

1 medium onion, minced

6 strips bacon, chopped

1 stalk celery, minced

½ cup chopped fresh spinach

½ cup chopped mushrooms

1 medium apple, diced

8 tablespoons (1 stick) butter

3 cups chicken stock

1½ teaspoons poultry seasoning

½ cup raisins (optional)

4 cups toasted croutons or stuffing mix

½ cup macadamia nuts, chopped

Salt and pepper to taste

Sauté the onion, bacon, celery, spinach, mushrooms, and apple in butter for 5 to 8 minutes or until the onion looks translucent. Add the chicken stock and poultry seasoning, and bring to a boil. Add raisins (if desired) and cook 3 minutes, or until soft. Remove from heat. Add croutons or stuffing mix and macadamia nuts. Stir, adjust seasoning with salt and pepper, and set aside until cooled to room temperature.

Upcountry Bean Sauce

(Makes about 12 cups)

2 or 3 ham hocks
6 cups water
6 cups chicken stock
2 cloves fresh garlic, minced
1 15-ounce can kidney beans, drained and rinsed
2 cups tomato sauce
2 medium carrots, diced
4 stalks celery, diced
2 medium onions, diced
½ cup chopped fresh cilantro
½ bunch watercress, cut into 1-inch pieces
3 potatoes, peeled and diced
Salt and pepper to taste

Put the ham hocks in a large stockpot, cover with water and chicken stock, and bring to a boil. Reduce the heat, add the garlic, and simmer, covered, for 3 hours, or until ham hocks are tender. Add everything else, and cook for 20 minutes more, or until vegetables are soft. Adjust seasoning with salt and pepper. If necessary to thicken, finely grate 1 raw potato into the sauce for the last 5 minutes of cooking.

Backyard-Style Barbecued Ribs

(Serves 4)

This is not a grill recipe, since the ribs aren't cooked over hot coals. The term barbecued is used because of the spicy barbecue-style sauce. When cooked right, ribs will induce barbecue sauce–ringed smiles from anyone adventurous enough to try them. I like to marinate ribs, wrap them in foil, and throw them in the oven.

2 pounds pork spareribs, preferably baby back ribs
¼ cup soy sauce
2 tablespoons minced fresh garlic
2 tablespoons peeled and minced fresh ginger
1 tablespoon chili powder
1 tablespoon coarsely ground black pepper
1 teaspoon salt
½ cup chopped fresh cilantro
Backyard Barbecue Sauce (see recipe on page 238)
Tailgate Teri Sauce (see recipe on page 184)

Preheat oven to 350°F.

Rub the ribs with soy sauce, garlic, ginger, chili powder, black pepper, salt, and cilantro. Wrap ribs in foil, and oven-bake for 1 hour turning once. Open foil and baste frequently with backyard barbecue sauce.

To serve, drizzle with a mixture of equal parts backyard barbecue sauce and tailgate teri sauce.

Backyard Barbecue Sauce

(Makes 3 cups)

1 15-ounce can tomato sauce
1 cup packed brown sugar
1 cup minced onions
¼ cup vinegar
¼ cup honey
1 tablespoon minced fresh garlic
1 tablespoon steak sauce
1 teaspoon liquid smoke
1 teaspoon chili powder
1 teaspoon coarsely cracked black pepper
½ teaspoon ground cumin
¼ teaspoon dry mustard
1 cinnamon stick

In a medium saucepan, combine all ingredients. Bring to a boil, reduce the heat, then simmer for 1 hour. Strain, and store in the refrigerator.

Hale'iwa Barbecued Pork Ribs

(Serves 4 to 6)

The reason I call this Hale'iwa barbecued pork ribs is that we used to go to Hale'iwa Beach Park on Sunday drives and have barbecues. It was important that we had the ribs marinated and cooked ahead of time so we didn't have to spend all day over the coals. We'd just throw them on the grill, brush them with sauce, and as soon as they heated through we'd have a delicious, quick meal.

2 whole slabs pork ribs, cut into sections of 3 ribs each
½ cup sea salt or kosher salt
4 cloves fresh garlic
1 finger fresh ginger, peeled
2 green onions
Hale'iwa Barbecue Sauce (see recipe on page 240)

Place the ribs in a stockpot and cover with water. Start with ½ cup sea salt, and keep adding until the water tastes salty, then add the garlic, ginger, and green onions. Bring to a boil. Reduce the heat and let simmer 45 minutes to 1 hour, or until ribs are tender.

Meanwhile, prepare the barbecue sauce. When the ribs are tender, remove from the stockpot and let cool. Cover tightly and store in refrigerator until ready to barbecue. Brush with Hale'iwa barbecue sauce and grill over hot coals on a hibachi until heated through. Continue to baste the ribs with the barbecue sauce as they cook.

Hale'iwa Barbecue Sauce

(Makes 3 to 3½ cups)

1 teaspoon red chili pepper flakes
2 15-ounce cans tomato sauce
2 cups packed brown sugar
½ cup vinegar
½ cup honey
2 cups minced onions
2 teaspoons liquid smoke
2 teaspoons chili powder
1 teaspoon coarsely cracked black pepper
2 tablespoons steak sauce
½ teaspoon dry mustard
1 cinnamon stick
1 cup canned crushed pineapple
1 tablespoon minced fresh garlic

Combine all ingredients in a saucepan, bring to a boil, reduce heat, and simmer for 1 hour. Strain.

"No Huhu" Pork Chops and Scalloped Potatoes

(Serves 4)

"No huhu" means don't cry, don't fuss. I call this dish no huhu because it's so easy to make. Pop it in the oven, tidy up the house, and in 65 minutes uncover moist pork chops and scalloped potatoes.

1 tablespoon vegetable oil
4 lean pork chops
1 medium onion, julienned
1 can (14½ ounces) chicken stock
1 cup milk
½ cup sour cream
2 tablespoons chopped fresh parsley
4 cups thinly sliced potatoes, peeled if desired
Salt and pepper to taste

Preheat the oven to 350°F. Butter a casserole dish large enough to hold the chops in a single layer.

Heat the oil in a skillet over medium-high heat and brown the chops on both sides, along with the onion. Set aside.

Make a sauce by blending the chicken stock, milk, sour cream, and parsley.

Place a layer of potatoes in the casserole, sprinkle with salt and pepper, and pour over some of the sour cream sauce. Continue making alternating layers of potatoes and sauce; top with the chops and browned onions.

Cover tightly and bake for 1 hour and 15 minutes.

Ginger Shoyu Pork

(Serves 8)

This is like shoyu chicken—real simple, real easy. You have to pay attention, though, and stir it now and then. The emphasis here isn't on the meat. Everything revolves around the spicy, aromatic sweetness of the ginger. Did you know that gingerroot helps prevent colds? It's a remedy my grandparents on the Choy side always recommended. Serve this with hot rice and steamed vegetables, Chinese cabbage, or mustard cabbage. Here's to your health!

1 tablespoon canola oil

2 cloves fresh garlic, crushed

4 pounds lean boneless pork butt, all visible fat trimmed, cut into 3-inch cubes

1 cup soy sauce

1 cup fat-free chicken stock

1 cup packed brown sugar

4 slices (½ inch thick) fresh ginger, peeled and bruised

In a 5-quart pot, heat the oil over medium-high heat and brown the pork for 3 to 5 minutes. Stir in the garlic and cook for 30 seconds, then add the remaining ingredients. Bring to a boil, reduce heat to very low, and simmer uncovered for 1 hour or until tender, turning pork occasionally.

North Shore Ham Hocks with Mung Beans and Eggplant

(Serves 12)

Filipino people arrived to work on the sugar plantations, and, like folks from other nations, brought their culture and cuisine. This recipe, one of my favorites, came from a Filipino family that lived in the small town of Kahuku on the north shore of Oʻahu. It's one of those great dishes where you look in the rice pot and ask, "Do we have enough rice to go with all this food?" Although the recipe calls for the narrow, straight Asian eggplants, you can substitute the ubiquitous round variety.

> 1 cup dried split mung beans
> 2½ pounds smoked ham hocks
> 4 cups or more fat-free chicken stock
> ½ medium onion, diced
> 1 small ripe tomato, sliced
> 3 cloves fresh garlic, minced
> 2 medium Asian eggplants or 1 medium purple eggplant,
>   cut into 2-inch cubes
> Salt and pepper to taste

Rinse the mung beans well. In a pot, cook the beans in 3 cups of water over medium heat for 20 minutes or until soft. If the water evaporates, add ⅛ cup more to avoid burning the beans.

In a large pot, bring the ham hocks and chicken stock to a boil, then simmer partially covered for 1 hour. Add the beans, onion, tomato, and garlic, and bring to a boil. Add the eggplant and cook 5 to 10 minutes. Season with salt and pepper. Be careful to remove bones from the ham hocks before serving.

Local Boy Smoked Pork

(Serves 1)

*I*t's either the sweet-and-sour flavor of the sauce in this stir-fry, or the fact that the dish takes all of ten minutes to cook, but local boys all over Hawai'i love this food. I don't know, maybe it's the whiskey. Be careful not to add whiskey over an open flame because it will ignite. Serve this over hot rice.

1 tablespoon vegetable oil
6 ounces ham steak, julienned
1 sweet onion, julienned
2 tablespoons soy sauce
1 tablespoon brown sugar
1 shot (1½ ounces) whiskey

Garnish:
1 tablespoon chopped green onion

Heat the oil in a heavy skillet or wok. Add the ham and brown. Add the onion and cook about 2 minutes. Add the soy sauce and brown sugar. Take the pan off the heat and stir in the whiskey. Cook another 2 minutes. Sprinkle with green onion.

Honomalino Lamb with Satay Sauce

(Serves 8)

*I*n Honomalino, located on the western part of the Big Island, the lambs are raised on grasses and macadamia leaves. It's not necessary to use a Honomalino lamb to make this recipe, it's just my favorite. I've dressed the meat up with Asian embellishments, a spicy marinade and a coconut-laced peanut sauce that give it a special 'ono (delicious) taste.

> *2 to 2½ pounds boneless lamb loin, trimmed of fat*
> *Honomalino Marinade (see recipe below)*
> *Satay Sauce (see recipe on page 246)*

Rub lamb with the Honomalino marinade mixture, and refrigerate for 4 to 6 hours, turning lamb occasionally. Broil lamb 4 to 6 minutes per side for medium-rare or until cooked to your taste. Slice and place on serving platter. Drizzle with satay sauce.

Honomalino Marinade

(Makes ½ cup)

2 tablespoons soy sauce
1 tablespoon granulated sugar
2 tablespoons hoisin sauce (sweet-spicy soybean-garlic sauce)
2 tablespoons canola oil
1 tablespoon minced fresh garlic
1 tablespoon peeled and minced fresh ginger
1 tablespoon chopped fresh cilantro
1 tablespoon minced fresh basil
½ teaspoon red chili pepper flakes
Salt and pepper to taste

Combine all ingredients.

Satay Sauce
(Makes 1½ cups)

2 tablespoons canola oil
½ cup minced onion
1 teaspoon minced fresh garlic
1 teaspoon peeled and minced fresh ginger
1 cup minced fresh basil
¾ cup peanut butter
2 tablespoons orange juice
2 teaspoons granulated sugar
½ teaspoon chili-garlic sauce, or ¼ teaspoon red chili pepper flakes
1½ cups coconut milk

Heat the oil in a saucepan and sauté the onion, garlic, ginger, and basil for 5 minutes, until the onion is translucent. Stir in the peanut butter, orange juice, sugar, and chili-garlic sauce or pepper flakes. Cook on low heat for 15 minutes, stirring occasionally. Stir in the coconut milk and cook until heated through. Cool to room temperature.

Asian Lamb Chops with Rotelli

(Serves 4 to 6)

I've been very blessed with this dish—one of the most successful in our restaurants. Basically, I've taken Chinese methods and flavorings, added a twist, and come up with this award-winning recipe.

Asian Marinade (see recipe below)
2 or 3 rib lamb chops per serving, 8 to 18 chops total
Rotelli with Vegetable Cream Sauce (see recipe on page 248)

Garnish:
Sprigs of fresh basil

Massage Asian marinade into the chops for 5 to 10 minutes, then let the chops marinate for 4 to 6 hours in the refrigerator.

Broil chops to perfection (about 2 to 3 minutes per side for medium-rare, or to your liking). Serve in large pasta bowls with 2 to 3 lamb chops on top of the pasta.

Asian Marinade

(Makes 2½ to 3 cups)

½ cup soy sauce
¾ cup minced fresh garlic
1 tablespoon peeled and minced fresh ginger
2 cups packed brown sugar
½ teaspoon red chili pepper flakes
½ cup minced fresh basil
½ cup minced fresh cilantro
Salt to taste

Combine all the ingredients.

Rotelli with Vegetable Cream Sauce

(Makes 4½ cups)

1 tablespoon butter

1 tablespoon olive oil

1½ tablespoons minced fresh garlic

1 medium carrot, julienned

2 medium zucchini, julienned

2 cups shiitake mushrooms, julienned

½ cup coarsely chopped fresh cilantro

1 16-ounce package rotelli

1 quart heavy cream or half and half

Salt and pepper to taste

¾ cup grated Parmesan cheese

In a large saucepan, heat the butter and olive oil over medium-high heat and cook the garlic for about 1 minute, without browning. Add the vegetables and cilantro and stir-fry for 2 to 3 minutes. Set aside.

Bring a large pot of salted water to a boil, add the rotelli, and cook till almost al dente, following package directions. Drain the pasta, add to the vegetables in the saucepan, and stir-fry for another minute. Add the cream, bring to a boil, then immediately reduce to a simmer. Adjust seasoning with salt and pepper. Just before serving, fold in the Parmesan cheese and let cook for 1 minute.

Island Braised Lamb Shanks

(Serves 3 or 4)

Braising, a European term, is a tenderizing technique that utilizes moist heat when cooking. Braising is different from boiling and poaching in one important respect: the meat is browned well before adding the liquid that forms the essential steam that cooks the meat. Aromatic ingredients such as herbs and vegetables are added to the liquid and provide the long, moist, tenderizing treatment that produces the well-flavored and delicious piece of meat. In this recipe, I include Chinese five-spice powder, cilantro, dry sherry, ginger, and soy sauce to flavor the lamb shanks.

3 or 4 meaty lamb shanks (about 3 pounds)
3 tablespoons vegetable oil
4 cloves fresh garlic, minced
8 cups chicken stock, or enough to cover meat
½ teaspoon Chinese five-spice powder
½ cup chopped fresh cilantro
5 tablespoons dry sherry
2 tablespoons brown sugar
1 finger fresh ginger, peeled and sliced
5 tablespoons soy sauce
½ cup julienned onion
½ cup julienned celery
½ cup julienned red bell pepper
½ cup julienned yellow bell pepper
¼ cup cornstarch blended with 3 tablespoons water for thickening

In a large heavy kettle, brown the lamb shanks in half the oil (reserving 1 tablespoon of oil for later use) until golden brown, about 6 to 8 minutes over medium-high heat. Stir in the garlic, then cover the meat with chicken stock. Add the five-spice powder, cilantro, sherry, brown sugar, ginger, and soy sauce. Bring to a boil, cover, and place in a preheated 350°F oven. Bake for about 1 to 1½ hours, or until very tender.

Remove the lamb and strain the stock. Set the lamb aside and keep warm.

In a large skillet, heat the remaining tablespoon of oil over medium-high heat and stir-fry the onion, celery, and peppers for 2 or 3 minutes, then add the stock and bring to a boil. While it's boiling, stir in the cornstarch mixture, and cook until thickened.

Place the shanks on a platter and cover with the vegetable-sauce mixture.

Side Dishes

Side dishes are vital to a successful meal. They give your guests a bonus, an extra burst of flavor that enhances your carefully prepared entree. People remember an unbelievable meal not only for the main dish but also for the side dishes. They are, in fact, a highlight for me.

Eating in Hawai'i is endlessly fascinating because we have so many types of side dishes that originated in so many diverse cultures, from Southeast Asian pickled, steamed, and stir-fried vegetables, to Portuguese eggplant, Japanese tempura, Korean kim chee, Hawaiian chicken lu'au, and good ol' American baked beans and mashed potatoes.

Local flavors are combinations of ethnic ingredients that have been blended into a new culinary style that is uniquely Hawaiian. They are the smells and tastes that I remember from small-kid time, locked into ginger and soy sauce, into the crispiness of stir-fried vegetables, into the aroma of magical herbs like hot Hawaiian chili peppers and lemongrass. They make me want to go back for that second, third, and fourth serving—when I'm down to the last bite and staring into my empty bowl, and my stomach is saying "full" but I still crave more. Now that's flavor.

I've included in this section some truly 'ono side dishes, like Kahuku Corn Smashed Potatoes, Sesame Ginger Snap Peas, and Hibachi Tofu. For me these extraordinary extras define the term "local flavor."

I like adding a little citrus to my recipes. Orange juice—whether in concentrate or fresh doesn't matter—adds a real nice, mellow flavor. So does fresh-squeezed lemon or lime juice. Remember, it's really important to taste your food while you cook and when you're done cooking, just to make sure it measures up to your refined palate. It's your special touch that will turn these recipes into culinary memories for those you serve.

Cooking creatively carries on the local tradition of blending and sharing. Let the ingredients share their flavors and you'll find more friends flocking to your kitchen to savor your incredible meals.

Black Goma Asparagus

(Serves 4)

Goma (sesame seeds) come in creamy white, yellow, reddish, or black varieties. I use all types of these tiny, flat seeds, but my favorite by far are the nutty-flavored black goma. You can find them in packages in the Asian sections of your supermarket.

1 pound asparagus
3 slices peeled fresh ginger
¼ cup chicken stock
1 tablespoon soy sauce
½ teaspoon granulated sugar
2 tablespoons vegetable oil
½ teaspoon salt

Garnish:
1 teaspoon black goma (black sesame seeds)

Wash the asparagus; snap off and discard the tough ends. Cut the stalks diagonally in 1½-inch sections. If the asparagus is young and tender, blanch the stalks (but not tips) by immersing quickly in boiling water and rinsing immediately under cold running water. Mature asparagus should be parboiled in salted water for 1 to 2 minutes, removed as soon as it begins to turn bright green, rinsed immediately in cold water, and drained. Do not blanch or parboil the tips.

Mince or crush the ginger. Combine chicken stock, soy sauce, and sugar. Heat the oil in a wok over medium-high heat; when it's almost smoking, add the salt and ginger and stir a few times. Add the asparagus and stir-fry until heated through. You may have to adjust the heat to prevent scorching.

Add the broth mixture and heat quickly. Simmer covered over medium heat for 2 to 3 minutes. Sprinkle with black goma and serve immediately.

Asian Bean Sprout Salad

(Serves 4 to 6)

*T*his is a very exotic slaw-style side dish. The flavors are typically Japanese, thanks to the vinegar, soy sauce, and sugar. I always like a little crunch in my food, so the sesame seeds are from me.

½ package (6 ounces) bean sprouts
3 tablespoons white sesame seeds
2 tablespoons vinegar
½ teaspoon granulated sugar
1 teaspoon soy sauce

Rinse the bean sprouts in cold water. Dip in boiling water for 1 minute and drain. In a heated pan, toast the sesame seeds until lightly browned. Grind the seeds, using a sesame seed grinder, or mash with a spoon. Mix remaining ingredients. Add to the bean sprouts and toss.

Bok Choy Broccoli

(Serves 6)

*B*ok choy is also known as celery cabbage. The Western variety I recommend is the broad and compact napa. This type of green contains quite a bit of moisture. This recipe for bok choy pairs its delicate flavor with that of the more domineering broccoli. It's great with fish dishes.

2 tablespoons vegetable oil
1 medium onion, thinly sliced
1 tablespoon peeled and grated or minced fresh ginger

2 cloves fresh garlic, crushed

½ teaspoon salt

3 cups broccoli florets, sliced

1 pound bok choy (napa cabbage), coarsely chopped

2 tablespoons lemon juice

1½ teaspoons granulated sugar

1 tablespoon soy sauce

Heat the oil in a wok or skillet over medium-high heat until it's almost smoking. Add the onion, ginger, garlic, and salt. Stir-fry for 2 minutes (do not let the garlic burn). Add the broccoli florets and bok choy, and stir-fry for 1 minute. Add the lemon juice, sugar, and soy sauce, and stir-fry for 3 minutes, or until crisp-tender. Serve immediately.

Chinese Cabbage Toss

(Serves 4 to 6)

This light "salad" is quick and easy to make, and goes well with heavy meat dishes. It's a salad only in the Western sense of the word. In the Asian tradition of cooking, this is a vegetable side dish.

2 pounds Chinese white cabbage, or bok choy (substitute fresh spinach)

1 teaspoon salt

2 teaspoons granulated sugar

2 tablespoons soy sauce

2 tablespoons vegetable oil

1½ teaspoons sesame oil

Cut the cabbage into strips 3 inches long by ½ inch wide, and blanch in boiling water for 2 minutes, then drain. Dry well, and place in a large bowl. Add salt, sugar, soy sauce, and oils. Toss well and serve.

Island-Style Coleslaw

(Serves 6 to 8)

This is a very tangy slaw, made with won bok (a Chinese cabbage). It's all right to substitute celery cabbage or head cabbage. For crunchy coleslaw, cut the cabbage in half and soak it in salted ice water for about 1 hour; drain well. Chill the cabbage and slice into thin strips. This is a great side for barbecues or picnics. It travels well.

¼ cup chopped green bell pepper
4 cups shredded won bok (or other cabbage)
¼ bunch watercress, chopped
8 stuffed olives, sliced
½ teaspoon dry mustard
1 teaspoon celery seed
2 tablespoons granulated sugar
3 tablespoons salad oil
⅓ cup vinegar
1 tablespoon chopped pimiento
Salt and pepper to taste

Place the green pepper, won bok, watercress, and olives in a large bowl. Cover and chill. Combine the other ingredients in a jar. Cover. Before serving, shake the jar and pour the dressing over the vegetables. Toss until combined.

Ginger Carrots

(Serves 6)

Gingerroot is one of the more dramatic spices I've worked with. This pungent aromatic is a staple in Asian cuisine. I've laced these carrots with ginger and sweetened them with brown sugar to give them a spicy, sugar-glaze quality.

6 large carrots
3 tablespoons butter
¼ teaspoon salt
1 tablespoon peeled and grated fresh ginger
2 tablespoons brown sugar

Cut the carrots into bite-sized pieces. Put in a sauté pan with ⅓ cup of water; cover and steam for 10 to 12 minutes or until carrots are tender and water has almost evaporated. Add the remaining ingredients and stir for a minute or two, until carrots are glazed.

Macadamia Nut Eggplant

(Serves 6)

I really enjoy the rich, refreshing flavor of macadamia nuts; they add a bit of elegance to any dish. Serve these eggplants with fish or chicken. They are a little heavy for a full-flavored beef or pork meal.

3 medium eggplants
⅓ cup vegetable oil
1 onion, minced
1 clove fresh garlic, minced
Salt and pepper to taste
1 tomato, peeled and chopped
1 teaspoon Worcestershire sauce
2 eggs, lightly beaten
1 cup macadamia nuts, chopped
½ cup fine soft buttered bread crumbs

Cut the eggplants in half lengthwise and scoop out the insides, leaving about a ¼-inch-thick shell. Mince the pulp and set aside.

Heat the oil in a skillet and cook the onion and garlic for about 5 minutes, until tender. Add the minced eggplant and cook slowly until lightly browned and almost tender. Season with salt and pepper. Add the tomato and Worcestershire; simmer for 3 minutes. Remove from heat and let cool slightly. Stir in the eggs and macadamia nuts. Mix well.

Stuff the eggplant shells with the mixture and top with bread crumbs. Set in a greased shallow roasting pan. Bake at 375°F for 25 minutes, or until eggplant shells are tender.

Pan-Fried Spicy Eggplant

(Serves 4)

This hot and spicy vegetarian dish is a favorite with everyone—people who prefer a no-meat diet and people who just love good food. In Indonesia, the garlic-chili paste used in this recipe is called "sambal." They use it as a condiment, the way salsa is used in Mexico—to spice up every meal. Because of the sambal, I suggest you serve this dish with rice. It helps tone down the heat.

3 tablespoons olive oil

2 cloves fresh garlic, minced

2 medium Asian eggplants or 1 medium purple eggplant, peeled
   and cut into 1-inch sections

2 tablespoons soy sauce

1½ tablespoons brown sugar

1 tablespoon hot Asian chili paste (sambal oelek)

1 cup chicken stock

⅛ teaspoon white pepper

In a wok, heat the oil and add the garlic, eggplant, soy sauce, brown sugar, and chili paste. Sauté for 2 to 3 minutes. Add the chicken stock and white pepper. Cover and simmer for 8 to 10 minutes.

Serve immediately.

Quick Snow Peas

(Serves 4)

Snow peas are also known as Chinese peas, pea pods, and sugar peas. They are very tender and require very little cooking. In fact, you want them to be crunchy but warmed through. Stir-fry the peas and serve them with a teriyaki-based chicken, beef, or fish, and steamed rice. This recipe is so tasty I sometimes eat it as an entree.

> 2 tablespoons vegetable oil
> 4 cups fresh snow peas, trimmed and strings removed
> 2 cloves fresh garlic, minced
> 1½ teaspoons soy sauce
> 1½ teaspoons oyster sauce
> 2 tablespoons chicken broth

Heat the oil in a wok or skillet over medium-high heat. Stir-fry the snow peas for 1 minute. Reduce the heat and continue to stir-fry for 30 seconds. Drain off excess oil. Sprinkle the snow peas with garlic, soy sauce, oyster sauce, and chicken broth. Simmer gently for 1½ minutes.

Sesame-Ginger Snap Peas

(Serves 8)

When I hear "snap peas" I think of this recipe—sweet, crispy, tender sugar snap peas speckled with black goma (sesame) seeds, with a hint of ginger. . . . You can turn this into a vegetarian entree by omitting the pork and serving it with tofu. Throw the tofu into the wok at the last minute to heat through. It's great.

Vegetable oil for deep-frying

1½ pounds fresh sugar snap peas, trimmed, strings removed

1 tablespoon sesame oil

2 tablespoons peeled and minced fresh ginger

2 medium cloves fresh garlic, minced

1½ teaspoons minced green onion

2 tablespoons minced smoked pork

2 tablespoons soy sauce

2 teaspoons rice wine vinegar

2 teaspoons brown sugar

1 teaspoon cornstarch

¼ cup chicken stock, at room temperature

Garnish:

Black goma (black sesame seeds)

In a wok or pan, heat 2½ inches of vegetable oil until it is very hot, about 365°F. Make sure the peas are dry. Blanch them in the oil in batches for 30 seconds. Drain on paper towels.

In a separate wok, heat the sesame oil and sauté the ginger, garlic, green onion, and smoked pork for 4 minutes. Add the soy sauce, vinegar, and brown sugar, and bring to a boil. Mix the cornstarch and chicken stock to dissolve cornstarch; stir the mixture into the wok until the sauce is thickened and clear. Fold in the sugar snap peas.

Garnish with black goma (sesame seeds) that have been toasted in a dry skillet.

Stuffed Peppers, Asian Style

(Serves 4)

This dish can be a meal in itself. The peppers are very tasty, and the filling gives you that satisfying "I'm full, but not stuffed" feeling. I have some friends who are vegetarians. We had them over for dinner and I served these stuffed peppers. They were a *big hit*!

8 medium red or yellow bell peppers

2 tablespoons vegetable oil

3 green onions, chopped

1 teaspoon minced fresh garlic

1 small finger fresh ginger, peeled and minced

2 tablespoons chopped fresh cilantro

2 ounces fresh bean sprouts

2 tablespoons (or more to taste) soy sauce

1 can (8 ounces) water chestnuts, drained, rinsed, and chopped

3 cups cooked rice

1 cup cooked and diced vegetables of your choice

1 egg, beaten

Salt and pepper to taste

Drop the peppers in a large pot of boiling water and parboil for 5 minutes. Remove and cool. Slice off the top ½ inch of each pepper and scoop out seeds and membranes. If the peppers won't stand upright, cut a thin slice from the bottom (without making a hole) to level them. Set aside.

Heat the oil in a wok or skillet and stir-fry the onions, garlic, ginger, and cilantro for 3 to 4 minutes, until the onions are wilted. Add the bean sprouts and soy sauce, and cook just until sprouts wilt. Remove from the heat.

Add the water chestnuts, rice, cooked vegetables, egg, salt, and pepper. Toss together until well mixed. Add more soy sauce, if desired. Spoon the mixture into the bell pepper cases.

Place in a baking dish containing ½ inch of hot water. Cover with foil and bake at 350°F for 30 minutes. Uncover and bake another 15 to 20 minutes, or until peppers are tender.

Fresh Island Sautéed Spinach

(Serves 4 to 6)

This vegetable side dish is so easy. You throw all of the ingredients in a pan, sauté, and serve. There. Now you don't have to read the directions. But I know that most people read the directions first and the headnote last. So I'll repeat the directions in the body of the recipe.

2 tablespoons butter
2 tablespoons fresh garlic, minced
2 pounds fresh spinach, well washed
Salt and pepper to taste
Toasted sesame seeds to taste

Throw all the ingredients into a large skillet and sauté about 5 minutes, while stirring, until the spinach is wilted but still bright green. Serve.

Choy Sum with " 'Onolicious" Sauce

(Serves 4)

For a taste of the Orient, try this unusual and healthful dish. You can substitute other greens—like spinach or kale— for the choy sum, and celery cabbage or napa cabbage for the ung choy. The " 'Onolicious" Sauce was created with cabbages in mind.

1 teaspoon cooking oil
1 bunch ong choy (water spinach or swamp cabbage),
   or napa cabbage
1 bunch choy sum (or substitute spinach or kale)
" 'Onolicious" Sauce (see recipe on page 264)

Fill a pot half full of water. Bring to a fast boil. Add 1 teaspoon of oil to the boiling water. Add the vegetables and cook for 1 minute or until just wilted. Drain. Rinse under cold running water. Drain. Squeeze to remove excess water. Cut into 2-inch lengths. Arrange on a platter and pour on the " 'Onolicious" sauce.

" 'Onolicious" Sauce

(Makes about ¼ cup)

1 tablespoon soy sauce
2 tablespoons mirin (Japanese sweet rice wine)
1 teaspoon sesame oil
1 teaspoon oyster sauce
1 teaspoon granulated sugar

Mix well.

Chicken Lu'au—My Mother's Favorite

(Serves 8)

My mom taught me how to do this. Every year we have a big Hawaiian lu'au, and the Chicken Lu'au has to be done the Choy family way. It's a great side dish for my Quick and Easy Shoyu Chicken or Traditional Backyard Beef Teriyaki. I asked my mom if I could give you this recipe. She said I could, if I made sure it was just the way she taught me. (You can substitute fresh spinach for the taro leaves. Just don't tell her that I told you to do it.)

2 tablespoons butter
½ medium onion, chopped
¾ pound boneless, skinless chicken breast, cubed

1 cup chicken stock

1 cup coconut milk

1 pound fresh lu'au (taro) leaves or spinach, steamed and chilled

½ teaspoon salt

In a large saucepan, heat the butter and sauté the onions about 5 minutes, until translucent. Add the chicken and cook 3 minutes, stirring frequently. Add the chicken stock, coconut milk, cooked lu'au (or spinach), and salt. Simmer for 20 minutes or until chicken is cooked.

Hibachi Mixed Vegetables

(Serves 4)

These marinated vegetables are wonderful just off the grill. Sometimes they fall through the spaces during cooking. I usually use a grid or grilling mesh when barbecuing small pieces of food like shellfish or vegetables. It's just much easier—less frustrating.

1 teaspoon chopped fresh garlic

¼ teaspoon black pepper

¼ teaspoon chili sauce

1 teaspoon chopped fresh cilantro

1 teaspoon chopped fresh thyme leaves

1 tablespoon white wine

1 tablespoon vegetable oil

1 tablespoon sesame oil

¼ teaspoon soy sauce

¼ teaspoon oyster sauce

1 zucchini, sliced thickly on the diagonal

1 yellow squash, sliced thickly on the diagonal

1 red bell pepper, cut into wedges

6 shiitake mushrooms, stems removed

Make a marinade by combining the first 10 ingredients. Combine the squash, bell pepper, and mushrooms in a bowl, mix in the marinade, and let stand for ½ hour. Cook over a charcoal broiler or hibachi until just tender.

Kahuku Corn Smashed Potatoes
(Serves 6 to 8)

Kahuku, once a plantation town near the northern tip of Oʻahu, struggled after the sugar mill closed in the 1970s. Some plantation workers' families leased plots from the private estate that owned the land, and started farms in fields once used to raise sugar cane. Today they harvest and sell some of the best corn and juiciest watermelons in the world. There really isn't anything as sweet as eating Kahuku corn on a warm summer evening. This mixture of corn and potatoes is a kuaʻaina (backcountry) treat, even if you live in the big city.

3 pounds potatoes, peeled and cut into 1-inch cubes
1½ teaspoons salt
8 tablespoons (1 stick) unsalted butter
1 large onion, diced
½ teaspoon ground cumin
5 cloves garlic, peeled and minced
2¼ cups fresh corn kernels
¾ cup milk
Salt and pepper to taste

Garnish:
1½ teaspoons finely chopped fresh cilantro

Place the potatoes in a pot. Cover with water and add the salt. Bring to a boil and cook until tender.

Meanwhile, heat the butter in a small skillet and sauté the onion, cumin, and garlic until the onion is translucent, about 3 to 4 minutes. Add the corn and cook for 2 more minutes. Add the milk, and simmer for 1 to 2 minutes, then season with salt and pepper to taste.

Remove the potatoes from the heat and drain. Mash the potatoes and add the corn mixture. Serve hot.

Sweet Potato Casserole

(Serves 12)

Every Thanksgiving my classmate Norman Masuto would give me the really big off-grade sweet potatoes he grew on his family farm in the North Shore community of Kahuku on the island of Oʻahu. I serve this casserole instead of candied yams for our holiday feast. It's a delightful break from tradition with a little Island flair. Try it; you'll like it so much it might even start a new tradition.

6 to 8 medium sweet potatoes or yams
¾ cup packed brown sugar
8 tablespoons (1 stick) butter
1 16-ounce can crushed pineapple, drained
½ cup coconut milk

Place the sweet potatoes in their jackets in a steamer basket over 1½ inches of boiling water. Steam, covered, for 25 minutes or until tender. Peel and cut in ⅜-inch-thick slices. In a buttered casserole dish, make a layer of half the sweet potato slices, half the brown sugar, half the butter (dot with thin pats), and half the pineapple. Repeat the layers. Pour coconut milk over all. Bake at 350°F for 20 to 25 minutes. Remove from the oven, let stand for 5 minutes, and serve.

Hibachi Tofu

(Serves 4)

One afternoon, while barbecuing in the backyard, I got this idea. I went into the kitchen, brought out a tub of tofu, and put it in the marinade I was using for the meat I was cooking, then threw the tofu on the grill. It turned out pretty tasty. I perfected the flavoring, and now I have another option for a barbecue side dish.

1 tablespoon chopped fresh garlic
¼ teaspoon ground black pepper
¼ teaspoon chili sauce
1 teaspoon chopped fresh cilantro
1 teaspoon chopped fresh basil
1 tablespoon salad oil
1 teaspoon sesame oil
¼ teaspoon soy sauce
1 block firm tofu, sliced into 4 sections

In a small bowl, combine all ingredients except the tofu. Mix well. Coat the tofu with the sauce and marinate for ½ hour. Cook over a hibachi or broiler until crispy. Be careful not to burn.

Spicy Wok Tofu

(Serves 6)

Tofu is really interesting. You can do so many things with it. It's a very bland food, so it borrows the seasoning and flavors from other ingredients. If you want, you can leave the whole tofu in a block, pour the spicy sauce over it, and dig in.

1 20-ounce block firm tofu
3 tablespoons canola oil
½ cup ground chicken or turkey
Spicy Wok Sauce (see recipe below)
2 teaspoons cornstarch
2 teaspoons cold water

Garnish:
1 green onion, chopped
1 tablespoon chopped fresh cilantro
1 teaspoon sesame oil

Cut the tofu into ½-inch cubes, and blanch 30 seconds in boiling water. Drain immediately.

In a wok, heat the oil and stir-fry the ground chicken or turkey until well browned. Add the spicy wok sauce and tofu; boil 3 minutes. Mix the cornstarch and water; add to the wok and stir until sauce thickens.

Garnish with green onion, cilantro, and sesame oil drizzled over all.

Spicy Wok Sauce

(Makes 1¼ cups)

1 cup chicken stock
2 tablespoons soy sauce
1 tablespoon bottled black bean sauce with chili
1 teaspoon chopped fresh garlic
1 teaspoon salt, or to taste
½ teaspoon peeled and minced fresh ginger

In a mixing bowl, combine all ingredients.

Lu'au-Style Cheese Cannelloni

(Serves 4)

I have had so many people ask me for a really good vegetarian lasagne-type dish. Here is a meatless one, using cheese and cream. It's not low-fat, but it is no-meat, and it's definitely *really good*.

16 large tubes cannelloni pasta
1 pound lu'au (taro) leaves or fresh spinach, washed thoroughly
⅛ teaspoon baking soda
10 ounces ricotta cheese
2 cups freshly grated Parmesan cheese
5 ounces goat cheese
½ teaspoon minced fresh garlic
⅓ cup chopped and toasted macadamia nuts
Salt and pepper to taste
White Sauce (see recipe on page 271)

Heat a large pot of salted water for the pasta. When the water boils, put in the cannelloni one at a time, stir, and cook over medium-high heat. When the cannelloni are half done (after 5 or 6 minutes for commercial pasta, or 2 minutes for fresh pasta), remove, and plunge into cold water. Drain and spread out on kitchen towels.

Prepare lu'au (taro) leaves by parboiling for 8 minutes in water and baking soda. Drain in a sieve, squeeze dry, and chop very fine. If using spinach, cook 2 minutes, drain, squeeze dry, then chop very fine.

While the pasta is cooking, put the chopped taro leaves or spinach into a bowl. Mix well with ricotta cheese, about half the Parmesan cheese, the goat cheese, garlic, half the toasted macadamia nuts, and salt and pepper to taste.

Preheat the oven to 350°F. Thoroughly butter a shallow ovenproof baking dish that is large enough to hold the cannelloni in a single layer. Fill the cannelloni with the spinach-cheese-nut mixture and arrange in the dish. Sprinkle with the remaining Parmesan cheese and cover with white sauce. Sprinkle with remaining toasted macadamia nuts.

Bake, uncovered, for about 20 minutes, or until the sauce is bubbling and the surface is lightly colored. Serve immediately.

White Sauce

(Makes 2 cups)

2 tablespoons butter
2 tablespoons all-purpose flour
2½ cups half and half
Salt and white pepper to taste
½ cup macadamia nuts, toasted and chopped

Melt the butter in a heavy saucepan over low heat. Stir in the flour and cook gently, stirring constantly, for 2 or 3 minutes. Gradually add the half and half, whisking until smoothly blended. Increase the heat and continue whisking while the sauce comes to a boil.

Reduce the heat to very low and simmer, uncovered, for about 15 minutes, stirring occasionally to prevent the sauce from developing a top skin or sticking to the bottom of the pan. Season with salt and pepper. Fold in the macadamia nuts, reserving 2 tablespoons for sprinkling over the top of the cannelloni. Whisk again until the sauce is smooth.

Manicotti Kilauea

(Serves 8)

This dish is a variation on lasagne. We have a cheese mixture, a tomato-based sauce, pasta, and more cheese. Change is a good thing, and in this case it's delicious, too.

Sausage and Ono Sauce (see recipe on page 272)
Cheese Filling (see recipe on page 273)
½ pound manicotti (16 shells)

Garnish:
Freshly grated Parmesan cheese

Prepare the sausage and ono sauce and set aside. Prepare the cheese filling. Preheat the oven to 375°F.

Boil the manicotti shells according to package directions. Drain and, when cool, stuff them with cheese filling.

Spoon half the sausage and ono sauce into a 13 × 9-inch baking pan. Arrange half the stuffed shells in one layer on top of the sauce. Spoon all but ¾ cup of the remaining sauce over the shells, and top with the rest of the shells in another layer. Finish with the ¾ cup reserved sauce, and sprinkle with Parmesan cheese.

Bake for 30 minutes.

Sausage and Ono Sauce

(Makes about 7½ cups)

1 pound Italian sausages

1 pound ono (wahoo) or firm, mild fish of your choice, diced

1 medium onion, minced

4 cups canned tomato purée

1 6-ounce can tomato paste

1 teaspoon chopped fresh opal basil or sweet basil

1 teaspoon granulated sugar

Salt and pepper to taste

1 cup water

Remove skin from the sausage. Place the sausage in a skillet and break up with a wooden spoon while browning well. Remove and reserve. Discard all but 1 tablespoon of fat, and quickly sauté the ono and onion, just until the fish loses its translucency.

Stir in the browned sausage, tomato purée, tomato paste, basil, sugar, salt, pepper, and water. Cover and simmer over low heat from 45 minutes to 1 hour.

Cheese Filling

(Makes about 2 cups)

1½ *pounds ricotta cheese*
½ *pound firm goat cheese, crumbled*
½ *pound mozzarella cheese, grated*
1 *tablespoon chopped fresh dill*
1 *tablespoon chopped fresh cilantro*
1 *teaspoon chopped fresh basil*
½ *teaspoon salt*

In a large bowl, combine all the ingredients and mix well.

Chinese Pasta Primavera

(Serves 8)

Pasta is a very interesting dish. When Marco Polo toured China, he fell in love with noodles and brought the concept back to Italy. But when the Italians tried to make Chinese noodles, they were limited by the flour and methods available in Italy, which were very different from those in China. That's why Italian pasta is different from Chinese noodles. This is my way of blending both Chinese and Italian influences in a hearty vegetarian pasta dish.

1 pound linguine
1 tablespoon olive oil
1 tablespoon butter
1 medium red bell pepper, cut into strips
1 medium yellow bell pepper, cut into strips
2 medium zucchini, trimmed but not peeled, and sliced
½ pound broccoli florets
½ pound asparagus, cut into 1-inch pieces
½ pound whole sugar snap or snow peas, trimmed
6 shallots or green onions, thinly sliced
1 clove fresh garlic, minced
¼ cup chopped fresh cilantro
2 tablespoons chopped fresh Thai basil or sweet basil
Salt and pepper to taste
1 tablespoon soy sauce.

Garnish:
¼ cup freshly grated Parmesan cheese

Fill a large pot with water, and begin heating it for the pasta.

Heat the oil and butter in a large skillet or wok, and stir-fry the vegetables, onions, and garlic for about 3 minutes. Add the cilantro and basil and cook another minute, or until vegetables are done to your taste—they should be a little crunchy.

When water boils, add linguine, and cook according to package directions; it should be al dente.

Season the vegetables with salt and pepper, mix with soy sauce, toss with pasta, and sprinkle with Parmesan cheese.

Kona Fisherman's Wife Pasta

(Serves 4 to 6)

I live in Kona, on the Big Island of Hawai'i, and have many friends who are expert fishermen. This recipe came from a friend's wife. She serves this side dish to complement the fish her husband brings home. They live on the slopes of Hualalai volcano, and grow the most beautiful macadamia nut trees. I added the opal basil leaves because of their pungent aroma and the beautiful purple color. You can substitute Thai or sweet basil, whichever is more readily available.

2½ teaspoons salt
30 fresh opal basil leaves, wiped clean with a soft cloth
½ cup freshly grated Parmesan cheese
1 cup coarsely chopped macadamia nuts
⅓ cup olive oil
1 pound bow-tie pasta

Heat water with 2 teaspoons salt in a large pot. While waiting for it to boil, place the basil, cheese, the remaining ½ teaspoon salt, and the nuts in a large mortar and pound to a pulp. Slowly add the olive oil, stirring. If you don't have a mortar, use a blender on low.

When the water boils, add the bow-tie pasta. Stir to keep pasta from sticking together, and cook until it's al dente. Drain, then place the pasta in large bowl and mix well with nut sauce. Serve at once.

Honaunau Farmer's Spaghetti

(Serves 4)

*I*n the small agricultural and fishing communities on the Big Island, farmers work the land as well as the ocean—planting their seeds in season, and fishing in their spare time. It's a great life, and when I'm not traveling or running my restaurants, I like to sit with them and live their lives through their stories. This pasta dish came about on one of those "talk story" evenings. I sometimes make the sauce using chicken breast strips and sometimes with fish chunks. Either way, this dish cooks up fast, is full of flavor, and is always a favorite.

2 tablespoons vegetable oil
1 medium onion, cut into thin slices
2 boneless skinless chicken breast halves, cut into thin strips
⅔ cup thinly sliced fresh mushrooms
1 medium carrot, julienned
2 basil leaves, finely chopped
3 small ripe tomatoes, peeled, quartered, seeded, and cut into strips
¾ cup whole sugar snap or snow peas, trimmed
1 cup black olives, sliced
Salt and pepper to taste
1 pound spaghetti
¾ cup freshly grated Parmesan cheese

Put a large kettle of salted water on to boil (approximately 1 gallon per pound of pasta).

Meanwhile, heat the oil in a wok and stir-fry the onion and chicken over medium heat for 3 to 4 minutes, or until the onion is translucent and the chicken loses its pink color. Add the mushrooms and cook for 2 minutes over low heat. Add the carrot, basil, and tomatoes, cover, and simmer slowly for 15 minutes. Fold in the peas and black olives and cook just until heated through. Adjust seasoning with salt and pepper. Set the sauce aside and keep warm.

Cook the spaghetti the way you like it, drain, and turn onto a large preheated dish.

Pour the sauce over the spaghetti, add the Parmesan, mix well, and serve.

Desserts

I *have loved desserts forever. I believe they are like fireworks at the* end of the great event called dinner. Or they can bring a certain sparkle and flair to any occasion, no matter how ordinary or mundane.

I take great care to offer a variety of flamboyant desserts and confections in my restaurants. I know a dessert is a hit when, at the end of the day, my dessert cupboard is empty. Some of our customers arrive late in the evening—after taking in a show or concert—for dessert and coffee. They say it's the best way to end a fun night out. One young man said that if he wants to impress his date, he brings her to my restaurant and orders my Chocolate, Chocolate-Chip Cheesecake. He swears that he's not trying to manipulate his lovely partner, but he always gets a second date—it works every time.

Hawai'i boasts a wonderful variety of exotic dessert flavors and textures—the tropical fruit tang of mango, papaya, guava, pineapple, and banana; the crunch of macadamia nuts and toasted coconut; and the aromatic richness of Island-grown coffee. Although some of the fruits are imported seasonally to the mainland United States, most of these ingredients are available year-round in Asian markets and in specialty sections of major grocery stores.

I'm often amazed at how much trouble a cook or chef will go through to develop a mouth-watering dessert. Over the years I've collected and created some really winning dessert recipes, beautiful to look at and just exploding with flavor. And most are surprisingly simple to make.

My favorite dessert is my wife Carol's Easy Banana Pie. It's unreal good. The best. Every time I tell her that, she kisses me, so this dessert is twice sweet. The other recipes I strongly recommend in this section are Minaka's MacNut Brownie, the Liliko'i Chiffon Cream Pie, and my mom's favorite: Haupia Profiteroles.

Each of these recipes has been vigorously tested and approved by thousands of my restaurant customers. Try them all, and pick the ones that best suit your taste. One woman said, "I would rather take home half of my entree than stuff myself and miss out on one of your desserts."

Go for it, and have fun.

Apple Crisp

(Serves 8)

Crisp, a very old dessert, is a deep-dish pie (usually made with fruit) topped with a thick crust. This apple crisp recipe can be made using any other seasonal fruit such as peaches, blackberries, or plums. The origin of this type of dessert is somewhere in the farmlands of rural Europe. My apple crisp is topped with a sweet, crunchy streusel layer that is browned to a heavy crust. Serve it hot with vanilla ice cream. I add slivered almonds sometimes, just for an added crunch.

> 8 Granny Smith apples
> 1½ cups packed brown sugar
> 1 cup all-purpose flour
> 1 teaspoon ground cinnamon, or to taste
> Streusel (see recipe below)

Core and peel the apples; slice into sixteenths. Mix the brown sugar, flour, and cinnamon. Sprinkle over the apple slices. Mix well and place in an even layer in a buttered deep-dish pie plate.

Make streusel. Top apple mixture heavily with streusel. Bake at 350°F for 45 to 50 minutes, until golden brown.

Streusel

> 1 stick (¼ pound) butter, cut into pieces
> ⅔ cup granulated sugar
> ¾ cup all-purpose flour
> ¼ teaspoon ground cinnamon

Mix butter and sugar till partially creamy. Add cinnamon, then add flour slowly. Mix until crumbly. Do not overmix.

Hibachi Bananas Foster

(Serves 6)

This is a really exciting dish to prepare. Any time you have flames leaping out of a pan, you're sure to cause some excitement. I need to caution you here. Please be careful. Only experienced flambé cooks should try the flambé step. And make sure the ocean or some other body of water is close, in case the flambé gets too big!

> 8 tablespoons (1 stick) unsalted butter
>
> 1 cup packed dark brown sugar
>
> ¼ cup banana liqueur
>
> 6 ripe bananas, sliced and doused with lemon juice to
>   prevent discoloration
>
> 3 or 4 splashes 151-proof rum
>
> Vanilla ice cream (optional)
>
> Whipped cream (optional)
>
> Toasted macadamia nuts (optional)

In a sauté pan over low heat, melt the butter until it bubbles lightly. Stir in the brown sugar and cook until the mixture bubbles again. Stir in the banana liqueur and banana slices, and transfer the mixture to a disposable aluminum pan. Wrap tightly with foil, and pack for a picnic.

At the picnic: Place the foil-wrapped pan on a hot hibachi, and grill until you can smell sugar cooking and caramelizing on the bananas. Do not burn the sugar—remove the foil to monitor cooking. When the sugar mixture glazes nicely over the bananas, splash with rum. Use tongs to tilt the pan slightly toward the embers so the sauce will ignite. The flame will disappear quickly, as soon as the alcohol burns off.

If desired, spoon flambéed bananas over vanilla ice cream, and top with whipped cream and toasted macadamia nuts.

This dessert can be prepared at home in a sauté pan on a gas stove; if on an electric stove, use a lighter or match to flambé the rum.

Hibachi Pineapple Spears

(Serves 4)

My brother Patrick developed this recipe one afternoon. We'd taken a bunch of pineapple spears to the beach with us for the kids, who were more interested in catching crabs in the tidepools. So, after we grilled the chicken, Patrick wrapped the pineapple in foil and put it on the hibachi. These tasty treats disappeared fast when the kids got their hands on them.

2 pounds fresh pineapple, cut into thin spears
4 tablespoons brown sugar
4 tablespoons (½ stick) butter
Freshly ground pepper (optional)

Lay 3 or 4 pineapple spears on each of 4 pieces of foil. Top the fruit with a sprinkling of light brown sugar and a small butter dollop. Seal foil packets. Grill on both sides until the sugar melts. Open the foil and, if desired, top the fruit with a little freshly ground pepper.

Mango Bread

(Makes 2 loaves)

I love mango bread. Here in the Islands, it's a tradition to make it and give it away. You can make French toast with it. You can toast it. It's fun sitting around peeling mangoes. If that doesn't sound fun, you can substitute mashed banana, grated carrot, or diced papaya in place of mango.

2 cups all-purpose flour

2 teaspoons baking soda

1 teaspoon baking powder

2 teaspoons cinnamon

3 eggs, well beaten

¾ cup canola oil

1½ cups granulated sugar

2 cups peeled and diced fresh mango

½ cup raisins

½ cup macadamia nuts or walnuts, chopped

½ cup grated coconut

Preheat the oven to 350°F. Grease and flour two 9 × 5-inch loaf pans.

Sift the flour, baking soda, baking powder, and cinnamon into a small bowl.

In a large mixing bowl, combine the eggs, oil, and sugar. Combine with dry ingredients and blend well. Fold in the mango, raisins, macadamia nuts or walnuts, and coconut. Pour into the loaf pans and bake for 45 to 60 minutes, or until the bread is golden brown.

To test if bread is done, insert a toothpick in the center of the loaf. When it comes out clean, the bread is done. Let the loaves cool in the pans for 10 to 15 minutes; then unmold and let cool completely on racks.

Burnt Crème with Kona Coffee

(Serves 6)

Some of my neighbors grow Kona coffee trees in their yards, and a few of the trees have started sprouting up along the roadside in vacant areas. The coffee beans are the most cherished in the world, and they've literally gone wild here in our rich volcanic soil. This doesn't devalue them at all. Nothing is quite so comforting as the glorious smell of Kona coffee brewing. I wanted to showcase the flavor in a dessert, and this burnt crème is perfect.

2 cups heavy cream

6 eggs

½ cup plus 6 teaspoons granulated sugar

6 tablespoons brown sugar

1½ teaspoons freeze-dried Kona coffee granules

2 teaspoons vanilla extract

Preheat the oven to 350°F.

In a heavy saucepan, heat the cream over low heat until bubbles form around the edges.

In a mixing bowl, combine the eggs, ½ cup granulated sugar, the brown sugar, and the coffee granules; whisk until slightly thickened. Gradually whisk the scalded cream into the egg mixture. Stir in vanilla.

Pour the mixture into six 6-ounce custard cups. Arrange the cups in a roasting pan and place in the oven. With the oven door ajar, pour enough hot water into the roasting pan to come halfway up the cups. Bake for 45 minutes, or until set.

Refrigerate until well chilled. Place the cups on a baking sheet and sprinkle each with about 1 teaspoon sugar. Slide under a preheated broiler, as close as possible to the heat source. Broil, watching closely, until the topping is melted and bubbly. Chill before serving.

"Always Tastes Great" Macadamia Nut Bread Pudding
(Serves 16)

Bread pudding is always a favorite. It's one of those "comfort foods" that warms the soul as well as the stomach. When I was young, my mother baked bread. Every so often she made an extra loaf. It took me a while to notice, but whenever she did that we had leftover bread and, on the second day, incredible bread pudding for dessert. I added macadamia nuts to her recipe. I don't think she'd mind.

2 cups day-old bread, cut into cubes
1½ cups heavy cream
1 cup diced dried papaya (or substitute raisins or other dried fruit)
2 tablespoons all-purpose flour
¾ cup granulated sugar
3 eggs, beaten
½ cup chopped macadamia nuts
4 tablespoons (½ stick) butter, melted
1 teaspoon vanilla extract
½ teaspoon salt
Dash of cinnamon

Soak the bread in the cream. Dust the papaya lightly with flour to keep the fruit pieces from sticking together. Combine the remaining ingredients with the bread mixture. Pour into a buttered 9 × 9 × 2-inch baking dish. Bake uncovered for 45 minutes at 375°F.

Serve this bread pudding right out of the oven, topped with vanilla ice cream.

Coconut Bread Pudding

(Serves 8)

Bread pudding originated in bakeries as a way to use up day-old goods. Adding a custard-style mixture of eggs, sugar, and milk to diced bread cubes moistened the bread into a hearty, dense pudding. Frontier families enjoyed this delicious dessert whenever there were surplus loaves. Coconut Bread Pudding is a staple dessert at my Breakfast, Lunch, & Crab restaurant in Iwilei. We top the pudding with a scoop of ice cream (sometimes vanilla, sometimes coconut). If you want to test this dessert out before you make it, come on down.

3 eggs
¾ cup granulated sugar
4 cups milk
6 tablespoons coconut milk
8 cups diced bread—about ½-inch cubes
½ cup toasted macadamia nuts, chopped
½ cup toasted coconut flakes

Garnish (per serving):
2 tablespoons coconut syrup
Whipped cream
Pineapple, diced
Toasted macadamia nuts, chopped
Toasted coconut flakes

Whisk the eggs and sugar together. Add the milk and coconut milk; mix thoroughly. Set the custard mixture aside.

Layer the bread, macadamia nuts, and coconut flakes in a 13 × 9-inch pan. Pour the custard mixture evenly over the top. Let the custard soak into the bread. Bake at 325°F for 45 minutes to 1 hour, until a toothpick inserted near the center comes out clean.

To serve, drizzle about 2 tablespoons of coconut syrup over each portion. Top with a swirl of whipped cream. Sprinkle with diced pineapple, macadamia nuts, and coconut flakes.

Minaka's MacNut Brownie

(Serves 6)

I really enjoy a good, crunchy-crusted, gooey brownie. So when my friend Minaka brought these brownies to a Christmas party, I asked her for the recipe. In my restaurants I top the brownies with two scoops of vanilla ice cream and a thin stream of chocolate syrup. It's a real treat.

4 ounces dark or semisweet chocolate
8 tablespoons (1 stick) butter
3 eggs
1¼ cups granulated sugar
1 teaspoon vanilla extract
1 cup sifted all-purpose flour
¼ cup macadamia nuts, diced

Preheat the oven to 325°F. Butter an 8-inch square baking pan.

Melt the chocolate and butter in a double boiler over simmering water. Whip the eggs with sugar and vanilla for 5 to 10 minutes, until thick and pale yellow in color. Gradually stream the melted chocolate into the egg mixture, whipping constantly. Fold the flour into the batter, then pour into the prepared pan. Sprinkle macadamia nuts on top. Bake for 20 to 25 minutes or until an inserted toothpick comes out *almost* clean. Cool. Cut into 12 bars. Top with vanilla ice cream before serving.

Hilo Haupia Squares

(Serves 24)

These squares are really, really 'ono (delicious). The macadamia nut cookie crust adds a nice, crisp texture to offset the creamy haupia (coconut pudding). I like to oven-toast some flaked coconut on a dry baking sheet in a preheated 325°F oven until lightly browned, then sprinkle it over the top. Crunch, crunch!

> Macadamia Cookie Crust (see recipe below)
> Haupia Mixture (see recipe on page 288)

Pour the haupia over the baked macadamia cookie crust. Chill until firm. Garnish with coconut flakes and fresh strawberries. To serve, cut into squares.

Macadamia Cookie Crust

(Makes 3 cups)

2 sticks (½ pound) butter
2 cups all-purpose flour
¼ cup packed light brown sugar
½ cup macadamia nuts, finely chopped

Preheat the oven to 350°F.

In a medium mixing bowl, cut the butter into the flour with a pastry blender until the mixture resembles coarse crumbs. Stir in the brown sugar and macadamia nuts; mix well. Press the dough into a 13 × 9-inch baking pan. Bake for 15 minutes or until lightly browned.

Haupia Mixture

(Makes 4½ to 5 cups)

2 cans (12 ounces each) frozen coconut milk, thawed
2 cups milk
1 cup granulated sugar
½ cup cornstarch

Garnish:
1 cup toasted sweetened flaked coconut
8 ounces fresh strawberries, chopped (optional)

In a large saucepan, mix the coconut milk with the milk. In a bowl, mix the sugar with the cornstarch and stir into the unheated coconut milk and milk mixture. Cook over medium heat, stirring frequently, until the mixture boils. Immediately remove from the heat.

Pineapple-Coconut Yum Yum

(Serves 10 to 20)

I call this a Yum Yum because it's more than just yummy, it's twice that good. I take it out of the oven and let it set for about 5 minutes, then cut and serve with a scoop of vanilla ice cream. Maybe I should call it Pineapple-Coconut Yum Yum Yum.

Preheat the oven to 350°F.

Bottom Crust:
2 sticks (½ pound) butter, softened
⅔ cup granulated sugar
½ teaspoon vanilla extract

1½ cups all-purpose flour

1 cup macadamia nuts, chopped

To make the crust, cream the butter and sugar until fluffy. Add the vanilla, then stir in the flour and macadamia nuts. Press into the bottom of a 13 × 9-inch pan and bake for 10 minutes at 350°F.

Filling:

1 cup granulated sugar

1 tablespoon cornstarch

1 20-ounce can crushed pineapple with juice (2½ cups)

½ cup shredded coconut

To make the filling, combine the sugar and cornstarch in a small saucepan. Add the crushed pineapple with juice. Cook over medium heat until thickened. Add the coconut and pour over the crust.

Topping:

½ cup granulated sugar

¼ cup all-purpose flour

8 tablespoons (1 stick) cold butter, cut into 8 pieces

2 cups rolled oats

For the topping, combine sugar, flour, and butter in a bowl. With a pastry cutter or 2 knives, blend the mixture until the butter is the size of peas. Stir in the oatmeal. Sprinkle the topping evenly over the filling. Pat down firmly. Bake at 350°F for about 35 minutes, or until lightly browned.

Haupia Profiteroles

(Serves 4)

Profiteroles are miniature cream puffs, usually filled with ice cream or custard and sprinkled with powdered sugar. Mine have a haupia (coconut pudding) filling with a sprinkling of sweetened coconut flakes. A presentation option is to place three of the profiteroles on a plate. Make a rosette of whipped cream in the middle of the profiteroles and in between them on the outside. Place the fourth profiterole in the middle of the whipped cream. Stick a quarter strawberry on each of the rosettes. Then sprinkle with sweetened coconut flakes just before serving. I must admit, it's a little rich, so use it as a special dish for special occasions.

½ cup water
1 stick (¼ pound) butter
1 cup all-purpose flour
3 eggs
Haupia Mixture (see page 288)

Garnish:

Sweetened coconut flakes

In a large saucepan, bring the water and butter to a full boil. Turn heat off. Add the flour, stir until combined. Return to medium heat and stir vigorously until the batter forms a ball, about 3 minutes.

Place in a mixer on low speed. Mix until there is no more steam and the bowl is cool on the outside. Add the eggs one at a time. Mix thoroughly before adding the next egg. Beat the dough until it is shiny and smooth.

Using a pastry bag with a plain medium-size tip, pipe the batter in 1½-inch-diameter balls onto sheet pans lined with parchment paper. Bake at 400°F for 15 minutes, then lower heat to 325°F and bake for another 40 minutes. *Do not open the oven while profiteroles are baking, or they will collapse!* Cool.

Make haupia mixture. Pour into a glass bowl, and cover the haupia directly with plastic wrap. Cool overnight. When ready to serve, cut profiteroles in half and use a small ice cream scoop to fill the profiteroles with the filling.

Macadamia Nut Banana Cake

(Serves 4 to 6)

My wife Carol is the real dessert expert in our family. She makes the best turnovers and the best double-crusted pies in the world. I enjoy watching her bake, but she always kicks me out of the kitchen. She says baking is not like cooking—you can't just throw in a little of this and a little of that. She says it's more of a science. It has to be exact; you have to stick to the recipe. She's taught me a lot about baking. She makes Macadamia Nut Banana Cake to hand out for Christmas.

> *3½ sticks (⅞ pound) butter, softened*
> *2 cups granulated sugar*
> *4 cups sifted all-purpose flour*
> *1 tablespoon baking powder*
> *6 eggs, beaten*
> *2 tablespoons vanilla extract*
> *1 pound raw macadamia nuts, coarsely chopped*
> *1 pound firm bananas (preferably apple or finger bananas), chopped*

Preheat the oven to 250°F.

Cream the butter and sugar. Measure the sifted flour, then sift with baking powder. Add eggs and flour, alternately, to creamed butter-sugar mixture. Add vanilla and stir. Fold in the macadamia nuts and chopped bananas.

Pour the batter into a large, well-greased tube pan (the kind in which you make angel food cake). Before baking, place a pan of water on the oven rack below; the steam will keep the cake moist during cooking.

Bake at 250°F for 2 to 3 hours. Test with a toothpick. When the toothpick comes out clean, the cake is done.

Papaya Passion Fruit Cake

(Serves 6 to 8)

I realize you may have some difficulty getting fresh passion fruit at the local grocery store. The frozen variety will work just fine here. Remember that sugar has been added to the frozen passion fruit juice, so your icing will be sweeter. If you can't find passion fruit, either fresh or frozen, try lime or pineapple juice. The lime will make the icing much more tart, and the pineapple will make it quite sweet. You may want to adjust the sugar to suit your taste.

8 tablespoons (1 stick) butter, softened
1 cup granulated sugar
2 eggs, beaten
1 cup mashed papaya
2 cups sifted all-purpose flour
½ teaspoon cinnamon
½ teaspoon salt
¾ teaspoon baking powder
1 teaspoon baking soda
½ teaspoon ground allspice
½ teaspoon ground cloves
Passion Fruit Icing (see recipe on page 293)

Garnish:
½ cup macadamia nuts, chopped
½ cup grated coconut

Preheat the oven to 350°F. Grease and flour a 13 × 9-inch baking pan.

Cream the butter and sugar together until fluffy. Gradually add the beaten eggs and mashed papaya. Sift all the dry ingredients together and stir into the creamed butter mixture.

Pour into the prepared pan and bake for 25 minutes, or until a toothpick inserted in the center comes out clean. Cool in the pan. Ice with passion fruit icing and sprinkle with chopped macadamia nuts and coconut.

Passion Fruit Icing

(Makes 2 cups)

3 tablespoons butter, softened
2¼ cups confectioners' sugar
3 tablespoons fresh or frozen liliko'i (passion fruit) juice

Cream the butter and sugar until light and fluffy. Add the passion fruit juice, beating until the icing is smooth and stiff enough to spread.

Chocolate, Chocolate-Chip Cheesecake

(Serves 12)

*T*here's just no denying the high fat content in any cheesecake. The use of the basic ingredients—cream cheese, sugar, and eggs—make this one of the most calorically dense desserts known to man. But all of that aside, it's still one of the most requested treats in the United States. I periodically serve this cheesecake in my restaurants. It's very rich, and after eating a meal at a Sam Choy's, many of my patrons decide to share this dessert. One woman shared one with her husband, then bought another slice to take home and eat later.

Oreo Cookie Crust (see recipe on page 295)
2 pounds cream cheese, at room temperature
1½ cups granulated sugar
⅓ cup unsweetened cocoa powder
6 eggs
1½ cups chocolate chips
Ganache (see recipe on page 295)

Make the cookie crust and allow to cool. Preheat the oven to 300°F.

Cream the cream cheese, sugar, and cocoa together. Beat in the eggs one at a time. Fold in the chocolate chips. Pour over the Oreo cookie crust. Bake for 1½ to 2 hours, until the outer edge of the cake is set. Chill for at least 4 hours, then remove from the pan and glaze with the ganache.

Chill for ½ hour, then cut into 12 slices and serve.

Oreo Cookie Crust

(Makes one 9-inch pie crust)

2 cups Oreo cookie crumbs (centers removed and
   chocolate cookies crushed)
½ cup granulated sugar
8 tablespoons (1 stick) butter, melted

Mix the crumbs, sugar, and butter. Grease a 10-inch springform pan. Press the crumbs firmly into the bottom of the pan. Bake at 350°F for 10 minutes or until the crust is firm.

Ganache

(Makes 2½ cups)

1 cup heavy cream
2 cups chocolate chips, plus additional for decorating

Bring the cream to a boil. Pour cream over 2 cups of chocolate chips and stir until smooth.

Place the chilled cheesecake on a cooling rack. Place cooling rack on a cookie sheet. Pour warm ganache over the cheesecake to glaze. Decorate by pressing chocolate chips on the edges of the cake.

Easy Banana Pie

(Serves 4 to 8)

Y ou can use any type of banana for this pie. I prefer apple bananas because of their dense meat and tart taste. That's just a personal thing. It may be because I grow them in my backyard. Make sure you dip the bananas in lime juice or lemon juice before putting them in the pie filling mixture. The citric acid stops the bananas from turning brown.

1 8-ounce package cream cheese, softened
1 cup sour cream
3 tablespoons granulated sugar
3 cups sliced bananas, dipped in lime juice or lemon juice
Graham Cracker Crust (see recipe below)

Garnish:

Whipped cream

Blend the cream cheese and sour cream. Add the sugar, and mix well. Stir in the bananas.

Pour into the graham cracker crust. Freeze until firm. Remove from the freezer 5 minutes before serving. Top with whipped cream.

Graham Cracker Crust

(Makes 1 pie crust)

1 cup fine graham cracker crumbs
2 tablespoons granulated sugar
3 tablespoons butter, melted

Combine the ingredients and press firmly into an unbuttered 9-inch pie plate by pressing down with another pie plate. Chill until firm, about 45 minutes.

Liliko'i Chiffon Cream Pie

(Serves 6 to 8)

*I*t is very important that you use fresh yellow liliko'i (passion fruit) juice for this recipe. If you use frozen juice, reduce the amount of sugar added to the gelatin mixture from ½ cup to ¼ cup.

1 tablespoon unflavored gelatin

¼ cup cold water

4 eggs, separated

½ teaspoon salt

½ cup fresh liliko'i (passion fruit) juice (see headnote)

1 cup granulated sugar

1 teaspoon grated lemon rind

1 baked 9-inch pie shell

Garnish:

Whipped cream

Enough toasted, shredded coconut to sprinkle on top

To soften the gelatin, mix with ¼ cup cold water. Let stand for 5 minutes, then heat in the top part of a double boiler until the liquid becomes translucent.

In a saucepan, beat the egg yolks until thick; add the salt, liliko'i juice, and ½ cup of the sugar. Mix well.

Cook over low heat until thickened, about 10 minutes, stirring constantly. Add the gelatin mixture and stir until dissolved. Remove from the heat. Stir in the lemon rind and cool until slightly congealed. Beat the egg whites with the remaining ½ cup sugar until stiff peaks form. Gently fold into the liliko'i mixture.

Pour the filling into a cooled, baked pie shell and chill until firm. Top with whipped cream and sprinkles of toasted coconut.

Macadamia Nut Pie

(Serves 8)

Now *this* is a dessert—rich macadamia nuts suspended in a sweet, creamy pie filling and topped with fluffy whipped cream. Serve it with a good hot cup of Kona-blend coffee.

3 eggs
⅔ cup granulated sugar
1 cup light corn syrup
2 cups macadamia nuts, coarsely chopped
2 tablespoons butter, melted
1 teaspoon vanilla extract
1 unbaked 9-inch pie shell

Garnish:

Whipped cream (optional)
2 tablespoons chopped macadamia nuts

Preheat the oven to 325°F.

Beat the eggs with the sugar and corn syrup. Stir in the macadamia nuts. Add the butter and vanilla, and blend well.

Pour the mixture into the pie shell. Bake for 50 minutes, or until the crust is golden and the center is somewhat set. Test by shaking gently. Let cool, then chill.

Garnish with a swirl of whipped cream, if desired, and a sprinkling of chopped macadamia nuts.

Papaya Sherbet

(Serves 4 to 6)

I can watch the sun set over the Pacific Ocean from my lanai at home. This recipe was born from a need to cool off during a warm summer evening as the sun was going down. As I sat there dipping into my Papaya Sherbet, watching the sun turn the clouds into reddish orange fluffs, I realized that the papaya was the same color. I almost named this recipe Kona Sunset Sherbet.

> 2½ cups sliced papaya
> 1 cup granulated sugar
> 1 tablespoon fresh lemon juice or lime juice
> 2 tablespoons gelatin
> ½ cup cold water
> 2 cups heavy cream

Mash the papaya, add the sugar, and cook for 5 minutes in a saucepan, stirring constantly. Remove from the heat and strain through a sieve. Add lemon or lime juice.

Soak the gelatin in cold water for 5 minutes, and heat in a double boiler until the liquid is translucent. Add to the papaya mixture and stir well. Cool, and chill for 2 hours.

Add 1½ cups of the cream and freeze until slushy. Whip the remaining ½ cup of cream to soft peaks and fold into the mixture. Freeze again.

Ginger-Pineapple Sherbet

(Serves 4 to 6)

You know how much I love ginger. So I guess it's no surprise that I would try to find a way to put ginger in a dessert. It really adds a wonderfully spicy flavor to this tart sherbet.

1 cup granulated sugar
½ cup pineapple juice
1 tablespoon fresh lemon juice or orange juice
1 tablespoon peeled and grated fresh ginger
2 cups light cream

Mix all ingredients in a bowl. Place in the freezer until partially frozen, then mix well with a wooden spoon, or beat with a whisk. Return to the freezer until frozen solid.

Three-Fruit Sherbet

(Serves 8)

I freeze the fruit purée until it's like slush, then whip it with a whisk and refreeze. I like to go through this process three times so it comes out really smooth. It's great for the hottest times of the summer.

1 ripe medium mango, peeled and pit removed
1½ 6-ounce cans liliko'i (passion fruit juice) concentrate
1 13-ounce can pineapple chunks with syrup
1 cup instant nonfat milk powder
1 tablespoon granulated sugar

In a food processor or blender, combine all the ingredients, and blend well. Pour into a pan, and freeze until slushy. Beat with a whisk and return dessert to the freezer. If desired, repeat the process twice more. Freeze until solid.

Mango Guava Sorbet

(Serves 10)

Here's a good way to use an overabundance of mangoes. We always have plenty of common mangoes in Kona. People bring them by the boxes. Some sell, some give.

2 large overripe mangoes, peeled and cut into 1-inch cubes
1 6-ounce can frozen guava nectar concentrate, thawed
Sugar to taste

Purée all the ingredients in a food processor or blender. Freeze for 45 minutes or until icy.

Remove the mixture from the freezer, whip with a wire whisk, then refreeze for another 45 minutes.

Remove the mixture from the freezer and machine process for 30 seconds. Refreeze until ready to serve.

Drinks

One of the wonderful things about Hawai'i is the feeling of celebration that permeates the air. From the moment the Hawaiian sun god La rises above the mountains on his daily journey across the sky to the instant he descends below the ocean horizon, our islands vibrate with a call to relax. It's not uncommon for one local to say to another, "Brah, it's pau hana time. Kick back."

This is just part of a culture that basks in an eternal feeling of summertime. The waves, trade winds, sunshine, and sandy beaches call to us to take a day off. Everybody who visits here is on vacation. It can be difficult sometimes to have to work while others play.

I thought you might like a section on tropical drinks, a little oasis that can transport you and your guests to Ka'anapali or Waikiki. Wherever you are, the sunsets will be laced in gold and highlighted in amethyst purple.

The drinks included here can all be served "virgin" or not. For some gatherings a little Kahlúa is perfect, while at other times alcoholic drinks just won't work. You choose.

For those of you unfamiliar with making layered drinks, here's a tip. When the recipe calls for you to "float" a liqueur like Midori on the top of the drink, take a teaspoon or tablespoon (depending on the size of the glass), hold it upside down above the drink, and pour the liqueur over the crown of the spoon, allowing it to flow in an umbrella effect into the glass. This action will disperse the liqueur so it falls evenly and remains separated from the liquid beneath it. Very impressive. You'll feel like a seasoned bartender. I hope these little beverages top off your special occasions, and put smiles on the faces around your table.

Bermuda Triangle

(Serves 1)

1 ounce vodka
1 ounce pineapple juice
1 ounce orange juice
1 ounce grenadine
1 ounce sweet & sour
1 ounce Midori liqueur

Garnish:
¼ slice of pineapple
1 maraschino cherry

Fill a hurricane glass with ice, then begin to build the drink. Start with vodka, then add pineapple juice, orange juice, grenadine, and top with sweet & sour. Float with Midori, or top with ¼ slice of pineapple and a maraschino cherry.

Guava Colada from the Valley

(Serves 1)

1 ounce light rum
1 ounce pineapple juice
2 ounces guava juice concentrate
1 ounce Coco Lopez coconut syrup
1 ounce half and half

Garnish:
¼ slice of pineapple
1 orchid

Fill a blender one-third full of ice. Add all the ingredients and blend until slushy. Pour into a hurricane glass and garnish with ¼ slice of pineapple and an orchid.

Haupia with a Kick "Oh Yeah"

(Serves 1)

1 ounce light rum
2 ounces Coco Lopez coconut syrup
1 ounce half and half
Ice

Garnish:
1 orchid

Fill a blender one-third full of ice. Blend all the ingredients, then pour into a Viva Grande glass or ice tea tumbler and garnish with an orchid.

Kona Mac Freeze

(Serves 1)

1 ounce Kahlúa
1 ounce Kahana Mac Nut Liqueur
1 ounce half and half

Garnish:
3 tablespoons whipped cream
1 teaspoon ground macadamia nuts

Fill a blender one-third full of ice. Add all the ingredients and blend until creamy. Pour into a Viva Grande glass or ice tea tumbler to ¼ inch from the top. Add whipped cream and sprinkle with ground macadamia nuts.

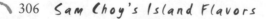

Lava Flow—Get It While It's Hot!

(Serves 1)

2 ounces strawberry purée
1 ounce light rum
1 ounce pineapple juice
1 ounce sweet & sour
1 ounce coconut syrup
1 ounce half and half

Garnish:
¼ slice of pineapple
1 orchid

Pour the strawberry purée into a 14-ounce hurricane glass. Fill a blender one-third full of ice and add all the other ingredients. Purée until slushy. Tilt the glass to the side and gently pour the blender ingredients down the inside of the glass, being careful not to disturb the strawberry purée.

Garnish with ¼ slice of pineapple and an orchid.

Loco Loco Mocha Mocha

(Serves 1)

Hershey's chocolate syrup
1 ounce Coco Rum
1 ounce Kahlúa
1 ounce half and half
3 ounces pineapple juice
1 ounce Kahlúacino

Garnish:
3 tablespoons whipped cream
Cocoa powder (for dusting)
1 maraschino cherry

Squirt Hershey's chocolate syrup all around the inner portion of a 14-ounce hurricane glass. Fill a blender one-third full of ice. Add all the ingredients and blend until creamy. Pour blended ingredients into a hurricane glass, leaving ¼ inch at the top. Cap with whipped cream and sprinkle with cocoa powder. Place a maraschino cherry in the middle of the whipped cream.

Over the Rainbow

(Serves 1)

1 ounce Malibu rum
2 ounces pineapple juice
2 ounces cranberry juice
1 ounce Midori liqueur

Garnish:
¼ slice of pineapple
1 orchid

Fill a hurricane glass with ice. Add all the ingredients except Midori. Float with 1 ounce of Midori liqueur, and garnish with ¼ slice of pineapple and an orchid.

Sam's North Shore Smoothie

(Serves 1)

1 ounce vodka
1 ounce orange juice
1 ounce cranberry juice
2 ounces strawberry purée
1 ounce grenadine syrup

Garnish:
3 tablespoons whipped cream
1 maraschino cherry

Fill a blender one-third full of ice. Add all the ingredients and blend. Pour the mixture into a Viva Grande glass and top with whipped cream. Garnish with a maraschino cherry.

Scorpion in a Glass

(Serves 1)

½ ounce light rum
½ ounce brandy
1 ounce orange juice
½ ounce Orgeat syrup

Garnish:
¼ slice of orange

Fill a blender one-fourth full of ice. Add all the ingredients and blend. Pour the mixture into a champagne flute and garnish with ¼ slice of orange.

Tropical Crab Itch

(Serves 1)

1 ounce curaçao
2 ounces orange juice
1 ounce Orgeat syrup
1 ounce dark rum

Garnish:
¼ slice of pineapple
1 orchid
1 back scratcher (optional)

Fill a blender one-third full of ice. Add the curaçao, orange juice, and Orgeat syrup. Blend until slushy and pour into a hurricane glass. Float with dark rum and garnish with ¼ slice of pineapple, an orchid, and a back scratcher!

You Are the Bestess

1 ounce Kahlúa
1 ounce Bailey's Irish Cream
1 ounce coconut syrup
½ ripe banana
1 ounce half and half

Garnish:
1 slice of banana
¼ slice of pineapple

Fill a blender one-third full of ice. Add all the ingredients and blend until creamy. Pour the mixture into a Riedel glass and garnish with a slice of banana and ¼ slice of pineapple.

Menus

Seafood Feast

APPETIZER	*Breaded Oysters with Wasabi Cocktail Sauce*
SALAD	*Shrimp-Stuffed Avocado with*
	Mango-Onion Dressing
ENTREE	*Island-Style Lobster Boil with Chili Peppers*
	& Other Things
SIDE DISH	*Hibachi Mixed Vegetables*
TROPICAL DRINK	*Tropical Crab Itch*

Tailgate Party

APPETIZERS	*Mochi Mochi Chicken*
	Hot, I Mean Hot, Miniature Beef Kabobs
SALAD	*O'ahu-Style Potato Salad*
ENTREES	*Tailgate Teri Steaks*
	Makawao Chicken Chili
DESSERT	*Hibachi Pineapple Spears*
TROPICAL DRINK	*Scorpion in a Glass*

Backyard Picnic

APPETIZERS	*Wok-Barbecued Shrimp with Pepper-Papaya-*
	Pineapple Chutney
	Spicy Chicken Wingettes
SALAD	*Easy Fruit Salad for the Beach*
ENTREES	*Kona Cuisine Seafood Brochettes*
	Traditional Backyard Beef Teriyaki
SIDE DISHES	*Island-Style Coleslaw*
	Sweet Potato Casserole
DESSERT	*Minaka's MacNut Brownie*

Hawaiian Grinds

APPETIZER	*Sam Choy's World Famous Marlin Poke*
SOUP	*Local Boy Beef Stew*
ENTREE	*Steamed Mahimahi Laulau*
SIDE DISH	*Chicken Lu'au—My Mother's Favorite*
DESSERT	*Hilo Haupia Squares*
TROPICAL DRINK	*Guava Colada from the Valley*

Dinner for Two

APPETIZER	*Ginger-Marinated Seared Sashimi*
SOUP	*Quick and "Tastes Good" Barley Soup*
ENTREE	*Quick and Easy Shoyu Chicken*
SIDE DISHES	*Black Goma Asparagus*
	Ginger Carrots
DESSERT	*Easy Banana Pie*
TROPICAL DRINK	*Over the Rainbow*

Potluck Dinner

SALAD	*"Wow the Neighbors" Seafood Salad*
SOUP	*Da Wife's Bean Soup*
ENTREES	*My Kids' Favorite Seafood Lasagne*
	'Onolicious Teri-Glazed Meatloaf
SIDE DISHES	*Kahuku Corn Smashed Potatoes*
	Stuffed Peppers, Oriental Style
DESSERT	*Coconut Bread Pudding*

Thanksgiving

APPETIZER	*Baked Brie with Macadamia Nuts*
ENTREE	*Sam's Special "Big-O" Thanksgiving Turkey*
SIDE DISHES	*Fresh Island Sautéed Spinach*
	Kahuku Corn Smashed Potatoes
	Sweet Potato Casserole
DESSERTS	*"Always Tastes Great" Macadamia Nut Bread Pudding*
	Apple Crisp

The Wow-Em Dinner

APPETIZER	*'Ahi and Shrimp Candy*
SOUP	*'Ula'ino Watercress Soup*
SALAD	*Macadamia Nut–Crusted Ono Caesar Salad*
ENTREE	*Honomalino Lamb with Satay Sauce*
DESSERT	*Hibachi Bananas Foster or Burnt Crème with Kona Coffee*
TROPICAL DRINK	*Bermuda Triangle*

Glossary

'Ahi—Hawaiian name for yellowfin, bigeye, or albacore tuna.

Ama ebi—very large shrimp, locally harvested off the coast of Kaua'i.

Arugula—also known as rocket. A member of the cabbage family, related to watercress, mustard, and radishes. Use with discretion. It has a very sharp flavor. (Substitute watercress.)

Asian eggplant—long, slender eggplant with purple, lavender, or green-colored skin.

Bamboo shoots—young, tender, ivory-colored shoots of the bamboo, used as a vegetable in Asia. Adds sweetness, delicacy, and crispness to dishes. Most commonly available canned, in the Asian sections of supermarkets. Always rinse before using.

Basil—aromatic plant native to India.

Bay scallops—delicate and sweet in flavor with lean, firm flesh. Very small; the meat is between ½ and ¾ inch thick.

Bean threads—thin, near-transparent strands (known as *harusame* in Japan), made from ground mung beans. Widely used in Northeast and Southeast Asia. Because of their neutral flavor, they readily absorb flavors of other foods. Also called cellophane noodles.

Big Island—named Hawai'i, also called the Island of Hawai'i. The largest and southernmost island in the Hawaiian chain.

Black beans—Chinese fermented and often salted soybeans; can be soaked in water to remove some saltiness. Used to flavor Chinese sauces.

Black goma—black sesame seeds.

Bok choy (bok choi)—sometimes called Chinese chard or white mustard cabbage. Has long white stalks with dark green leaves. Choose cabbage with smooth stalks and crisp leaves.

Butterfish—black cod with a strong flavor. (Substitute bluefish.)

Cannelloni—pasta tubes that are large enough to stuff.

Carpaccio—Italian word for thinly sliced raw meat preparations.

Celery seeds, whole—seeds of the celery plant. Sold in the spice sections of most supermarkets.

Chili-tamarind paste—tamarind, the fruit of a Southeast Asian legume, is made into a paste, and mixed with hot chili paste. Found in the Asian sections of most local supermarkets.

Chili oil—an orange-red oil that is extremely hot. Sold in dispenser bottles, used to "fire up" dishes. A popular condiment in Asian countries.

Chili powder—a combination of various spices and dried hot peppers. A popular combination is black pepper, cumin, oregano, paprika, cloves, and garlic. Found in the spice sections of supermarkets.

Chili sauce—made from cayenne pepper. Very popular in Latin America and India. (Substitute Tabasco.)

Chinese five-spice powder—pungent spicy Asian licorice flavoring made with Szechuan peppercorns, cinnamon, cloves, fennel seed, and star anise. Also called five-star spice.

Choy sum—a Chinese cabbage. (Substitute spinach or kale.)

Cilantro—Chinese parsley. The green leaves and stems of the coriander plant.

Clams—a variety of bivalve mollusks that belong to the Veneridae family. Sold fresh (either shelled or unshelled), fresh-frozen, or canned. When buying unshelled clams, make sure they are still alive. The shells of live mollusks are tightly sealed, or will close slowly when tapped. Choose clams that have a fresh smell, and avoid those that smell of ammonia.

Clam juice—the seasoned juices of cooked clams. Sold canned.

Coconut flakes—flakes from the coconut, sold sweetened or unsweetened in the baking sections of most superments. Dried grated unsweetened coconut is available in natural-food stores.

Coconut milk—rich, creamy liquid extracted by squeezing the grated meat of a coconut. Available fresh, canned, or frozen.

Coconut syrup—sold and served with maple and fruit syrups.

Coriander seeds—seeds of the coriander plant, closely related to caraway, fennel, dill, and anise, and sold with all major spices.

Cumin—seasoning used in curry and chili powders; from the parsley family.

Daikon sprouts—sprouts of the daikon, a white-fleshed Asian root that can grow to a length of 14 inches and weigh a hefty 4 to 5 pounds. Used in Japan for soups, pickles, or eaten raw.

Dashi—a clear, light Japanese fish broth. Sold as instant stock in granules or tea bags. (Substitute chicken stock.)

Dau see—salted fermented black beans.

Dill, fresh—an aromatic herb having fine leaves and small yellow flowers. Flavor combines well with vinegars to mellow the spiky taste.

Ehu—Hawaiian name for orange snapper.

Furikake—Japanese condiment of dried seaweed flakes and sesame seeds, available in the Asian sections of local supermarkets.

Fusilli—spiral pasta.

Ginger—spicy, pungent rhizome grown in tropical regions.

Guava concentrate, frozen—frozen juice concentrate from the guava. Sold in the frozen-foods section of most supermarkets.

Hapuʻupuʻu—grouper or sea bass. (Substitute: yellowfin tuna [ʻahi], red snapper, or mahimahi.)

Haupia—traditional Hawaiian coconut pudding. Today, any coconut pudding is called haupia.

Hibachi—small, portable, inexpensive Japanese outdoor grill used widely in backyards, on patios, and at beaches in Hawaiʻi.

Hijimi—spicy, Japanese pepper sprinkle.

Hoisin sauce—a sauce made with fermented soy beans, garlic, rice, salt, and sugar. The flavor is sweet and spicy.

Hot Asian chili paste—commercial preparation made of red chili peppers and sometimes garlic. Also called *sambal oelek*, or Chinese garlic-chili sauce. Available in the Asian sections of markets.

Hot chili peppers—small potently hot chili peppers grown and used widely in Hawaiʻi. Also known as Hawaiian hot chili peppers.

Hot mustard powder—see "Mustard, dry."

Hot pepper sauce—see "Chili sauce."

Imu—underground oven, the "earth oven" of ancient Hawaiʻi. A hole is dug in the ground and lined with fire-heated stones, banana stalks, and banana leaves. Usually a whole pig is cooked inside, along with other meats and vegetables.

Kaffir lime leaves—glossy, dark green leaves used for cooking. They look like two leaves that are joined end to end. Dried kaffir lime leaves, with a flora-citrus aroma, can be found in Asian markets. Fresh leaves, which have a more intense, fragrant aroma, are sometimes available.

Kamano—Hawaiian word for any large salmon or trout.

Kiawe chips—chopped wood from the algaroba or mesquite bushes. Kiawe is the Hawaiian word for mesquite.

Kiwi fruit—a fuzzy, edible "mist green" fruit (also called Chinese gooseberry) from a vine native to Asia and grown in New Zealand. Available seasonally.

Laulau—packages of ti leaves or banana leaves containing pork, beef, salted fish, or taro tops, baked in a ground oven (imu) or steamed. Lau means leaf.

Lemongrass—a citrus-scented grass that adds a distinctive lemon flavor and aroma to the cooking of Indonesia, Malaysia, Indochina, and Thailand. Its long, woody stalk grows from a base that resembles the white part of a green onion.

Liliko'i (passion fruit) juice—tangy, plum-sized, multiseeded tropical fruit. (Substitute orange juice.) Sold in frozen concentrate form. Find in freezer sections of supermarkets or Asian markets.

Lollo rossa—red curly lettuce of Italian origin.

Lomi—also called lomi lomi. Means to rub, squeeze, knead, or massage.

Lu'au—young taro leaves; cook thoroughly 50 to 60 minutes before eating; used in laulau; the word has come to mean a feast where laulau is traditionally served. (Substitute spinach leaves.)

Lychee—sweetly fragrant, inch-round fruits from the tropical lychee tree. Available fresh or canned in Asian sections of markets.

Macadamia nuts—round, oily nuts with a creamy, slightly crunchy texture; grow on trees mostly on the Big Island and in Australia.

Mahimahi—Hawaiian name for dolphinfish. Has firm, light pink flesh.

Mango—oval tropical fruit with golden-orange flesh and an enticing, aromatic flavor; skin color ranges from yellow-orange to burgundy to green; from a quarter pound in size; available in the produce sections of markets. (Substitute peaches or nectarines.)

Marlin—a large game fish with a long swordlike snout. Also known by its Japanese name, nairagi.

Mirin—Japanese sweet rice wine. (Substitute 1 tablespoon cream sherry or 1 teaspoon sugar for each tablespoon mirin.)

Mochiko—Japanese glutinous rice flour; available in the Asian sections of supermarkets and Japanese markets.

Mongo beans—dried and split mung bean. Can be found in the Asian sections of supermarkets, or in Asian markets.

Mushrooms—

> *chanterelle mushrooms*—have a cup-shaped yellow cap ranging from ¾ inch to 4 inches across. Found in produce sections of most well-stocked supermarkets.
>
> *oyster mushrooms*—grayish or tan. Found in Asian markets and some supermarkets. Have very disagreeable taste when raw. When slightly cooked, they have a mild flavor and succulent texture.
>
> *portobello mushrooms*—extremely large, dark brown mushrooms that are simply the fully mature form of the crimini mushroom or common culti-vated white mushroom. They can be found in gourmet produce markets as well as many supermarkets.

shiitake mushrooms—from Japan and Korea, these dense, dark mushrooms are usually dried, then soaked to moisten before using. Have a meaty flavor. Shiitake mushrooms are also sold fresh.

straw mushrooms—also known by their Japanese name, enoki. Cream-colored Japanese mushrooms with tiny round caps atop slender stalks up to 5 inches long. Sold in small plastic bags in Japanese markets, and in some supermarkets.

Mussels—bivalve mollusks sold in supermarkets frozen, previously frozen, or canned.

Mustard cabbage—also known as mustard greens. A relative of broccoli, brussels sprouts, kale, and kohlrabi.

Mustard, dry—also sold as powdered mustard. Mustard seeds are harvested, dried, and ground to form an aromatic powder used to flavor marinades, curries, dressings, and sauces. Available in either sweet or hot.

Nori—Japanese word for paper-thin sheets of seasoned, dried seaweed used for sushi. Available in Asian sections of supermarkets, or in Asian markets.

Ogo—Japanese name for Gracilaria seaweed.

Onaga—Japanese name for red snapper. The Hawaiian name is 'ula'ula. Red snapper has pink flesh.

Ong choy—swamp cabbage. Also called water spinach. (Substitute head cabbage.)

Onion powder—freeze-dried and ground onion. Sold in the spice sections of most supermarkets.

Ono—Hawaiian name for a large mackerel, also known in Hawai'i as wahoo. Flesh has a white flaky texture.

Opah—French name for moonfish. A very large, brightly colored, silvery, marine bony fish.

'Opakapaka—Hawaiian name for pink snapper.

Opal basil—purple basil.

Oysters—bivalve mollusks with thick, rough, irregular grayish or brownish shells. The top shell is larger and flatter than the lower one. Do not buy fresh unshelled oysters unless they are alive and full of water.

Oyster sauce—a thick brown sauce with the subtle flavor of oysters, made from oysters, brine, and soy sauce. Used in many stir-fried dishes.

Oysters on the half shell—oysters sold with the top shell removed. It's best to buy oysters fresh, and remove the shells before serving to ensure freshness.

Panko—Japanese coarse bread crumbs used for crunchy deep-fried coatings. (Substitute fine dry bread crumbs.)

Papaya—melonlike fruit with a smooth, yellow or orange flesh and a shiny green-to-yellow skin. Usually about 1 pound in weight.

Papaya, dried—freeze-dried meat of the papaya. Sold in produce sections of most supermarkets, or in Asian markets. (Substitute with other dried fruits.)

Paprika—a powder made from sweet red peppers that have been dried and finely ground. Paprika is a Hungarian word meaning sweet pepper.

Parmesan cheese—hard, dry cheese made from skimmed or partially skimmed cow's milk. It is sold in blocks, or grated and packaged. Most recipes call for it to be freshly grated.

Peanut oil—a clear oil pressed from peanuts, used in salads. Because of its high smoke point, it is prized for frying and deep-frying.

Pearled barley—barley grain that has undergone five to six polishing operations to create a grain that is uniform in size and shape. In the process, the grain is stripped of its germ.

Pineapple, fresh—the fruit of a tropical spear-leafed American bromeliad; its edible pulp consists of the flowers fused into a compound. The yellowish flesh is fibrous, sweet, and juicy, and near the darker-colored base sweeter and more tender than near the top. Available seasonally in the produce sections of most supermarkets.

Pineapple juice—juice of the fresh pineapple. Available in cans.

Poha—Yellow, cherry-sized fruit with a spicy pulp and lanternlike parchment covering; rare in Hawai'i; known elsewhere as cape gooseberry, ground cherry, or husk tomato.

Poke—Hawaiian word for slice; refers to a traditional Hawaiian dish of sliced raw seafood, fresh seaweed, Hawaiian salt, and Hawaiian red chili peppers.

Portuguese sausage—a popular meaty product with mild, medium, or hot spicing. (Substitute Italian sausage.)

Prosciutto—the Italian word for ham. Used to describe a ham that has been seasoned, salt-cured (not smoked), and air-dried. Prolonged cooking will toughen it.

Pupu—appetizer.

Radicchio—a red-leafed Italian chicory most often used as a salad green. When buying, look for leaves that are tender but firm, with a slightly bitter flavor.

Red cabbage—the red variety of regular "head" cabbage. Generally used in slaws.

Red chili pepper flakes—dried and crushed red chili peppers. Found in the spice sections of most supermarkets.

Red onion—also known as purple onion. Sold in most produce sections in supermarkets. Widely used in salads.

Rice noodles—made from rice pounded into flour. They look like long white hairs, are thin, brittle, and opaque, about 5 inches long, and have a distinctive flavor. Sold in the Asian sections of most supermarkets, or in Asian markets.

Rice wine vinegar—Japan's relatively mild rice vinegar, the type most often found in local supermarkets. Chinese rice vinegar—white, red, or black—has a stronger flavor.

Rock or sea salt—white or pink coarse sea salt traditionally harvested on Kaua'i; the pink tint is from 'alaea mud. (Substitute any organic rock salt.)

Sake—yellowish, slightly sweet Japanese rice wine.

Sambal oelek—Fiery-hot chili paste. A table condiment in Indonesia. Also known as hot Asian chili paste.

Sashimi—very thin slices of fresh raw fish. Traditional Japanese appetizer.

Scallions—another name for a variety of onion greens. Most commonly called green onions.

Scallops—popular bivalves. The hinged muscle is sold canned, frozen, or fresh (unshelled). Two major classifications: bay scallops and sea scallops.

Sea scallops—large scallops often used in Chinese stir-fry because of their size and delicate flavor.

Sesame oil—the seasoning oil of China, Japan, and Korea. A dense, flavorful oil pressed from toasted sesame seeds into an aromatic, golden brown oil. Use sparingly in cooking preparations, such as marinades, or in fresh preparations such as poke.

Sesame seeds—native of Indonesia and East Africa. Sold raw or roasted, with or without their hulls. Found in the spice sections of most supermarkets.

Shallots—more like a garlic than an onion, with a head composed of one or two cloves. Has a mild onion flavor. Sold in most gourmet produce sections in supermarkets.

Sherry—a fortified Spanish wine, amber in color; sold dry, medium-dry, or sweet. Used for drinking or cooking.

Soba noodles—Japanese thin buckwheat noodles. Also known as Japanese angel hair pasta.

Somen noodles—These delicate Japanese noodles are usually produced from hard wheat flour mixed with oil. Most somen are white, but you'll sometimes see a yellow variety that contains egg yolks.

Soy sauce—Dark, savory, and salty, soy sauce is one of the more versatile and frequently used Asian seasonings. Made of soy beans, flour, yeast, salt, and sugar; saltiness varies from brand to brand.

Snow peas—sweet, flat pea pods used in stir-fried dishes. These crisp, bright green vegetables are eaten whole. Break off the tips and pull backward to remove any strings. Available fresh in most supermarkets year-round. (Substitute sugar snap peas.)

Star anise—the reddish-brown, woody fruit of the Illicium verum, a small evergreen tree native to southeastern China. Also known as badian. Introduced to Europe by an English navigator in the late sixteenth century, this irregular, eight-pointed star is one of the spices used to create Chinese five-spice powder. Available in the Asian sections of local supermarkets.

Star fruit—also known as carambola. Sold seasonally in the produce sections of most supermarkets. Slice it horizontally to produce stars. (Substitute pears, apples, or other firm-meat fruit.)

Steamer basket—Asian bamboo steamer.

Sugar snap peas—delightfully sweet, edible pod pea, which is a cross between the English pea and the Chinese snow pea.

Sweet & sour—a flavoring widely used in cocktail drinks. Can be found in most grocery store liquor departments.

Sweet potato—the orange-colored edible root of a tropical American vine, often confused with the yam, which is starchier and less flavorful than the sweet potato.

Swordfish—a large marine game fish with a long extension of its upper jaw; also called broadbill. (Substitute marlin, or other firm white-meat fish.)

Szechuan peppercorns—wild berries from the prickly ash tree. (Substitute black peppercorns.)

Taro—nutritious, starchy tuber used for making poi, the traditional Hawaiian staple; more than 200 taro varieties are grown worldwide; steam, boil, or bake taro thoroughly 20 to 90 minutes, depending on size.

Tarragon—an herb, can be purchased either dried or fresh. (Always use fresh herbs if you have the choice.)

Teriyaki—Japanese sauce or marinade with soy sauce, sugar, and fresh ginger.

Thai basil—the basil herb grown in Siam. (Substitute with sweet basil.)

Thai chilies—also called bird's eye chilies. These chilies are very small and fiery hot; sold dried. (Substitute crushed red pepper; allow ¼ teaspoon for each chili.)

Thai fish sauce—a thin, salty, brownish gray sauce. Known as nam pla in Thailand, this particular type of fish sauce is much milder than the Japanese, Chinese, Burmese, or Vietnamese versions.

Thyme leaves—leaves from the aromatic plant native to the Mediterranean region. Most common is French thyme. Usually sold in the produce sections of supermarkets with the fresh herbs.

Ti leaves—leaves of a Polynesian and Australian woody plant of the agave family. (Substitute banana leaves, corn husks, or aluminum foil.)

Tofu—fresh soybean curd; bland and therefore versatile. Readily absorbs food flavors.

Uku—Hawaiian name for gray snapper.

Wasabi—hot green Japanese horseradish. Pungent root with an extremely strong, sharp flavor. Popular condiment for foods in Japan. Available in powder or paste in Asian markets.

Water chestnuts—tubers of a marsh plant with a crisp texture and sweet flavor. Available canned, or sold fresh in Chinese markets. Canned water chestnuts are offered whole or sliced. After opening can, rinse well, and peel before serving. To store, cover with cold water, and refrigerate for up to 2 weeks (changing water daily).

White miso—fermented soybean paste containing rice.

White pepper—from pepper berries picked when very ripe and completely red; soaked in salt water for a few days to dissolve outer shell, exposing the white inner seed. Corns are then dried. Much milder flavor than black pepper.

Wok—versatile round-bottomed pan universal in Chinese cookery; used with and without a cover for stir-frying, steaming, boiling, braising, and deep-frying.

Won bok—Chinese cabbage or napa cabbage.

Wonton wrappers—thin, wheat wrapping, usually sold in square sheets. Can be found in the Asian section of your supermarket. Keep refrigerated.

Index

'ahi
    cakes with wasabi aioli, 42–43
    new wave marinated salad, 66–68
    salad with creamy peanut dressing, 91–92
    and shrimp candy, 44
    stuffed, with Hana butter and papaya coulis, 149–50
aioli, wasabi, 43
"always tastes great" macadamia nut bread pudding, 284
anise beef brisket, braised, 219
appetizers, 13–53
    'ahi and shrimp candy, 44
    'ahi cakes with wasabi aioli, 42–43
    baked Brie with macadamia nuts, 15
    breaded oysters with wasabi cocktail sauce, 52–53
    "catch of the day" crispy seafood basket, 28–29
    Chinese scallops with chili-ginger oil and black beans, 49–50
    coconut macnut shrimp with guava sweet & sour sauce, 45–46
    crab-and-shrimp-stuffed shiitake mushrooms with mango béarnaise sauce, 17–18
    deep-fried mahimahi macadamia nut fingers, 30–31
    furikake-crusted sashimi, 38–39
    ginger-marinated seared sashimi, 40–41
    hot, I mean hot, miniature beef kabobs, 23–25
    Kilauea oysters, 51
    mochi mochi chicken, 19
    ono carpaccio with hot ginger-pepper oil, 41–42
    "pau Hana" hot chicken with cold ginger sauce, 22–23
    poke patties, 32–33
    Sam Choy's world-famous fried marlin poke, 34
    Sam's coconut sweet pork, 26–27
    seafood-stuffed nori fish rolls with tomato lomi, 35–37
    spicy chicken wingettes, 20–21
    spicy mango chutney, 16
    steamed "'onolicious" shrimp, 47
    wok-barbecued shrimp with pepper-papaya-pineapple chutney, 48–49
apple crisp, 279
Asian bean sprout salad, 254
Asian chicken marinade, 61
Asian creamy dressing, Sam Choy's original, 59
Asian lamb chops with rotelli, 247–48
Asian macadamia chicken salad with fried noodles, 60–61
Asian marinade, 247
Asian salad sauce, 70
Asian-style stuffed peppers, 262
asparagus
    black goma, 253
    fresh, and stir-fried U-10 shrimp, 128
    fresh, baked scallops au gratin with, 139–40
avocado
    Big Island bisque, 106
    shrimp-stuffed, with mango-onion dressing, 85–86

backyard-style barbecued ribs, 237–38
baked Brie with macadamia nuts, 15
baked coconut shrimp 'Anaeho'omalu Bay, 135–36
baked scallops au gratin with fresh asparagus, 139–40
baked teriyaki mahimahi, 157
baked whole snapper with coconut milk, 166–67
banana(s)
    easy pie, 296
    Foster, hibachi, 280
    macadamia nut cake, 291
barbecue marinades, 206
    chicken, 191
    shrimp, 76, 131
    wok, 48
barbecue sauces
    backyard, 238
    Hale'iwa, 240
barley soup, quick and "tastes good," 100–101

basil vinaigrette dressing, 82
bean(s)
    black, Chinese scallops with chili-ginger oil
       and, 49–50
    black, sauce, braised colossal shrimp with,
       137
    black, sauce, ginger clams with, 122
    da wife's soup, 102
    mung, North Shore ham hocks with eggplant
       and, 243
    upcountry sauce, 236
bean sprout salad, Asian, 254
béarnaise sauce, mango, 18
beef, 209–29
    Big Island short ribs, 221
    braised anise brisket, 219
    Hawaiian barbecued tri-tip steak, 215
    Hawaiian prime rib au jus, 211–12
    hot, I mean hot, miniature kabobs, 23–25
    Kamuela dry-rub tenderloin, 212–13
    Lana'i ranch pot roast, 220–21
    local boy stew, 113
    lu'au stew, 112
    marinades, 218, 225
    'onolicious teri-glazed meat loaf, 226–27
    Papa Choy's tomato, 224–25
    pepper stir-fry, 223
    pulehu rib eye, 213–15
    stir-fried, with Honaunau snow peas, 222
    tailgate teri steaks, 216–17
    traditional backyard teriyaki, 217–18
bella mushroom salad, 89–90
Bermuda triangle, 305
best crabmeat soup with taro, 109
beverages, see drinks
Big Island avocado bisque, 106
Big Island beef short ribs, 221
bisques
    Big Island avocado, 106
    cold papaya, mango, and cape gooseberry,
       105
blackened snapper with tropical salsa,
    154–55
blackening mix, 155
bok choy broccoli, 254–55
braised anise beef brisket, 219
braised colossal shrimp with black bean sauce,
    137
braised ginger-honey chicken, 182
bread, mango, 282
breaded oysters with wasabi cocktail sauce,
    52–53
bread puddings

coconut, 285
    macadamia nut, 284
Brie, baked with macadamia nuts, 15
broccoli bok choy, 254–55
broccoli seafood soup, cream of, 107
brochettes, Kona cuisine seafood, 174
broth, lemongrass, 100
brownie, Minaka's macnut, 286
burnt crème with Kona coffee, 283
butter, ginger pesto, 121
butterfish, simmered shoyu-sugar, with
    vegetables, 151
butter log, Hana, 149
butter sauce, shiitake sherried, 185

cabbage, Chinese, toss, 255
Caesar salad
    dressing, 72
    macadamia nut-crusted ono, 70–72
cakes
    chocolate, chocolate-chip cheesecake, 294–95
    macadamia nut banana, 291
    papaya passion fruit, 292–93
calamari marinade, 120
calamari stir-fry, 119–20
candy, 'ahi and shrimp, 44
cannelloni, lu'au-style cheese, 270–71
cape gooseberry, papaya, and mango bisque,
    cold, 105
carpaccio, ono, with hot ginger-pepper oil,
    41–42
carrots, ginger, 257
"catch of the day" crispy seafood basket, 28–29
catfish, pan-fried, with Sam's sweet & sour
    sauce, 152–53
cheesecake, chocolate, chocolate-chip, 294–95
cheese cannelloni, lu'au-style, 270–71
cheese filling, 273
chicken
    Asian macadamia salad with fried noodles,
       60–61
    braised ginger-honey, 182
    breast, with shiitake sherried butter sauce,
       184–85
    broiled garlic breast, sunshine salad with,
       62–63
    Christopher's stir-fried, 195–96
    hekka, 198–99
    hibachi breasts, 186
    Ka'u lime, 189
    lemon, 187
    lu'au—my mother's favorite, 264–65
    macadamia nut breasts with tropical

marmalade, 190–91
Makawao chili, 197
mochi mochi, 19
Paniolo fajitas, 200–201
"pau Hana" hot, with cold ginger sauce, 22–23
quick and easy shoyu, 183
roasted, with macadamia nut stuffing, 179–80
spicy braised, with ginger, 181
spicy wingettes, 20–21
stir-fried, with sweet peppers and onions, 194–95
sweet-and-sour breasts with tropical fruits, 191–93
tofu with watercress, 201–2
wok, with eggplant and hot peppers, 203
chiffon cream pie, liliko'i, 297
chili, Makawao chicken, 197
chili-ginger oil, 50
   Chinese scallops with black beans and, 49–50
chili peppers & other things, Island-style lobster boil with, 124
Chinese cabbage toss, 255
Chinese pasta primavera, 274–75
Chinese scallops with chili-ginger oil and black beans, 49–50
chocolate, chocolate-chip cheesecake, 294–95
chowder, Sam Choy's South Point, 110–11
choy sum with "'onolicious" sauce, 263–64
Christopher's chicken marinade, 196
Christopher's stir-fried chicken, 195–96
chutneys
   pepper-papaya-pineapple, 49
   spicy mango, 16
cilantro salmon steaks, 156
cioppino, cool summer night, 98–99
citrus dressing, spicy, 37
clams
   ginger, with black bean sauce, 122
   steamer, with ginger pesto butter, 120–21
cocktail sauce, wasabi, 53
coconut
   baked shrimp 'Anaeho'omalu Bay, 135–36
   bread pudding, 285
   cream sauce, 168
   cream sauce, ginger pesto-crusted snapper with, 167–68
   cream spinach sauce, 160
   cream spinach sauce, crusted mahimahi with, 159–60
   -ginger sauce, 173

-ginger sauce, seared albacore tuna with, 172–73
macnut shrimp with guava sweet & sour sauce, 45–46
milk, baked whole snapper with, 166–67
-pineapple yum yum, 288–89
Sam's sweet pork, 26–27
shrimp filling, 136
spinach lu'au sauce, 169
coffee, Kona, burnt crème with, 283
cold papaya, mango, and cape gooseberry bisque, 105
coleslaw, Island-style, 256
condiments
   blackening mix, 155
   chili-ginger oil, 50
   coconut shrimp filling, 136
   dry seasoning salt, 213
   ginger pesto, 59
   ginger pesto butter, 121
   hijimi rémoulade, 127
   papaya coulis, 150
   papaya-pineapple marmalade, 76–77
   pepper-papaya-pineapple chutney, 49
   spicy mango chutney, 16
   spicy vine-ripened tomato relish, 127
   tempura batter, 29
   tomato dressing, 90
   tomato lomi, 36
   tropical marmalade, 31
   wasabi aioli, 43
   wiki-wiki rub, 202
   see also marinades; salsas; sauces
cool summer night cioppino, 98–99
Cornish game hens, Island-style barbecued, 206
corn smashed potatoes, Kahuku, 266–67
coulis, papaya, 150
crab
   best soup with taro, 109
   -and-shrimp-stuffed shiitake mushrooms with mango béarnaise sauce, 17–18
   tomato, 123
cranberry sauce, 205
cream sauces
   coconut, 168
   coconut spinach, 160
   dill, 166
   vegetable, rotelli with, 248
cream soups, 105–11
creamy Asian dressing, Sam Choy's original, 59
creamy peanut dressing, 92
   'ahi salad with, 91–92
crème, burnt, with Kona coffee, 283

crumb crust mixture, 234
crunchy Hale'iwa mahimahi, 158
crusted mahimahi with coconut cream spinach sauce, 159–60
cucumber vinaigrette, sweet-and-sour, 39
curried scallops, stir-fried, 140

da wife's bean soup, 102
deep-fried mahimahi macadamia nut fingers, 30–31
desserts, 277–301
    apple crisp, 279
    burnt crème with Kona coffee, 283
    chocolate, chocolate-chip cheesecake, 294–95
    coconut bread pudding, 285
    easy banana pie, 296
    ganache, 295
    ginger-pineapple sherbet, 300
    graham cracker crust, 296
    haupia profiteroles, 290
    hibachi bananas Foster, 280
    hibachi pineapple spears, 281
    Hilo haupia squares, 287–88
    liliko'i chiffon cream pie, 297
    macadamia cookie crust, 287
    macadamia nut banana cake, 291
    macadamia nut bread pudding, 284
    macadamia nut pie, 298
    mango bread, 282
    mango guava sorbet, 301
    Minaka's macnut brownie, 286
    Oreo cookie crust, 295
    papaya passion fruit cake, 292–93
    papaya sherbet, 299
    passion fruit icing, 293
    pineapple-coconut yum yum, 288–89
    three-fruit sherbet, 300–301
dill cream sauce, 166
    opah macadamia nori with, 165–66
    paradise shrimp scampi over linguini with, 138–39
dill vinaigrette, 66
dips and dipping sauces
    hot mustard, 27
    my dad's favorite, 134
    Nihoa, 132
    spicy sashimi, 41
    see also sauces
dressings
    Asian salad sauce, 70
    Caesar salad, 72
    creamy peanut, 91–92
    fruit slaw, 94

    mango-onion, 86
    Sam Choy's original Asian creamy, 59
    spicy citrus, 37
    tomato, 90
    see also vinaigrettes
drinks, 303–11
    Bermuda triangle, 305
    guava colada from the valley, 305
    haupia with a kick "oh yeah," 306
    Kona mac freeze, 306
    lava flow—get it while it's hot!, 307
    loco loco mocha mocha, 308
    over the rainbow, 308–9
    Sam's North Shore smoothie, 309
    scorpion in a glass, 310
    tropical crab itch, 310
    you are the bestess, 311
dry seasoning salt, 213
duck
    "dry" marinade, 207
    Sam Choy's award-winning roast, 207

eggplant
    macadamia nut, 258
    North Shore ham hocks with mung beans and, 243
    pan-fried spicy, 259
    wok the chicken with hot peppers and, 203

fajitas, Paniolo chicken, 200–201
fish, 147–75
    poke patties, 32–33
    raw, for sashimi and poke, 10–11; see also poke; sashimi
    Sam's amazing no-fat steamed vegetables and, 175
    seafood-stuffed nori rolls with tomato lomi, 35–37
    selection and purchase of, 9–10
    stock, 111
    substitutions for, 11–12
    see also seafood; specific fish
five-spice marinade, 44
fried onions, 215
fried oysters with spicy, vine-ripened tomato relish, 126–27
fruit(s)
    easy salad for the beach, 93
    Hilo tropical slaw, 94
    sherbet of three, 300–301
    slaw dressing, 94
    spicy salsa, 171

tropical, sweet-and-sour chicken breasts
  with, 191–93
  see also specific fruits
furikake-crusted sashimi, 38–39

ganache, 295
garlic
  broiled chicken breast, sunshine salad with,
    62–63
  chicken marinade, 63
  ginger slivers, and fried shrimp, wok-fried
    red lettuce and red oak salad with, 86–87
  shrimp with spinach, red peppers, and oyster
    mushrooms, 132–33
ginger
  -boiled fresh shrimp with my dad's favorite
    dipping sauce, 133–34
  carrots, 257
  -chili oil, 50
  clams with black bean sauce, 122
  -coconut sauce, 173
  cold sauce, 23
  cold sauce, "pau Hana" hot chicken with,
    22–23
  -honey braised chicken, 182
  -honey scallops and shrimp, baby romaine
    lettuce with, 88
  marinade, 40
  -marinated seared sashimi, 40–41
  -pepper oil, hot, 42
  pesto, *see* pesto, ginger
  -pineapple sherbet, 300
  scallops with colorful soba noodles, 78–80
  seared scallops with tomato-chanterelle lomi,
    141–42
  -sesame snap peas, 260–61
  shoyu pork, 242
  slivers, garlic, and fried shrimp, wok-fried
    red lettuce and red oak salad with, 86–87
  spicy braised chicken with, 181
  spicy marinade, 79
  steamed mussels, 125
glazes
  special teriyaki, 214, 218
  tailgate teri, 227
  teriyaki, 25
glossary, 317–25
goma, black, asparagus, 253
gooseberry, cape, papaya, and mango bisque,
  cold, 105
graham cracker crust, 296
grilled foods, *see* hibachi cooking; pulehu
guava colada from the valley, 305

guava mango sorbet, 301
guava sweet & sour sauce
  coconut macnut shrimp with, 45–46
  Sam Choy's, 46

Hale'iwa barbecued pork ribs, 239–40
Hale'iwa barbecue sauce, 240
ham hocks with mung beans and eggplant,
  North Shore, 243
Hana butter, stuffed 'ahi with papaya coulis and,
  149–50
Hana butter log, 149
haupia
  Hilo squares, 287–88
  with a kick "oh yeah," 306
  mixture, 288
  profiteroles, 290
Hawaiian barbecued shrimp salad with
  papaya-pineapple marmalade, 75–77
Hawaiian barbecued tri-tip steak, 215
Hawaiian prime rib au jus, 211–12
hekka marinade, 199
herb salsa, tropical, 163
herb sauce, 162
hibachi cooking
  bananas Foster, 280
  chicken breasts, 186
  Hale'iwa barbecued pork ribs, 239–40
  Hawaiian barbecued shrimp salad with
    papaya-pineapple marmalade, 75–77
  hot, I mean hot, miniature beef kabobs,
    23–25
  hot marinade, 186
  Kona cuisine seafood brochettes, 174
  lasagne-style tofu salad, 57–59
  mixed vegetables, 265–66
  Nihoa shrimp kabobs, 130–32
  pineapple spears, 281
  tofu, 268
  traditional backyard beef teriyaki, 217–18
hijimi rémoulade, 127
Hilo haupia squares, 287–88
Hilo tropical fruit slaw, 94
Honaunau farmer's spaghetti, 276
honey-ginger chicken, braised, 182
honey-ginger scallops and shrimp, baby romaine
  lettuce with, 88
honey-lime vinaigrette, 74
  poached snapper salad with, 73–74
honey wasabi sauce, 29
Honomalino lamb with satay sauce, 245–46
Honomalino marinade, 245
hot, I mean hot, miniature beef kabobs, 23–25

hot ginger-pepper oil, 42
    ono carpaccio with, 41–42
hot hibachi marinade, 186
hot kabob marinade, 24
hot mustard dip, 27

Island braised lamb shanks, 249–50
Island seafood stew, 114–15
Island-style barbecued Cornish game hens, 206
Island-style coleslaw, 256
Island-style lobster boil with chili peppers
    & other things, 124

kabobs
    hot, I mean hot, miniature beef, 23–25
    hot marinade, 24
    Nihoa shrimp, 130–32
Kahuku corn smashed potatoes, 266–67
Kamuela dry-rub tenderloin, 212–13
Ka'u lime chicken, 189
Ka'u macnut-crusted roast loin of pork with
    tropical marmalade, 233–34
Kilauea oysters, 51
Kona coffee, burnt crème with, 283
Kona cuisine seafood brochettes, 174
Kona fisherman's wife pasta, 275
Kona mac freeze, 306

lamb, 231, 245–50
    Asian chops with rotelli, 247–48
    Honomalino, with satay sauce, 245–46
    Island braised shanks, 249–50
Lana'i ranch pot roast, 220–21
lasagne, my kids' favorite seafood, 143–45
lasagne-style hibachi tofu salad, 57–59
laulau, steamed mahimahi, 161–62
lava flow—get it while it's hot!, 307
lemon chicken, 187
lemongrass broth, 100
    wok-seared jumbo shrimp in, 99–100
lemon-pepper mahimahi salad, 69–70
lemon sauce, 188
lettuce
    baby romaine, with honey-ginger scallops
        and shrimp, 88
    red, and red oak salad, wok-fried, with
        ginger slivers, garlic, and fried shrimp,
        86–87
liliko'i chiffon cream pie, 297
lime chicken, Ka'u, 189
lime-honey vinaigrette, 74
linguini, paradise shrimp scampi with dill cream
    sauce over, 138–39

lobster, Island-style boil with chili peppers
    & other things, 124
local boy beef stew, 113
local boy smoked pork, 244
local-style osso bucco with shiitake mushrooms,
    228–29
loco loco mocha mocha, 308
lomi, tomato, 36
lomi, tomato-chanterelle, 142
lu'au beef stew, 112
lu'au chicken—my mother's favorite, 264–65
lu'au-style cheese cannelloni, 270–71
lu'au-style spinach salad with ginger pesto
    sauce, 83–84

macadamia nut(s)
    Asian chicken salad with fried noodles,
        60–61
    baked Brie with, 15
    banana cake, 291
    bread pudding, 284
    chicken breasts with tropical marinade,
        190–91
    coconut shrimp with guava sweet & sour
        sauce, 45–46
    cookie crust, 287
    creamy soup, 108
    -crusted ono, 71
    -crusted ono Caesar salad, 70–72
    -crusted roast loin of pork with tropical
        marmalade, 233–34
    deep-fried mahimahi fingers, 30–31
    eggplant, 258
    Kona freeze, 306
    Minaka's brownie, 286
    opah nori with dill cream sauce, 165–66
    pie, 298
    sesame crust, 160
    stuffing, 180
    stuffing, roasted chicken with, 179–80
mahimahi
    baked teriyaki, 157
    crunchy Hale'iwa, 158
    crusted, with coconut cream spinach sauce,
        159–60
    deep-fried macadamia nut fingers, 30–31
    lemon-pepper salad, 69–70
    steamed laulau, 161–62
Makawao chicken chili, 197
mango
    béarnaise sauce, 18
    béarnaise sauce, crab-and-shrimp-stuffed
        shiitake mushrooms with, 17–18

332 Index

bread, 282
guava sorbet, 301
-onion dressing, 86
-onion dressing, shrimp-stuffed avocado
    with, 85–86
papaya, and cape gooseberry bisque, cold,
    105
salsa, 130
salsa, smoked shrimp with, 129–30
spicy chutney, 16
manicotti Kilauea, 271–73
marinades
    Asian, 247
    Asian chicken, 61
    barbecue, 206
    barbecue shrimp, 131
    beef, 225
    calamari, 120
    chicken barbecue, 191
    Christopher's chicken, 196
    "dry" duck, 207
    five-spice, 44
    garlic chicken, 63
    ginger, 40
    hekka, 199
    Honomalino, 245
    hot hibachi, 186
    hot kabob, 24
    Maui moa, 192
    mochi mochi, 19
    new wave, 68
    paradise, 139
    pua'a, 233
    pulehu beef, 214
    Sam's simple soy, 195
    seafood, 172
    seafood soy sauce, 31
    shrimp barbecue, 76
    spicy fajita, 200–201
    spicy ginger, 79
    spicy soy, 78
    steak, 218
    tofu, 58
    wok barbecue, 48
marlin, Sam Choy's world-famous fried poke, 34
marmalades
    papaya-pineapple, 76–77
    tropical, 31
Maui fisherman's soup, 97–98
Maui moa marinade, 192
meat loaf, 'onolicious teri-glazed, 226–27
menus, 313–15
Minaka's macnut brownie, 286

mocha mocha, loco loco, 308
mochi mochi chicken, 19
mochi mochi marinade, 19
mushroom(s)
    bella salad, 89–90
    breast of chicken with shiitake sherried
        butter sauce, 184–85
    oyster, garlic shrimp with spinach, red
        peppers and, 132–33
    seared ginger scallops with tomato-
        chanterelle lomi, 141–42
    shiitake, crab-and-shrimp-stuffed, with
        mango béarnaise sauce, 17–18
    shiitake, local-style osso bucco with,
        228–29
    shiitake sauce, 229
    shiitake sherried butter sauce, 185
mussels, ginger steamed, 125
mustard dip, hot, 27
my dad's favorite dipping sauce, 134
    ginger-boiled fresh shrimp with, 133–34
my dad's ong choy and pork soup, 104
my dad's tomato beef, 224–25
my kids' favorite seafood lasagne, 143–45
my mother's favorite chicken lu'au, 264–65

new wave marinade, 68
new wave marinated 'ahi salad, 66–68
Nihoa dipping sauce, 132
Nihoa shrimp kabobs, 130–32
no-fat mashed potatoes, 205
no-fat steamed fish and vegetables, 175
no-fat stuffing, 205
"no huhu" pork chops and scalloped potatoes,
    241
noodles
    colorful soba, gingered scallops with, 78–80
    fried, Asian macadamia chicken salad with,
        60–61
nori
    opah macadamia, with dill cream sauce,
        165–66
    seafood-stuffed fish rolls with tomato lomi,
        35–37
North Shore ham hocks with mung beans and
    eggplant, 243
nut(s), see macadamia nut

O'ahu-style potato salad, 90–91
oils
    chili-ginger, 50
    hot ginger-pepper, 42
ong choy and pork soup, my dad's, 104

onion(s)
    fried, 215
    -mango dressing, 86
    stir-fried chicken with sweet peppers and,
        194–95
ono
    carpaccio with hot ginger-pepper oil, 41–42
    macadamia nut-crusted, 71
    macadamia nut-crusted, Caesar salad, 70–72
    and sausage sauce, 272
    stir-fried, and Hawaiian hot peppers, 164
"'onolicious" sauce, 264
'onolicious teri-glazed meat loaf, 226–27
opah macadamia nori with dill cream sauce,
    165–66
Oreo cookie crust, 295
osso bucco with shiitake mushrooms, local-style,
    228–29
over the rainbow, 308–9
oysters
    breaded, with wasabi cocktail sauce, 52-53
    fried, with spicy vine-ripened tomato relish,
        126–27
    Kilauea, 51

Pacific seafood pasta salad, 81–82
pan-fried catfish with Sam's sweet & sour sauce,
    152–53
pan-fried spicy eggplant, 259
Paniolo chicken fajitas, 200–201
Papa Choy's tomato beef, 224–25
papaya
    coulis, 150
    coulis, stuffed 'ahi with Hana butter and,
        149–50
    mango, and cape gooseberry bisque, cold,
        105
    passion fruit cake, 292–93
    -pepper-pineapple chutney, 49
    -pineapple marmalade, 76–77
    -pineapple marmalade, Hawaiian barbecued
        shrimp salad with, 75–77
    sherbet, 299
paradise marinade, 139
paradise shrimp scampi with dill cream sauce
    over linguini, 138–39
passion fruit icing, 293
passion fruit papaya cake, 292–93
pasta
    Asian macadamia chicken salad with fried
        noodles, 60–61
    gingered scallops with colorful soba noodles,
        78–80

Honaunau farmer's spaghetti, 276
Kona fisherman's wife, 275
lu'au-style cheese cannelloni, 270–71
manicotti Kilauea, 271–73
my kids' favorite seafood lasagne, 143–45
Pacific seafood salad, 81–82
paradise shrimp scampi with dill cream sauce
    over linguini, 138–39
primavera, Chinese, 274–75
rotelli with vegetable cream sauce, 248
patties, poke, 32–33
"pau Hana" hot chicken with cold ginger sauce,
    22–23
peanut dressing, creamy, 92
pepper
    -ginger oil, hot, 42
    -lemon mahimahi salad, 69–70
    -papaya-pineapple chutney, 49
    -papaya-pineapple chutney, wok-barbecued
        shrimp with, 48–49
peppers
    beef stir-fry, 223
    Hawaiian hot, stir-fried ono and, 164
    hot, wok the chicken with eggplant and, 203
    red, garlic shrimp with spinach, oyster
        mushrooms and, 132–33
    stuffed Asian style, 262
    sweet, stir-fried chicken with onions and,
        194–95
pesto, ginger, 59
    butter, 121
    butter, steamer clams with, 120–21
    -crusted snapper with coconut cream sauce,
        167–68
    sauce, 84
    sauce, lu'au-style spinach salad with, 83–84
pies
    easy banana, 296
    liliko'i chiffon cream, 297
    macadamia nut, 298
pineapple
    -coconut yum yum, 288–89
    -ginger sherbet, 300
    hibachi spears, 281
    -papaya marmalade, 76–77
    -pepper-papaya chutney, 49
poached salmon with spicy fruit salsa, 170–71
poached snapper salad with honey-lime
    vinaigrette, 73–74
poaching liquids, 65, 74, 82, 134, 171
poke, 13–14
    fish for, 10–11
    patties, 32–33

patty mixture, 33
Sam Choy's world-famous fried marlin, 34
traditional seasoning sauce, 33
pork, 231–44
    backyard-style barbecued ribs, 237–38
    ginger shoyu, 242
    Hale'iwa barbecued ribs, 239–40
    Ka'u macnut-crusted roast loin with tropical marmalade, 233–34
    local boy smoked, 244
    "no huhu" chops and scalloped potatoes, 241
    North Shore ham hocks with mung beans and eggplant, 243
    and ong choy soup, my dad's, 104
    Sam's coconut sweet, 26–27
    'Ulupalakua stuffed loin with upcountry bean sauce, 234–36
potato(es)
    Kahuku corn smashed, 266–67
    no-fat mashed, 205
    O'ahu-style salad, 90–91
    scalloped, "no huhu" pork chops and, 241
poultry, 177–207
    Island-style barbecued Cornish game hens, 206
    Sam Choy's award-winning roast duck, 207
    Sam's special "Big-O" Thanksgiving turkey, 204–5
    see also chicken
profiteroles, haupia, 290
pua'a marinade, 233
puddings, bread
    coconut, 285
    macadamia nut, 284
pulehu
    beef marinade, 214
    Hawaiian barbecued tri-tip steak, 215
    rib eye, 213–15
    see also hibachi cooking
pupu, 13

quick and easy shoyu chicken, 183
quick and "tastes good" barley soup, 100–101
quick snow peas, 260

relish, spicy vine-ripened tomato, 127
rémoulade, hijimi, 127
ribs, barbecued
    backyard-style, 237–38
    Hale'iwa, 239–40

rotelli, Asian lamb chops with, 247–48
rotelli with vegetable cream sauce, 248

sake sauce, 199
salads, 55–94
    'ahi, with creamy peanut dressing, 91–92
    Asian bean sprout, 254
    Asian macadamia chicken, with fried noodles, 60–61
    baby romaine lettuce with honey-ginger scallops and shrimp, 88
    bella mushroom, 89–90
    Chinese cabbage toss, 255
    easy fruit, for the beach, 93
    entree, 57–84
    gingered scallops with colorful soba noodles, 78–80
    Hawaiian barbecued shrimp, with papaya-pineapple marmalade, 75–77
    Hilo tropical fruit slaw, 94
    Island-style coleslaw, 256
    lasagne-style hibachi tofu, 57–59
    lemon-pepper mahimahi, 69–70
    lu'au-style spinach, with ginger pesto sauce, 83–84
    macadamia nut-crusted ono Caesar, 70–72
    new wave marinated 'ahi, 66–68
    O'ahu-style potato, 90–91
    Pacific seafood pasta, 81–82
    poached snapper, with honey-lime vinaigrette, 73–74
    shrimp-stuffed avocado with mango-onion dressing, 85–86
    side, 85–94
    soba, 80
    spicy soy shrimp, 77–78
    sunshine, with broiled garlic chicken breast, 62–63
    wok-fried red lettuce and red oak, with ginger slivers, garlic, and fried shrimp, 86–87
    "wow the neighbors" seafood, 64–66
salmon, poached, with spicy fruit salsa, 170–71
salmon steaks, cilantro, 156
salsas
    mango, 130
    spicy fruit, 171
    tropical, 155
    tropical herb, 163
salt, dry seasoning, 213
Sam Choy's award-winning roast duck, 207
Sam Choy's guava sweet & sour sauce, 46
Sam Choy's original Asian creamy dressing, 59

Sam Choy's South Point chowder, 110–11
Sam Choy's world-famous fried marlin poke, 34
Sam's amazing no-fat steamed fish and
    vegetables, 175
Sam's coconut sweet pork, 26–27
Sam's North Shore smoothie, 309
Sam's simple soy marinade, 195
Sam's special "Big-O" Thanksgiving turkey,
    204–5
Sam's sweet & sour sauce, 153
sashimi
    fish for, 10–11
    furikake-crusted, 38–39
    ginger-marinated seared, 40–41
    spicy dipping sauce, 41
satay sauce, 246
    Honomalino lamb with, 245–46
sauces
    Asian salad, 70
    black bean, ginger clams with, 122
    coconut cream, 168
    coconut cream spinach, 160
    coconut-ginger, 173
    cold ginger, 23
    cranberry, 205
    dill cream, 166
    ginger pesto, 84
    Hale'iwa barbecue, 240
    herb, 162
    honey wasabi, 29
    lemon, 188
    mango béarnaise, 18
    "'onolicious," 264
    sake, 199
    Sam Choy's guava sweet & sour, 45–46
    Sam's sweet & sour, 153
    satay, 246
    sausage and ono, 272
    shaka shoyu, 202
    shiitake mushroom, 229
    shiitake sherried butter, 185
    spicy chicken, 21
    spicy wok, 269
    spinach coconut lu'au, 169
    stir-fry, 225
    sweet-and-sour, 193
    tailgate teri, 184
    teriyaki, 217
    traditional poke seasoning, 33
    upcountry bean, 236
    vegetable cream, rotelli with, 248
    wasabi cocktail, 53
    white, 271

    see also condiments; dips and dipping sauces;
        marinades
sausage and ono sauce, 272
sautéed snapper with spinach coconut lu'au
    sauce, 168–69
scallops
    baby romaine lettuce with honey-ginger
        shrimp and, 88
    baked au gratin, with fresh asparagus,
        139–40
    Chinese, with chili-ginger oil and black
        beans, 49–50
    gingered, with colorful soba noodles, 78–80
    seared ginger, with tomato-chanterelle lomi,
        141–42
    stir-fried curried, 140
scorpion in a glass, 310
seafood
    "catch of the day" crispy basket, 28–29
    cool summer night cioppino, 98–99
    cream of broccoli soup, 107
    Island stew, 114–15
    Kona cuisine brochettes, 174
    marinade, 31, 172
    Maui fisherman's soup, 97–98
    my kids' favorite lasagne, 143–45
    Pacific pasta salad, 81–82
    selection and purchase of, 9–10
    -stuffed nori fish rolls with tomato lomi,
        35–37
    stuffing, 36
    "wow the neighbors" salad, 64–66
    see also fish; shellfish
seared albacore tuna with coconut-ginger sauce,
    172–73
seared ginger scallops with tomato-chanterelle
    lomi, 141–42
sesame-ginger snap peas, 260–61
sesame/macnut crust, 160
shaka shoyu sauce, 202
shellfish, 117–45
    selection and purchase of, 9–10
    see also seafood; specific shellfish
sherbets, 299–301
sherried shiitake butter sauce, 185
shoyu
    ginger pork, 242
    quick and easy chicken, 183
    shaka sauce, 202
    -sugar butterfish, simmered, with vegetables,
        151
shrimp
    and 'ahi candy, 44

and-crab-stuffed shiitake mushrooms with mango béarnaise sauce, 17–18

baby romaine lettuce with honey-ginger scallops and, 88

baked coconut 'Anaeho'omalu Bay, 135–36

barbecue marinade, 76, 131

batterless deep-fried, 87

coconut macnut, with guava sweet & sour sauce, 45–46

colossal, braised with black bean sauce, 137

fried, ginger slivers, and garlic, wok-fried red lettuce and red oak salad with, 86–87

garlic, with spinach, red peppers, and oyster mushrooms, 132–33

ginger-boiled fresh, with my dad's favorite dipping sauce, 133–34

Hawaiian barbecued salad with papaya-pineapple marmalade, 75–77

Nihoa kabobs, 130–32

paradise scampi with dill cream sauce over linguini, 138–39

smoked, with mango salsa, 129–30

spicy soy salad, 77–78

steamed "'onolicious," 47

stir-fried U-10, and fresh asparagus, 128

-stuffed avocado with mango-onion dressing, 85–86

wok-barbecued, with pepper-papaya-pineapple chutney, 48–49

wok-seared jumbo, in lemongrass broth, 99–100

side dishes, 251–301

Asian bean sprout salad, 254

black goma asparagus, 253

bok choy broccoli, 254–55

chicken lu'au—my mother's favorite, 264–65

Chinese cabbage toss, 255

Chinese pasta primavera, 274–75

choy sum with "'onolicious" sauce, 263–64

fresh Island sautéed spinach, 263

ginger carrots, 257

hibachi mixed vegetables, 265–66

hibachi tofu, 268

Honaunau farmer's spaghetti, 276

Island-style coleslaw, 256

Kahuku corn smashed potatoes, 266–67

Kona fisherman's wife pasta, 275

lu'au-style cheese cannelloni, 270–71

macadamia nut eggplant, 258

manicotti Kilauea, 271–73

pan-fried spicy eggplant, 259

quick snow peas, 260

salads, 85–94

sesame-ginger snap peas, 260–61

spicy wok tofu, 268–69

stuffed peppers, Asian style, 262

sweet potato casserole, 267

simmered shoyu-sugar butterfish with vegetables, 151

smoked shrimp with mango salsa, 129–30

smoothie, Sam's North Shore, 309

snap peas, sesame-ginger, 260–61

snapper

baked whole, with coconut milk, 166–67

blackened, with tropical salsa, 154–55

ginger pesto-crusted, with coconut cream sauce, 167–68

poached, salad with honey-lime vinaigrette, 73–74

red, with tropical herb salsa, 162–63

sautéed, with spinach coconut lu'au sauce, 168–69

snow peas

Honaunau, stir-fried beef with, 222

quick, 260

soba noodles, colorful, gingered scallops with, 78–80

soba salad, 80

soups and stews, 95–115

beef lu'au, 112

best crabmeat with taro, 109

Big Island avocado bisque, 106

clear, 97–105

cold papaya, mango, and cape gooseberry bisque, 105

cool summer night cioppino, 98–99

cream, 105–11

creamy macadamia nut, 108

da wife's bean, 102

fish stock, 111

Island seafood, 114–15

lemongrass broth, 100

local boy beef, 113

Maui fisherman's, 97–98

my dad's ong choy and pork, 104

quick and "tastes good" barley, 100–101

Sam Choy's South Point chowder, 110–11

seafood cream of broccoli, 107

Ula'ino watercress, 103

wok-seared jumbo shrimp in lemongrass broth, 99–100

South Point chowder, Sam Choy's, 110–11

soy marinades

Sam's simple, 195

seafood, 31

spicy, 78

soy shrimp salad, spicy, 77–78
spaghetti, Honaunau farmer's, 276
special teriyaki glaze, 214, 218
spices, marinade of five, 44
spicy braised chicken with ginger, 181
spicy chicken sauce, 21
spicy chicken wingettes, 20–21
spicy citrus dressing, 37
spicy fajita marinade, 200–201
spicy fruit salsa, 171
    poached salmon with, 170–71
spicy ginger marinade, 79
spicy mango chutney, 16
spicy sashimi dipping sauce, 41
spicy soy marinade, 78
spicy soy shrimp salad, 77–78
spicy wok sauce, 269
spicy wok tofu, 268–69
spinach
    coconut cream sauce, 160
    coconut lu'au sauce, 169
    coconut lu'au sauce, sautéed snapper with, 168–69
    fresh Island sautéed, 263
    garlic shrimp with red peppers, oyster mushrooms and, 132–33
    lu'au-style salad with ginger pesto sauce, 83–84
squid, calamari stir-fry, 119–20
steak marinade, 218
steamed fish and vegetables, Sam's amazing no-fat, 175
steamed mahimahi laulau, 161–62
steamed mussels, ginger, 125
steamed "'onolicious" shrimp, 47
steamer clams with ginger pesto butter, 120–21
stews, see soups and stews
stir-fried dishes
    beef with Honaunau snow peas, 222
    calamari, 119–20
    chicken with sweet peppers and onions, 194–95
    Christopher's chicken, 195–96
    crunchy Hale'iwa mahimahi, 158
    curried scallops, 140
    ono and Hawaiian hot peppers, 164
    Papa Choy's tomato beef, 224–25
    pepper beef, 223
    U-10 shrimp and fresh asparagus, 128
stir-fry sauce, 225
stock, fish, 111
streusel, 279

stuffed 'ahi with Hana butter and papaya coulis, 149–50
stuffed peppers, Asian style, 262
stuffings
    macadamia nut, 180
    no-fat, 205
    seafood, 36
    'Ulupalakua, 235
sunshine salad with broiled garlic chicken breast, 62–63
sweet-and-sour chicken breasts with tropical fruits, 191–93
sweet-and-sour cucumber vinaigrette, 39
sweet-and-sour sauce, 193
    guava, Sam Choy's, 46
    Sam's, 153
sweet potato casserole, 267

tailgate teri glaze, 227
tailgate teri sauce, 184
tailgate teri steaks, 216–17
taro
    beef lu'au stew, 112
    best crabmeat soup with, 109
tempura batter, 29
teriyaki
    baked mahimahi, 157
    glaze, 25
    'onolicious teri-glazed meat loaf, 226–27
    sauce, 217
    special glaze, 214, 218
    tailgate teri glaze, 227
    tailgate teri sauce, 184
    traditional backyard beef, 217–18
three-fruit sherbet, 300–301
tofu
    chicken with watercress, 201–2
    hibachi, 268
    lasagne-style hibachi salad, 57–59
    marinade, 58
    spicy wok, 268–69
tomato beef, Papa Choy's, 224–25
tomato crab, 123
tomato dressing, 90
tomato lomi, 36
    -chanterelle, 142
    -chanterelle, seared ginger scallops with, 141–42
    seafood-stuffed nori fish rolls with, 35–37
tomato relish, spicy vine-ripened, 127
tropical crab itch, 310
tropical fruits, sweet-and-sour chicken breasts with, 191–93

tropical fruit slaw, Hilo, 94
tropical herb salsa, 163
    red snapper with, 162–63
tropical marmalade, 31
    Ka'u macnut-crusted roast loin of pork with, 233–34
    macadamia nut chicken breasts with, 190–91
tropical salsa, 155
    blackened snapper with, 154–55
tuna, seared albacore, with coconut-ginger sauce, 172–73
turkey, Sam's special "Big-O" Thanksgiving, 204–5

Ula'ino watercress soup, 103
'Ulupalakua stuffed pork loin with upcountry bean sauce, 234–36
'Ulupalakua stuffing, 235
upcountry bean sauce, 236

vegetable(s)
    Chinese pasta primavera, 274–75
    cream sauce, rotelli with, 248
    hibachi mixed, 265–66
    Sam's amazing no-fat steamed fish and, 175
    simmered shoyu-sugar butterfish with, 151
    see also side dishes; specific vegetables
vinaigrettes
    basil dressing, 82
    dill, 66

honey-lime, 72
sweet-and-sour cucumber, 39
wasabi, 58–59

wasabi
    aioli, 43
    aioli, 'ahi cakes with, 42–43
    cocktail sauce, 53
    cocktail sauce, breaded oysters with, 52–53
    honey sauce, 29
    vinaigrette, 58–59
watercress, chicken tofu with, 201–2
watercress soup, Ula'ino, 103
white sauce, 271
wife's bean soup, 102
wiki-wiki rub, 202
wok cooking
    barbecued shrimp with pepper-papaya-pineapple chutney, 48–49
    barbecue marinade, 48
    chicken with eggplant and hot peppers, 203
    fried red lettuce and red oak salad with ginger slivers, garlic, and fried shrimp, 86–87
    seared jumbo shrimp in lemongrass broth, 99–100
    spicy tofu, 268–69
"wow the neighbors" seafood salad, 64–66

you are the bestess, 311